ASPECTS
OF
SHAKESPEARE

ASPECTS

OF

SHAKESPEARE

Being

BRITISH ACADEMY LECTURES

By

L. ABERCROMBIE, E. K. CHAMBERS
H. GRANVILLE-BARKER, W. W. GREG
E. LEGOUIS, A. W. POLLARD
C. F. E. SPURGEON, A. THORNDIKE
AND J. D. WILSON

Oxford
AT THE CLARENDON PRESS
1933

OXFORD UNIVERSITY PRESS
AMEN HOUSE, E.C. 4
LONDON EDINBURGH GLASGOW
LEIPZIG NEW YORK TORONTO
MELBOURNE CAPETOWN BOMBAY
CALCUTTA MADRAS SHANGHAI
HUMPHREY MILFORD
PUBLISHER TO THE
UNIVERSITY

PRINTED IN GREAT BRITAIN

PREFACE

THE provision of an annual Shakespeare Lecture, on a foundation instituted by a generous donor, has been for more than twenty years one of the functions of the British Academy. With one or two exceptions, the lectures given, besides appearing in the *Proceedings* of the Academy, were published at the time as pamphlets by the Oxford University Press. The suggestion has been made by the Delegates of the Press, and was cordially accepted by the Council of the Academy, that a certain number of the more recent lectures should be reissued as a volume, and thus be more easily and more widely accessible, while they would also acquire enhanced value from being read in connexion with one another. This volume accordingly contains the nine lectures given in the years 1923–31. The prefixed list of titles indicates their scope. Their authors, all recognized experts as well as accomplished scholars, have had the opportunity of revising the text of their lectures as originally published, and modifying it or adding notes where they felt that to be desirable. But the alterations or additions actually made are few and slight.

The range of subjects here handled, though wide, is only a small portion of the whole field of Shakespearian studies. That field is indeed limitless, and its fertility is inexhaustible. It continues to attract to its cultivation an increasing number of trained scholars and students. Their labours, even when minutely technical, all converge upon a common object—knowledge of Shakespeare; comprehension of his work and entrance into his world.

There may be little likelihood of substantial increase in documentary evidence bearing directly on Shakespeare's life and activities: on the extent to which he collaborated with others; on the vicissitudes of the text of his plays; on the dates of their composition and production; or on the interpretations given them, from his own time until now, on the stage and in literature. But the story of the facts, the interpretation of the evidence, continues to proceed. Textual criticism is conducted with scientific method. Our acquaintance with Shakespeare's environment becomes almost daily fuller and more intimate; very specially our knowledge of the Elizabethan–Jacobean theatre and of the general movement of dramatic art in the period during which Shakespeare was an actor, a producer, and a playwright. The mythology which had accumulated round him is being cleared away. Less regard is paid to fantastic theories. The exploration of origins is receding to its proper plane. The perils of aesthetic comment are better realized: so are the more disastrous dangers of theoretic reconstruction of Shakespeare's own personality, his views and doctrines and spiritual experiences. The real problems are being faced, under more skilled guidance and with greater intelligence. It is only thus that we can arrive at appreciation of Shakespeare as an artist, and of his work as art, as an undiminished vital force in the life, thought, and art of the present day. Students of Shakespeare and his world—alike the world in which he lived and the world which he created—may receive from the contents of this volume not only information but illumination. A much wider circle will also, it may be hoped, find them alike instructive and interesting.

J. W. MACKAIL.

December 1932.

CONTENTS

THE FOUNDATIONS OF SHAKE-
SPEARE'S TEXT[1]

By ALFRED W. POLLARD, C.B., F.B.A.

THIS annual Shakespeare lecture in previous years has been given by distinguished students and critics of literature who have concerned themselves mostly with the larger questions of Shakespeare's art, and year by year, as I have sat waiting in the audience, I have wondered how the lecturer who was about to address me would find anything fresh to say, where so much had already been said and written. Because Shakespeare is so inexhaustible my predecessors always *have* found something fresh to say, and yet I imagine that when each man braced himself to his task that difficulty presented itself to him as a real one. My own trouble is of a different kind. We are celebrating this year the Tercentenary of the publication of Shakespeare's Plays in the Folio Edition of 1623, and it is my privilege to ask your attention this afternoon to such problems as: what was the task which Heminge and Condell, the collectors and gatherers of the plays, and Edward Blount and William Jaggard their publishers, set before them ? what materials were at their disposal ? what use did they make of them ? and how far can we be satisfied with the result ? My trouble is that to some of these questions it is only possible at this moment to offer answers avowedly tentative and incomplete, because, as regards the Folio, so little work has yet been done along the lines in which I hope to interest you. Those lines are in their origin bibliographical, the method followed in bibliography being first to get all the information possible from the book itself and

[1] Read April 23, 1923. Save for two slight changes for clearness, the text of this lecture is here reprinted as originally published in 1923. A postscript calls attention to some statements I should now modify. A. W. P. (1932).

then to interpret this information in the light of all we know as to the methods of book-production at the time that it was printed and published. Of late years a good deal of useful work has been done in clearing up the problems of the single plays printed in small quarto before the publication of the Folio in 1623. That work has been done mainly by sorting the Quartos into groups and not only studying each quarto individually, but studying it also as a member of its group. Forty years or so ago, in prefaces to some of the Facsimiles of the early Quartos issued under the direction of Dr. Furnivall, real progress was made by the late Peter Augustus Daniel in determining the relation of the quarto editions of single plays to the texts of the same plays as they appear in the Folio. Mr. Daniel had the advantage of building on the foundations laid by the editors of the (old) Cambridge Shakespeare, Messrs. Clark and Glover and Wright. But he advanced knowledge greatly, both in accuracy and extent, and we can only regret that he was not entrusted with the task of editing *all* the facsimiles. On the Folio as a whole, more especially on the plays which had not previously appeared in quarto editions, little work that can be reckoned final has yet been completed, and until we can group the plays according to the sources from which they appear to be derived, and then test this grouping scene by scene, not much permanent progress can be made. Finally, in addition to all this work, there remains (to borrow the not very happy phrase applied to Biblical research) the Higher Criticism of Shakespeare, the effort to discover not only what happened to his text at the hands of printers and publishers, but something at least of what happened to it from the time that each play was first 'plotted' till it became stabilized in a final form. As to that most difficult of all problems you will be relieved to hear that I propose to say only a very little this afternoon, and that little mainly by way of a plea for moderation and a refusal to press too far methods which (I am yet confident), if cautiously used, should be fruitful of good results.

Our problem then is the Foundations of Shakespeare's Text. What are our materials, the necessary materials, for investigating it ? The foundations of Shakespeare's text must have been laid in his study and in the playhouse. Any fragment of text which can be shown to be derived from Shakespeare or from the playhouse requires investigation. Until a text can be shown to be so derived it cannot be admitted as evidence. Applied to our problems, this rules out all editions subsequent to 1623. On the face of them these are reprints, and until it can be shown that where they differ from the editions from which they are reprinted, these differences are the result of a new recourse to Shakespeare's manuscripts or to the playhouse copies, they do not concern us, though they have their own interest.

We are left then with the Folio of 1623, and the forty-four editions of sixteen different single plays issued before it appeared, from the *Titus Andronicus* of 1594 to the *Othello* of 1622. Among these editions of single plays we find that for *Romeo and Juliet* and for *Hamlet* we have for each play two texts so different from each other as to be clearly derived from different sources. Treating these rival texts as distinct, we have then eighteen First Editions and twenty-six Reprints. We find that these twenty-six Reprints differ, each of them, in scores of lines from the First Editions from which they are derived. We examine these differences to see, not merely whether they are good or bad, but whether, when good, they must be due to a new consultation of Shakespeare's autograph or a copy of it, or may more reasonably be attributed to the cleverness of the printer's reader. In the case of each play we must consider this question both as regards each difference in itself and as regards each difference in relation to all the other differences. Moreover, while we must consider the evidence for each play by itself, we must also consider the evidence for all these twenty-six intermediate editions as a group. Taking the good readings introduced in these editions individually we find some whose goodness needs explanation, and explanations have been forthcoming, though I must not trouble you with examples this afternoon, interesting as they mostly are. Taking each Intermediate Edition by itself, in no single instance do we find evidence of the sort of care which could lead us to believe that its overseer had obtained access to any authoritative source. Taking the Intermediate Editions as a class we find that every time a play was reprinted, new errors were introduced, mostly many new errors, and that the few corrections are nearly always such as any moderately intelligent reader would naturally make for himself. As evidence of the words which Shakespeare wrote or of the words which were spoken by the actors engaged in his plays these Intermediate Editions are absolutely worthless, except where we possess only one or two copies of the First Edition. It is necessary to make that exception because, printing being a slow process in Shakespeare's day, corrections were sometimes made while a sheet of text was passing through the press, so that some of the copies printed would have a right reading, where others had a wrong one. A Second Edition might thus be printed from a copy of the First in which a correction had been made which does not appear in any copy of the First now extant. With this reservation, all the Intermediate Editions are worthless as to the words Shakespeare wrote or the actors spoke, and all the later Reprints, the third, fourth, and later editions, are worthless without any reservation at all.

For another purpose, however, the Intermediate Editions have one quite distinct value, that is as tests of the First Folio. They were in existence in 1623 when the Folio was printed. Every printer knows the convenience and comfort of printing from type instead of from manuscript, and while the printer would be better pleased to print from the latest quarto instead of from manuscript, the publishers of the Folio had two good reasons for paying sixpence for a printed text and sending it to the playhouse to be corrected, rather than copying the whole play afresh; firstly, they would have had to pay their copyist more, and secondly, he would probably have made more mistakes. It can be proved that even when, as in the case of *Richard III*, recourse was had to a radically different text, the copy which the Folio printer received was one of the late quartos, altered in accordance with the manuscript, and that readings, including obvious errors, which had originated with the Intermediate Quartos, thus got into the Folio, to the detriment of its authority. We must note also that this applies to punctuation as well as to words, that, for instance, the punctuation of *A Midsummer-Night's Dream* in the Folio, where it differs from that of the First Edition, is largely derived from the Quarto of 1619, and therefore cannot be authoritative. Thus in considering the authority of the Folio we must clearly deduct from it everything that can be shown to be derived from an edition itself of less authority than the First.

We are thus left with the eighteen First Quarto editions and the Folio (purged of any readings accepted from variants introduced into the later Quartos) as the twin Foundations of Shakespeare's text. What is the value of each of these ? We take the Quartos first, and here we can make a further sub-division by separating into a group by themselves four of the First Quarto editions: the 1597 *Romeo and Juliet*, the 1600 *Henry V*, the 1602 *Merry Wives of Windsor*, and the 1603 *Hamlet*. Two of these editions were quickly superseded by much superior texts, the *Romeo and Juliet* of 1599 and the *Hamlet* of 1604. Not one of the four was used in printing the Folio. Their texts are shorter by from a third to nearly a half than those printed in the Folio; they are full of absurdities, though also 'good in parts' —the parts, it has been suggested, which were played by a minor actor, through whose treachery sections of Shakespeare's text were placed at the disposal of an unscrupulous printer, or of an uninquiring printer through the agency of an unscrupulous publisher. In the Address to the Reader in the First Folio there is a well-known reference to buyers of Shakespeare's plays having previously been 'abus'd with diverse stolne and surreptitious copies, maimed and deformed by the frauds and stealthes of iniurious impostors, that expos'd them', and the comforting assurance is given that 'even those are now offer'd to your view cur'd, and perfect of their limbes'. It is submitted that this reference is not only explained, but *completely* explained, by the existence of these four bad texts, for each of which a radically different one was substituted in the Folio, and that there is no reason whatever to apply the epithets 'stolne and surreptitious' to any of the remaining First Quartos, which are of an entirely different character, and came into the world of books in a markedly different way.

The four quartos to which the epithets 'stolne and surreptitious' obviously apply I have ventured to call uncompromisingly the Bad Quartos, but I have already admitted that they are 'good in parts', and it has even been thought that they throw more light on the evolution of Shakespeare's plays than any other documents we possess. The other fourteen Quartos it is convenient to call, equally sweepingly, the Good Quartos, though the goodness of some of them is painfully obscured by defects, which have too hastily been ascribed to the innate weakness or wickedness of all copyists and compositors who have had anything to do with Shakespeare's texts. It is better to confess that some of the flaws in these Good Quartos are the result of imperfections in Shakespeare's own work, and I have ventured to claim that some of these Good Quartos may actually have been set up from Shakespeare's autograph manuscripts.

The argument is that in the absence of evidence making it impossible, we are not entitled to assume that what *did* happen in the case of some plays by other playwrights did *not* happen to some plays by Shakespeare. In the case of some plays by other playwrights we find that it was the author's autograph manuscript which was first submitted to the censor and then used as a prompt copy and equipped with the notes and stage-directions necessary for this purpose. From the notes and stage-directions which

occur in some of the printed quartos, there is a high probability that these were printed from prompt copies, and if
what happened with other plays by other playwrights is
any guide to what happened to Shakespeare's, some of
these prompt copies were probably in his autograph.
Some of them, also, were probably *not*; but it may be
claimed that at every stage in the passage of a play from
Shakespeare's study the balance of probabilities is in
favour of optimism. Thus, firstly, when there was a risk
of piracy it would be foolish to increase that risk by making
a single needless transcript. Secondly, in view of the
insistence of the censor that a play should be acted in exact
conformity with the copy on which the licence was inscribed, the greatest proof of obedience on the part of the
players would be to put this inscribed copy in the hands
of the prompter as a guarantee against gag. Thirdly, as
a ready means of persuading the wardens of the Stationers'
Company that a play might be printed without special
'authority' being obtained for it, the production of the
manuscript on which the censor's licence was inscribed,
as the copy sent to the printer, would carry all before it.
On the other side I can think of no countervailing argument except that the owners of the play would not be
likely to let such a precious thing as a prompt copy out of
their hands. But if, in place of their manuscript prompt
copy, they could, within three or four weeks, get back
a printed copy which could be used for the same purpose
(and, in the case of *A Midsummer-Night's Dream*, we have
evidence that the printed copy was so used) this objection
is greatly weakened. Without labouring this point further,
I ask you to believe on the evidence of all the editors who
have largely relied on these editions, while mechanically
abusing them, that these fourteen good First Quartos form
a very solid section of our Foundations, sometimes supplying, sometimes rivalling, always at least supplementing the
texts found in the Folio, and for the most part carrying
with them the prestige of being based on versions used in
the playhouse while Shakespeare was still connected with

it. The producers of the Folio did not make the best use of this material. When later reprints were more easily obtainable they used these in preference to the originals, correcting them by the prompt copy which sometimes may have been of the original edition. In other cases, as in *Richard III*, they relied on a manuscript which they believed (in the case of *Richard III* wrongly) to be of higher authority. But the 'good' quartos have been re-covered, thanks to the enthusiasm of collectors, and as regards most of these fourteen plays for which we have a double text our position is exceptionally good.

If the managers of Shakespeare's company were able to supply good texts, in some cases possibly autograph texts, to the printers of the Quartos whom they probably disliked (regarding them only as a preferable, but still unpleasant, alternative to pirates), it may seem reasonable to believe that when they authorized and cordially authenticated a collected edition of Shakespeare's plays they would be able to do as well or better. It is here, ladies and gentlemen, that we reach the Third Act of our Pleasant Comedy of the Fate of Shakespeare's Plays. As an incurable optimist I refuse to believe that the fate of these plays can rightly be regarded as Tragic. I claim to lead you up gradually to a happy ending. But in a Shakespearian comedy, so often illustrative of the theme 'the course of true love never did run smooth', there is often a moment when tragic possibilities are so evident that only the description of a play as a comedy assures us of a happy ending. More than this, lest you accuse me of deceiving you, it must be remembered that the hero of a Shakespearian comedy is often a much more sober and disciplined person in the last act than in the first. He may have made mistakes and paid penalties; he may have run into dangers and difficulties and not escaped scot-free; and we may find that this is so with the hero of this lecture, Shakespeare's text. Our hero has begun well. The Good Quartos stand greatly to his credit. The attacks by the pirates have done no harm and have supplied valuable information. But we are now at the crisis of our Drama. We have to face two facts; the first, that the Globe Theatre was burnt down in 1613, and there is no agreement at present as to what damage was then done to the collection of prompt copies or other theatrical manuscripts in the company's possession; secondly, that in 1623 something like a dozen years had elapsed since the last of Shakespeare's plays had been written, and some thirty since the production of the earliest, and such knowledge as we possess of how plays written by other dramatists were handled does not encourage us to believe that by any means all of the manuscripts available in 1623 were in the same state as when Shakespeare put his last touches to them.

Both of these points are serious, and I must repeat with especial reference to them my plea for indulgence, on the ground that the work of investigation is far from complete. As regards the possible destruction of playhouse copies in the fire of 1613, alarm may at first sight seem superfluous. We know that many plays by Greek dramatists have been lost, because, while no manuscripts of them survive, quotations from them in the writings of other authors prove that they once existed. As far as I know we have no evidence of this or any other kind that any single play by Shakespeare has perished, the reference by Francis Meres (in his *Palladis Tamia* of 1598) to a *Loves Labours Won* being satisfactorily explained as pointing to *All's well that ends well* having been originally produced under the title which Meres quotes. If the Folio editors have delivered the goods, and *all* the goods, what need is there for pessimism? My pessimism does not, and cannot, extend to the survival of my hero. In the last act of a comedy he must appear, damaged perhaps, but presentable. But is he quite the man we thought? Somewhat against my will I have to own that there is more in a passage of Dr. Johnson's preliminary advertisement of his edition of Shakespeare than I was willing to admit eight years ago. In his highly imaginative picture of the misfortunes which had befallen the text of Shakespeare's plays, Johnson asserted that they had been 'printed at last from compilations made by chance or by stealth out of the separate parts written for the theatre', which he proceeds to write of as 'fragments so minutely broken and so fortuitously re-united'. I still think the words *by chance* and *fortuitously* the nearest approach to nonsense which the great Doctor ever made, but that the separate parts written for one of the actors who took the characters of Marcellus, Volte-mar, the Second Player, &c., in *Hamlet*, the Host in the *Merry Wives of Windsor*, and various parts of moderate importance in *Romeo and Juliet* and *Henry V* were one of the sources from which the piracies of these plays were put together is highly probable. More than this, there are three plays first printed in the Folio, the *Two Gentlemen of Verona*, *Merry Wives of Windsor*, and *Winter's Tale*, which, it has been plausibly maintained, were mainly or entirely put together from the Actor's parts reunited (*not* fortuit-ously) by means of the 'Plot' or list of the entrances of the various actors in each scene. The main evidence for this theory is that instead of the entrance of each actor being noted at its proper point, they are all massed together at the beginning of each scene. The text in these plays is by no means bad; as has been suggested, an actor's part is likely to have been legibly written and free from erasures. But there is no chance of a Shakespeare autograph in these 'Parts', and some risk both of omissions and gag. Our evidence as to their use as 'copy' for the Folio is cogent only for the three plays named, but it must be remembered that, if after 1613 it had been desired to revive a play which only survived in these 'Parts', a prompt-copy would have had to be constructed from them, and this, in the course of a few years, would have been gradually filled out with the necessary entrances and exits and other stage-directions. On the other hand, we have prompt-copies for the three parts of *King Henry VI*, which no one in 1613 would have been likely to trouble to reconstruct, if it had once perished, and there were certainly manuscripts of *Richard III* and some seven other plays first printed in Quarto. It is clear, therefore, that some manuscripts in addition to the theatrical 'Parts' survived, and it must always be remembered that we have no contemporary statement, such as has come down to us as to a later calamity of the same kind, that any manuscripts were destroyed at this fire. Save the peculiarity in the stage-directions of the three plays named, there is really no evidence on either side, and the only reasonable attitude is thus that which would certainly be adopted by a Fire Insurance Company, a refusal to admit any claim as to which specific evidence cannot be produced.

Another alternative to which recourse might have been had if and when any prompt-copies were destroyed has been surmised to exist in copies of plays made for private patrons of the stage. We gather from a preface and prologue by Thomas Heywood that from about 1605 there was a sufficient demand for plays in manuscript to encourage shorthand writers to take them down at the theatre. We gather also that, when the theatres were closed during the Civil War, Beaumont and Fletcher's plays (mainly prompt-copies) were temporarily in private hands and had to be bought back. The amateur of theatrical manuscripts seems to have had a real existence. We may imagine, if we please, that the text of *The Tempest* with its elaborate literary stage-directions and careful punctuations, may be a text of this class, prepared for some play-loving courtier who had seen it acted at Whitehall and was willing to pay for a copy for his private reading, and again willing to lend it when the original text was lost. Here also we may be thankful for what we have, and yet admit that a prompt-copy might have been better. I believe, however, that even when full allowance has been made for both these possibilities the possibility of plays printed from players' parts, and the possibility of plays printed from fair copies made for private patrons, any theory which assumes a large destruction of prompt-copies in the fire of 1613 raises more difficulties than it explains.

Our second doubt, as to what may have happened to Shakespeare's plays between the time when he set his last personal touches to them and the handing over of the copy to the compositors in Jaggard's printing-house, is probably much the more serious of the two. To take the simplest case as an example: it is clear that Shakespeare, with all his amazing stage-craft, frequently wrote more lines than the actors were able to deliver in the time at their disposal. He himself, when emphasizing the brevity of plays, speaks of the 'two hours' traffic' of the stage. Perhaps in such a connexion two hours may stand for any time between two hours and three; but even granting this, it means that a play of 3,000 lines would have to be delivered at the rate of over a thousand lines an hour, and actors cannot deliver blank verse at the rate of much over a thousand lines an hour (especially if they insist on 'chanting' it) without risk of becoming incoherent. Yet *Henry IV*, *Troilus*, *Coriolanus*, *Lear*, *Othello*, and *Cymbeline* all exceed 3,300 lines; *Richard III* exceeds 3,600, *Hamlet* exceeds 3,900, and was probably performed in full as seldom in the seventeenth century as it is now, more probably still was never performed in full at all. Now if we take a case where we have both a quarto text and the Folio, for instance *Lear*, we find that both texts have been abridged, and that there are some eighty lines in the Folio which the Quarto omits, and some 190 lines in the Quarto which the Folio omits. How many lines there may have been in the original manuscript which *both* the Quarto and Folio omit no one can now tell. In the case of *Lear*, I think very few; but what about other plays, for instance, *Antony and Cleopatra* with its scenes of ten lines, of nine lines, of five lines, its two scenes of four lines ? Were these scenes always as short as this ? If you look at the scenes in *Lear* where the admirable 'Kent' explains successive situations to 'a Gentleman', and see how the Quarto has cut out some lines which the Folio retains and the Folio has cut out some which the Quarto retains, I think that you will surmise that in *Antony and Cleopatra* also there have been cuts. Please remember also that the Folio editor has been proved by Mr. Daniel to have had a copy of the First Quarto of *Lear* before him, and could have printed the lines cut out from the theatre's manuscript if he had pleased. But he did not please. We have to face the fact that the producers of the Folio preferred the acting-version used in the playhouse, and if lines written by Shakespeare were omitted from that, were content that they should perish. If that was a crime, they committed it.

Thus in all the longer plays by Shakespeare, speeches may have been curtailed to save time, and passages omitted because the players considered that they were ineffective in representation. But several of the plays are quite short. *The Tempest* has under 2,300 lines, *A Midsummer-Night's Dream* 2,173, *Macbeth* 2,100, *The Comedy of Errors* 1,777. It may seem, at first sight, as if plays as short as these could have offered no temptations to the abridger. Unhappily, the whole question as to the occasions on which exceptionally short plays were acted is still obscure. It has been suggested that they were in request for performances in the provinces, for performances at court, for performances in private houses, even possibly for performances in the public theatres in the short winter afternoons, or on Sundays. These are all plausible suggestions; but for lack of proof they remain suggestions and little more. Yet though the occasions are doubtful, it seems certain that (despite intermediate lengths) short plays and long plays were theatrically distinct, and that while some short plays (*A Midsummer-Night's Dream* I hope may be accounted one) were definitely planned as short, plays originally written as long were sometimes cut down to shortness, and plays originally written as short were occasionally expanded. It has been suggested with great plausibility that *The Tempest* was originally a much longer play than it now is, with the events which Prospero narrates to Miranda in the first Act represented in a series of scenes on the stage. There is even greater reason to believe that *dreadful* things have been done to *Macbeth*, the adjective

implying that not all of the changes made in *Macbeth*, perhaps not all of those made in *The Tempest*, were made by
Shakespeare. That is a grim thought, and there are possibilities grimmer still, possibilities of additions as well as
excisions. In the manuscript of the play of *Sir Thomas
More* (an extraordinarily useful manuscript to study) there
is a scene rewritten in a different hand, apparently for no
other reason than to put in a few conspicuously feeble
remarks by the Clown. Are there no additions of this kind
in the received text of Shakespeare ? What of *Macbeth* ?
Are all the Witch scenes Shakespeare's ? We have seen
how the text of *King Lear* was cut down alike in the Folio
and the Quarto. Was the Fool's 'prophecy' at the end of
Act III, sc. ii ever in Shakespeare's manuscript ? The Fool
has sung his song,

> He that has and a little tiny wit,
> With hey ho, the wind and the rain,
> Must make content with his fortunes fit,
> Though the rain it raineth every day.

Lear answers with the patience he ever shows to the Fool:
'True, my good boy', and bids the disguised Kent 'come
bring us to this hovel', and then we are to believe that
Shakespeare made the Fool stay behind and speak his
'prophecy':

> When priests are more in word than matter,
> When brewers mar their malt with water,

and the rest of it. It seems improbable.

I have already disclaimed any desire to enter this afternoon into the more difficult questions of the Higher
Criticism of Shakespeare. It was no part of the business
of his earliest printers to distinguish between what he took
from others and what was his own, or to mark by difference
of type the changes and additions he made in successive
rehandlings. In such a play as *Richard III*, the modern
editor of an unannotated text, whether he believes that
the Folio or (as surely he should) the Quarto represents
Shakespeare's latest text, has an impossible task of choosing

in cases of obscurity between two readings, both of which have authority. The four pirated texts give us hints of much more extensive changes than we find in *Richard III*, and in most of the plays, if we look closely enough into them, we shall find enough discrepancies, enough evidence of what seems imperfect revision, enough diversity of style, to tempt us to believe that Shakespeare wrote all his plays in the years of his dramatic apprenticeship and spent the rest of his working life in constantly rewriting them. That theory is not much more untenable than its opposite which envisages each play as the result of a continuous effort throughout so many weeks and then finished and done with. But discrepancies and loose ends and the reappearance of an earlier style in later plays can be explained in more ways than one. There is the possibility of rough drafts of plays, laid aside and developed later; the possibility, for which some evidence could be adduced, that Shakespeare's staying power as a dramatist was limited to half a play at a time, and that when he resumed work on it he may have been in a different mood and trusted too confidently to his memory; the possibility, lastly, that just as in dealing with the same situations Shakespeare expresses himself with curious similarity in plays of widely different dates, so when a generous lover has to be given a speech in a play as sombre as *King Lear* the speech shapes itself into the rhymes in which generous lovers pour out their passion in earlier plays. But all these considerations are this afternoon beside the point. They are problems for literary critics, problems for modern editors, but altogether outside the range of the actors, printers, and publishers who produced the First Folio. The charge a defender of these has to meet is that this edition is full of misprints, that in the longer plays lines and passages written by Shakespeare have been omitted, that in some of the shorter plays there has been drastic abridgement, and that now and again there seem to have been additions by other hands. It is a serious indictment. Some of you may be thinking that this Comedy of Shakespeare's text is not a Comedy at all, that the fate of his plays is tragic. Whoever thinks so is, to use a nice old-fashioned phrase, *sinning his mercies.* We have only to remember the fate of Marlowe's *Dr. Faustus,* now represented by a few fine speeches overladen with much alien buffoonery, or of the scanty and mangled texts of the plays of Greene and Peele, to recognize how great a miracle it is that Shakespeare's early work should have come down to us in so much better condition. These men were his immediate fore-runners. They had prepared their audience to expect something more than had previously been offered. By their popularity homes had been made for the drama, so that plays needed no longer to be performed at the Cross Keys or other inns. And yet it is possible that some of their best work would have been lost had it not been preserved in plays which Shakespeare rehandled. It is a great thing, a very great thing, that every play which Shakespeare wrote, or in which he had any considerable share, has come down to us, and come down in texts which, if here and there they present difficulties to students, who rightly wish to understand the exact sense in which every word is used in every passage, to the sympathetic reader, and still more to the sympathetic listener when the plays are acted or read, offer very few obstacles.

If any one persists in bewailing that the text of Shake-speare is not better than it is there is more to be said to him. If we go beyond the imperfections to the causes of the imperfections there is only one man to blame for them, and that is Shakespeare himself. If we are to blame any one, do not let it be the actors, or the printers, or the publishers. According to the standards of their day they all did extraordinarily well. Only if Shakespeare himself had lent a hand could they have done materially better. From 1594 onwards he was one of the two or three most important members of his Company. Quite a few years after 1594 he was already well to do. He ceased writing for the stage when he was about forty-six. After that he had some half a dozen years of leisure. Why did he not edit his own Plays and anticipate that volume of Ben Jonson's *Works* which appeared in the year of his own death? I think we may find two reasons, or perhaps two aspects of the same reason, which should content us. One of the impressions about Shakespeare which has been strongly forced on me, especially of late, is that he was all of one piece. He developed, but in his development he cast nothing away. His attitude towards life deepened, but his outlook remained the same. I think we may find this consistency in his attitude to his own work as a playwright. It was the well-attested custom of the time for a dramatist to sell his complete rights in his plays to one of the companies of actors, or to some agent acting on their behalf. The actors did what they pleased with the manuscript, abridged it, augmented it, caused it to be written in part or whole exactly as they pleased. It was the custom of the day and was accepted, for even the complaints of the dying Greene are of the inhumanity of the actors in leaving him to die lonely and destitute, rather than of any literary outrage. Shakespeare profited by this custom in his early days. He took over other men's plots, other men's drafts, other men's completed plays, and did to them what he was told, transmuting copper and silver into gold with an alchemy all his own. We applaud what he did, and invent fine phrases to glorify that which, in modern dramatists, we should regard as monstrous. I think at times it was a bit hard on the men whose work he used, and that from our latter-day point of view it is an act of piety, not only to them, but to Shakespeare, to give them credit for what we can trace of theirs. But it was the custom of the day thus to take over plots and ideas and rehandle and improve them. Shakespeare profited by it in his youth; he did not protest against it in his old age. He could have collected his own plays, expunged from them all that was not his, and prepared them for the press. As far as we know, or have any reason to guess, he did nothing of the kind. He had sold his work to the actors, and it was theirs to do with it what they would. He had seen no harm in trying to better other men's work; let other men better his—if they could. Because he took this course in his prosperous old age, the Ghost of Greene can have had no terrors for him. But the matter goes deeper than this. One dramatist of Shakespeare's day did collect his plays, and edit them himself and dignify his craft by calling them his Works— Ben Jonson. He, too, was consistent. As far as I know he borrowed no plot, took over no scene from any earlier writer. He was an original artist—and he did not forget it or let his audience forget it. He was in a marked degree a self-conscious artist, and his plays are full of his self-consciousness. Do we wish that Shakespeare's plays were more like Ben Jonson's? It has been contended that it is characteristic of the English race that its best work has always been done with a striking absence of any realization of what was being achieved. When we have builded our best, we have never quite understood what we were building. Surely in this Shakespeare was most character-istically one of his race. He was a self-conscious artist in his youthful Poems and Sonnets, and if these alone had survived he would have ranked high among his contem-poraries but hardly have been heard of in lands where English is a foreign tongue. He was utterly unself-conscious in his plays, and his plays have penetrated to the very ends of the earth. It was part of the price of this greatness that he should be careless of them and their fate.

But what a price it might have been! what a Tragedy. And what a magnificent reversal of the ill-fortune which threatened their destruction when, seven years after Shakespeare's death, the Folio appeared with thirty-six plays in it, so many of which had never been in print before! The adventurers were seven, rather a motley little crowd. Two old friends of the theatre, Heminge and Condell, anxious 'to keep the memory of so worthy a friend and fellow alive'; Edward Blount, the faithful friend of Marlowe; William Jaggard, who, as early as 1599, had set so high a value on Shakespeare's name that he had taken part in setting it on the title-page of *The Passionate*

Pilgrim, which contained but five poems of his, and those stolen; Isaac Jaggard, his son; John Smethwick, and William Aspley, who, in 1623, represented the original publishers of several of the Good Quartos, which we are bound to believe were honestly come by. What brought this motley little crew together? Probably Ben Jonson's volume of 1616 put the idea of a Shakespeare volume into men's minds. Shakespeare and Jonson were friends, but their friendship was compatible with a good deal of sparring, and their respective adherents doubtless sparred also. Jonson had collected his plays; why should not Shakespeare's be collected? But 1616, 1617, 1618 passed, and to the best of our knowledge nothing was done. In 1619, when still nothing had happened, William Jaggard seems to have planned with Pavier and Arthur Johnson and Nathaniel Butter, men whose traffic in Shakespeare's plays had been a good deal less reputable than that of those whom Aspley and Smethwick represented, a miscellany of all the plays they could collect by or attributable to Shakespeare. Ten plays were put into print, a curiously strange assortment: 2 and 3 *Henry VI*, not as they appear in the Folio with Shakespeare's final revision, but as printed in 1594 and 1595, with how much or how little of Shakespeare's work in them is never likely to be settled; *Pericles*, in which he had a hand; *A Yorkshire Tragedy*, with which it is incredible that he had anything to do; then five genuine plays, *The Merry Wives of Windsor*, *The Merchant of Venice*, *A Midsummer-Night's Dream*, *King Lear*, and *Henry V*, of which the first and last were reprints of the old piracies; then another play, *Sir John Oldcastle*, which Shakespeare can never have touched. *Henry V* was left anonymous as in the original piratical edition of 1600: on all the other plays, including *A Yorkshire Tragedy* and *Sir John Oldcastle*, Shakespeare's name was printed in full as that of the author. There is clear evidence in the continuous lettering of the sheets of the first three plays that it was originally intended to prefix some sort of collective title-page covering the whole miscellany. There is also bibliographical evidence that by the time *A Yorkshire Tragedy* was in hand this intention was abandoned, and all the last five plays bear the dates of earlier editions (*Henry V* a wrong date, 1608 instead of 1602), a recognized trick in reprinting books liable to be censored. What does it all mean and what has it to do with the First Folio? It means—among other things—that William Jaggard the printer, and the three publishers, Pavier, Johnson, and Butter, were convinced that Shakespeare's name would sell a miscellany even of this kind, and (as I view the evidence) that their unscrupulous faith convinced the honest men at the Globe Theatre that they must at last get to work. When men are hesitating to take up a venture there is no greater spur to action than to see some one else trying to forestall them, and this spur, I think, the volume of 1619 supplied to the organizers of the Folio. In an adventurous article in *The Literary Supplement* to *The Times* (22 March 1923) Mr. Crompton Rhodes has given reasons for believing that the players appealed to the Earl of Pembroke, then Lord Chamberlain, and that the Earl addressed a letter to the Master and Wardens of the Company of Stationers, advising them 'to take order for the stay of any further impression of any of the playes or interludes of his majesties servants without their consent'. But William Jaggard, Pavier, Johnson, and Butter were all men of some hardihood, difficult to suppress, and in the end Jaggard and his son, possibly after some arrangement with their friends, were given the printing of the Folio, and had the pleasure of superintending the setting up of the address 'To the great Variety of Readers, with its denunciation of the frauds and stealthes of iniurious impostors', which they could apply as they liked. We must thank Heminge and Condell for that touch of humour, and for much else besides. As the gatherers of the copy for the Folio, they exercised considerable care. No use was made of any of the Bad Quartos. The sadly late editions of some of the Good Quartos used to save copying were read with prompt-copies or other sources at the playhouse. Manuscripts of all the plays not already in print were hunted out. Ten years hence, I hope, we may know more than we do now as to what these manuscripts were. To-day we can only see that there were real difficulties to contend with and that in one way or another these difficulties were overcome. It was taken for granted that the stage-manager knew his business, and that the form in which each play had survived at the theatre was the form in which it should be preserved in print. There was some rough dividing into acts and scenes, but little other editing—a cause of thankfulness rather than regret. But somehow a text was produced which, however far short it falls of what specialists could wish, has yet been good enough to allow Shakespeare to become the most famous of Englishmen, and the delight of men and women all over the world. Surely these men also builded better than they knew.

Postscript (1932)

Mr. P. A. Daniel's conclusions, to which I allude on pp. 2 and 13, as to the printing of folio texts from late quartos, have been challenged as regards *King Lear*. On p. 7 and elsewhere I should have been wiser to write of 'copies derived from the theatre' rather than specifically of 'prompt-copies', though I think it unreasonable to expect Elizabethan texts for which the status of prompt-copies is claimed to show all the characteristics of the extant prompt-copies of twenty years later. As a possible exception to the statement on page 9 'we have no evidence that any single play by Shakespeare has perished', it might have been well to mention in a footnote *The History of Cardenio*, acted at Court in 1611 and entered on the Stationers' Register (9 Sept. 1653) by the bookseller-publisher Humphrey Moseley, as 'by Mr. Fletcher and Shakespeare', as to which see Sir E. K. Chambers, *William Shakespeare*, i. 539–42. The theory of 'assembled texts' mentioned on p. 10 has since been both extended and strongly disputed. The number of lines assigned to various plays on pp. 12 and 13 was based on the line-numbering in the 'Globe' edition which, as has been pointed out, owing to its narrow columns exaggerates the length of plays containing prose. Much more important than any of these small points are (i) the now pre-valent envisagement of the 'pirated' quartos as the product of actors stranded in the provinces putting together from memory (possibly in some cases with the aid of their 'parts'), plays in which they had acted, not with any immediate intention of selling their reconstructed texts for printing, but that they might have an additional play to act, and (ii) the addition to these 'bad' quartos, by Mr. Peter Alexander (*Shakespeare's Henry VI and Richard III*, Cambridge Univ. Press, 1929), of *The First Part of the Contention betwixt the two famous Houses of York and Lancaster* (1594) and *The true Tragedie of Richard Duke of York* (1595), as memorial reconstructions of the plays printed in the folio as *The Second* (and *Third*) *Part of King Henry VI*. If this explanation be accepted (as I have argued in my introduction to Mr. Alexander's book, that it should be), Shakespeare had much less cause to think of the Ghost of Greene than seemed probable when I was writing my lecture. We must look for other causes for his apparent lack of interest in the fate of his plays. But our grounds for thankfulness for the goodness of the materials for his text which have been preserved are now regarded as even greater than I contended.

THE DISINTEGRATION OF SHAKE-SPEARE[1]

By E. K. CHAMBERS, C.B.

THE rock of Shakespeare's reputation stands four-square to the winds of Time. But the waves of criticism beat perpetually about its base, and at intervals we must stand back and re-affirm our vision of the structural outlines. It is perhaps in itself a tribute to the wide appeal of the poet that so much of what is written about him is ill-informed and ill-balanced. Small minds are caught by, and fail to comprehend, that greatness and that variability. Hence the scouring of the *Dictionary of National Biography* for an alternative author, preferably aristocratic, of the plays. With these paradoxes I do not propose to concern myself. Doubtless they should be refuted, that the people be not deceived, but the task must be left to some one with a better temper for the patient anatomizing of human follies. This is but the spindrift on the face of the rock.

I propose to consider certain critical tendencies which, in their extreme manifestations, offer results hardly less perturbing than those with which the Baconians and their kin would make our flesh creep. This is the argument. Here are thirty-six plays handed down as Shakespeare's. You can put them in approximate chronological order, and arrive at a conception of the author's trend of development, both in mental outlook and in habits of diction and versification. But a closer analysis often reveals the co-existence in one and the same play of features belonging to different stages of the development, and sometimes of features which it is difficult to place in the line of development at all. Moreover, an examination of the texts shows

---

[1] Delivered in 1924. Save for the addition of three footnotes, this lecture is here reprinted as originally published in 1924.

such eccentricities and dislocations as to raise a doubt whether they can have come to us just as Shakespeare left them. Tracing these clues, our critics arrive at three results, on which varying degrees of stress are laid. Firstly, the extant texts, many of them not printed until several years after Shakespeare's death, have often been altered or abbreviated by other hands. Secondly, Shakespeare revised his plays, and the extant texts sometimes contain fragments of different recensions, in juxtaposition or overlay. Thirdly, the process of revision by Shakespeare was not confined to his own work; he also rehandled the work of other men, and left some or much of it standing in the texts. And if you ask how far this process of revision went, and whether it seriously qualifies the accepted Shakespearian authorship of the plays, you do not get reassuring answers. One man will tell you frankly that in many plays which you thought characteristically Shakespearian—*Richard II*, *Henry V*, *Julius Caesar*, for example—Shakespeare's part was quite subordinate. Another will fence with the issue, and explain that the conception of individual authorship is not altogether applicable to Elizabethan plays. The playing companies kept standing texts in their repertories, and one man after another brought them up to date, often over a long period of years, as theatrical needs required or literary fashions changed, so that a drama must really be thought of as an impersonal or communal affair, like a folk-lyric.

Well, you cannot brush away these speculations quite so easily as you can those of the Baconians. Keen wits are at work; well-equipped and painstaking minds have stated their theories—their heresies, if you will—and they demand scrutiny. We must follow the *Logos* where it leads. Obviously, one cannot take the matter far in an isolated lecture. Each of the impugned plays requires its individual examination. This must be based upon a patient analysis of the texts available. It must take account of what can be gleaned of the literary habits of the time; of the possibilities of sophistication latent in the activities of stage book-keepers and adapters, of copyists, of censors, of compositors and correctors of the press. The disintegrating critics give us no less; we owe them no less. I can only hope to make some general survey of the ground, and to chart some of the avenues of approach.

The traditional canon of the plays has a five-fold basis. Thirty-six plays were ascribed to Shakespeare in the First Folio. Thirteen of these had already been printed as his in quarto. Eleven had been ascribed to him by Francis Meres in 1598. Five are ascribed to him by other contemporaries.[1] This is external evidence. There is also such internal evidence as the plays themselves bear to the presence of a single 'shaping spirit of imagination'. It is, of course, primarily this internal evidence which the disintegrators, at this and that point, dispute. The external evidence they have merely to explain away. You can always explain away a historical record, with a sufficient licence of conjecture as to the *mala fides* of its origin. The earliest whisper against the authenticity of any play in the canon comes, I think, from Edward Ravenscroft. Ravenscroft adapted *Titus Andronicus* after the Restoration, and, when he printed it in 1687, said that he had been told by 'some anciently conversant with the stage' that the model was not originally Shakespeare's, 'but brought by a private author to be acted, and he only gave some master touches to one or two of the principal parts or characters'. We do not know who were Ravenscroft's informants. At least one old actor, William Beeston, whose father had been a 'fellow' of Shakespeare, and who may himself have known Shakespeare in his boyhood, survived to 1682. A true report is not, therefore, inconceivable. Eighteenth-century scepticism was not slow to seize upon this notion of revisional work by Shakespeare, and to give it a further extension. You find the substantial Shakespearian authorship of *Comedy of Errors*, *Love's Labour's Lost*, and oddly enough *Winter's Tale*, doubted by Pope (1725), of *Henry V*

---

[1] *Romeo and Juliet* and *Richard II* or *III*, by John Weever; *Hamlet*, by Gabriel Harvey; *Julius Caesar* and *Winter's Tale*, by Ben Jonson.

by Theobald (1734), of *Two Gentlemen of Verona* by Hanmer (1743), of *Richard II* by Johnson (1765), of *Taming of the Shrew* by Farmer (1767). It would be idle to raise the dust of the resultant controversies, in which the conservative side was taken by Edward Capell. The assailants were confident and impressionist. Ritson tells us that in *Two Gentlemen*, *Love's Labour's Lost*, and *Richard II*, 'Shakespeare's new work is as apparent as the brightest touches of Titian would be on the poorest performance of the veriest canvas spoiler that ever handled a brush'. The mutterings were largely silenced by the authority of Malone, who accepted Ravenscroft's account of *Titus Andronicus*, worked out the relation of 2 and 3 *Henry VI* to the *Contention* plays, took Shakespeare for their reviser, supposed *Henry VIII* to have undergone revision by a later hand, and beyond these only doubted *1 Henry VI*, the admission of which to the Folio he explained by Shakespeare's contribution of the Talbot scenes. Pope and the rest had been misled by inadequate attention to the chronology of the plays, which Malone was himself the first to study in detail, and by a consequent failure to distinguish between the criteria applicable to Shakespeare's juvenile and to his mature work. Malone's conclusions determined critical orthodoxy for the best part of a century. There were individual dissentients, notably Coleridge, who questioned much of *Richard III* and the 'low soliloquy' of the Porter in *Macbeth*, and declared in his table-talk, 'I think I could point out to half a line what is really Shakespeare's in *Love's Labour's Lost* and some other of the not entirely genuine plays'. Coleridge being Coleridge, it is needless to say that he never performed this task. Charles Knight (*c.* 1843) suggested that Shakespeare was only a reviser of *Timon of Athens*; James Spedding and Alfred Tennyson (*c.* 1850) fixed the second hand in *Henry VIII* as that of Fletcher; and William George Clark, and William Aldis Wright (1874) elaborated Coleridge's heresy about *Macbeth* by ascribing substantial interpolations in that play to Middleton.

Modern criticism of the canon, however, mainly owes its origin to F. G. Fleay, whose views, after fluttering the dove-cotes of the New Shakspere Society, were collected in his *Shakespeare Manual* (1876), thereafter underwent Protean transformations, and took final shape in his *Life and Work of Shakespeare* (1886). Fleay had read widely in dramatic literature, and had made a close study of the early texts, the diction, and particularly the versification, of Shakespeare. He came to distrust the received chronology, because it assigned single dates to plays which seemed to him to bear stylistic marks of more than one period. And he arrived at a theory of constant rehandling and of the coexistence in the texts of strata belonging to different dates. This he applied, at one time or another, and with frequent variations in the dates assigned, to thirteen of the thirty-six plays: *Comedy of Errors, Two Gentlemen, Love's Labour's Lost, Romeo and Juliet, Midsummer-Night's Dream, Richard II, Much Ado, Hamlet, Merry Wives, Twelfth Night, All's Well, Troilus and Cressida, Cymbeline.* As to the occasions of such revision he speaks with an uncertain voice. One group of plays may have been re-written, either for stage revival or for publication. Of another he suggests that fragments left unfinished at an early date were completed a decade later. But this notion is abandoned in favour of a supposed desire to replace work of an early coadjutor by Shakespeare's own. It is an easy step from Shakespeare as a reviser of Shakespeare to Shakespeare as a reviser of predecessors, Fleay distributed and redistributed *Henry VI, Richard III*, and *Titus Andronicus* among Shakespeare, Marlowe, Greene, Peele, Lodge, and Kyd; found much of Lodge and a little of Drayton in *Taming of the Shrew*, traces of Peele in *Romeo and Juliet*, traces of Kyd in *Hamlet*, debris of Dekker and Chettle in *Troilus and Cressida*. He pressed the doctrine of Middleton in *Macbeth*, but became doubtful about it; thought the second hand in *Timon* Tourneur's, and dropped him lightly for Wilkins; supposed the mask in *The Tempest* an interpolation by Beaumont. Perhaps his most revolutionary hypothesis was upon *Julius Caesar*, which he held to have been abridged and altered by Ben Jonson, as an appropriate return for an equally conjectural contribution by Shakespeare to a lost version of *Sejanus*. We approach the point where scholarship merges itself in romance. I desire to speak with respect and even kindness of Fleay, from whom, in common with many others, I derived an early stimulus to these studies. He was a man of fertile and ingenious mind. He laid his finger upon many of the bibliographical and stylistic features of the plays which loom large in current speculations. But he had a demon of inaccuracy, which was unfortunate, as he relied largely upon statistics. And he betrayed an imperfect sense of responsibility, both in advancing destructive notions without an adequate support of argument, and in withholding the explanations and justifications required by his own numerous and sometimes disconcerting changes of opinion. His self-confidence has hypnotized his successors, and many of his improvisations recur in the works of serious students, not to speak of those schoolbooks, compiled at starvation wages for competitive publishers, which do so much in our day for the dissemination of critical and historical error.

The mantle of Mr. Fleay has descended upon Mr. J. M. Robertson, who disposes its flying skirts into the decent folds of a logical system. His method of approach to his problems is uniform. It has three stages, upon each of which I shall have a cautionary note later. He begins with impressionist judgements. Certain passages do not answer to his conception of Shakespeare. Here is braggadocio, there an archaic stiffness, or flatness, or hackwork, or clumsy stage-craft, or pointless humour, or turgidity of thought, or falsity of moral sentiment. Or a whole play repels him. One reads like 'a mosaic of disparate parts'; in another he gets 'a strange feeling' about the general style. Then he proceeds to confirm his impressions by applying what he calls the 'inexorable' tests of treatment, style, and metrics; in particular, tests based upon the chronological phases of Shakespeare's blank verse. Finally, he settles down to look for 'clues' to the possible presence of alien hands; clues furnished by the use of words rare in Shakespeare's vocabulary, but traceable in the writings of other men; clues derived from characteristic tricks of phrase or tendencies in the handling of typical situations. It is all logical enough, given certain major premises, largely disputable. First you decide that Shakespeare cannot be present; then you look for the intruder. Mr. Robertson has now covered most of his ground, and tells us that, although he still has to dispose of *Cymbeline* and *The Tempest*, we are at a point where the 'idolater'—that is to say the man who believes in Shakespeare's authorship of the plays, more or less as they stand 'had probably heard what he would term "the worst" '. The worst, however, amounts to an alien invasion. In the front of a rather dim background of collaborations and revisions stand the two heroic figures, Marlowe and Chapman. I will disregard the ancient battle-fields of *Henry VI* and *Titus Andronicus*, for the campaign has now become more serious. If I understand Mr. Robertson aright, Marlowe, more than any other man, is predominantly the author of *Richard III*, *Richard II*, *Henry V*, *Julius Caesar*, and paradoxically enough *Comedy of Errors*, even in the forms in which they have reached us. Peele and Greene play minor parts, but the *Two Gentlemen* is substantially Greene's, and work of his remains embedded in *Taming of the Shrew* and *All's Well*. I gather that Peele is to be similarly revealed in *Cymbeline*. And both men, together with Kyd, Jonson, and the shades of many of Philip Henslowe's hungry troop of hack writers, Chettle, Dekker, Drayton, Heywood, and Munday, are evoked as possible contributors to a series of drafts and recasts, which the Marlovian work has undergone. Ultimately, of course, the Marlovian plays passed into the hands of Shakespeare, and they show traces of revision by him, which, however, was often limited to a little retouching or the insertion of particular speeches or scenes, 'substantially preserved' the

original *Richard II*, and even in *Henry V* did not amount
to 'vital rehandling'. Chapman, too, was among the intermediate manipulators of the earlier plays. But when
Marlowe passes out of the chronicle, Chapman becomes a
protagonist. His unquiet spirit flies like a lambent but
smoky flame over all the later part of the canon. He may
have inserted the mask into *The Tempest* after Shakespeare
left it. But in the main, his work underlies, rather than
overlies, Shakespeare's, in the form of drafts or contribu-
tions to drafts of plays, sometimes themselves mere recasts,
which Shakespeare afterwards rewrote as *Hamlet*, *Merry
Wives*, *All's Well*, *Measure for Measure*, *Troilus and
Cressida*, *Timon*, and *Pericles*. To Chapman I will return.
The complicated nature of Mr. Robertson's reconstructions and their relation to Fleay's may be illustrated by the
case of *Julius Caesar*. Marlowe is conjectured to have
written a sequence of three plays: a *Caesar and Pompey*,
a *Caesar's Tragedy*, a *Caesar's Revenge*. These passed to
the Admiral's men at the Rose, who revived *Caesar and
Pompey*, and *Caesar's Tragedy*, after some revision of the
latter by Chapman and Drayton, as their two-part *Caesar
and Pompey* of 1594–5. The first part was now laid aside
and rewritten later by Chapman as his *Caesar and Pompey*,
printed in 1631. Marlowe's original third play, *Caesar's
Revenge*, was perhaps recast by Dekker, Drayton, Middleton, Munday, and Webster, in the *Caesar's Fall* or *The
Two Shapes*, which they wrote for the Admiral's in 1602.
However this may be, the *Tragedy* and the *Revenge*, now
containing the work of from three to seven hands, were
transferred by the Admiral's to the Chamberlain's company, and were revised for the latter, still in a two-play
form, by Shakespeare. Finally, perhaps about 1607, the
two plays were compressed into the one now extant by
Ben Jonson, who added some touches of his own in a
characteristic anti-Caesarian vein. More of the present
substance is allowed to Shakespeare than in some of the
Marlovian plays retrieved from the canon by Mr. Robertson; but the primitive Marlowe still shows through the

overlay, notably in the speeches of Antony over the body of Caesar. It is entertaining to find that another recent critic, Mr. William Wells, also traces the origin of *Julius Caesar* to Marlowe. But he ascribes the revision, not to Chapman or to Jonson, but to Francis Beaumont, and only allows Shakespeare the first 57 lines of the play, lines which Mr. Robertson thinks un-Shakespearian. Evidently the disintegration of Shakespeare is an open career for talent.

Looking back over the results of Mr. Robertson's de-vastating offensive, I am tempted to quote my friend A. H. Bullen's comment upon a more modest raid. 'If this goes on', he said, 'Shakespeare will soon, like his own Lord Timon,

> be left a naked gull,
> Which flashes now a phoenix.'

Mr. Robertson will certainly reply that, even if witty, this is not fair. He is no despoiler of Shakespeare's authentic plumage. His eliminations touch nothing 'save inferior or second-rate work'; have not 'impugned one of the great plays as a whole, or a really great speech in any'. On the contrary, it is the sticklers for the canon who detract from Shakespeare's greatness. Battling for quantity, they sacri-fice quality. 'The *vin ordinaire* of the Elizabethan drama is for them indistinguishable from the vintage of the Master.' In particular, if they will not recognize Marlowe in *Richard II* or Greene in the *Two Gentlemen*, they are driven back on the alternative theory of a Shakespeare in bondage to a humiliating trick of mimicry, a 'parrot' Shakespeare, a 'sedulous ape'. This brings me to the first of my cautionary notes upon the successive steps in Mr. Robertson's critical progress. They are, you remember, three; the disquieting impressions, the 'inexorable' tests, the 'clues' to other men. I am sure that Mr. Robertson desires to exalt and not to depreciate Shakespeare. And that is precisely where the mischief lies. Our heresiarch, in fact, is himself an idolater. We have all of us, in the long run, got to form our conception of the 'authentic'

Shakespeare by means of an abstraction from the whole of the canon; there is no other material. Mr. Robertson abstracts through a series of rejections. He is repelled by childish work, by imitative work, by repetitive work, by conventional work, by unclarified work, by clumsy construction, by baldness or bombast. He idealizes. He looks for a Shakespeare always at the top of his achievement. This seems to me quite an arbitrary process. I cannot so read the record. Magic of phrase, lyrical impulse, pervasive humour, intuition of character, the clash of drama, a questing philosophy, a firm hold on the ultimate values of life: you are never far from one or other of these at any turn in Shakespeare. But these are not the whole warp and woof of the plays. We cannot be blind to the moments of artistic oblivion or carelessness, where the brain flags or the insight fails; to the trivial scenes where quibble speaks to the boxes or horse-play to the pit; to the exasperating scenes where psychological realism makes ugly nonsense of a romantic convention; to the perfunctory scenes which amount to no more than commonplace Elizabethan dramatic carpentry. We cannot leave these out of the account; if we do, we may get an ideal, but we lose Shakespeare. Of course I can construct apologies. There are inconsistencies of narrative and time-sequence. A practical playwright knows very well that these attract little attention on the stage, although they reveal themselves to the student poring over a printed text in his study. There are jests and wit-combats which do not seem to have the ghost of a laugh left in them. What is there so fleeting, so difficult to transmit from one age to another, as that phosphoric iridescence upon the surface of social life which we call wit? But I am not looking for apologies. I come to accept Shakespeare, not to praise him. Obviously there are things in the plays which any other Elizabethan could just as well, or just as badly, have written. They do not perturb me, as they perturb Mr. Robertson, to the point of searching for clues to another man. Perhaps Mr. Robertson will reply that I have not fully met his case; that it is not so much the passages of unmannered carpenter's work which give him pause, as passages which have a manner, but a manner which he cannot feel to be Shakespeare's, and does feel, when he analyses it, to be that of a Marlowe or of a Chapman. Here we are on more difficult ground. But it is part of the character of Shakespeare, as I read it in the canon, to be an experimentalist in style. I cannot regard the many phases through which his writing went in the short span of some twenty years as wholly due to a growth in which there was nothing deliberate. I discern abrupt beginnings and abrupt discontinuances. And he was receptive, as well as creative. I can suppose him experimenting in the manner of Marlowe, or even of poor Greene. And I can suppose him, much later, playing with stylistic elements, which had struck him in the work of Chapman, and ultimately dismissing them as, on the whole, unprofitable.

We come now to the 'inexorable' tests. These are largely metrical, based upon the familiar tables, compiled by Fleay and others, which put in statistical form the relative frequencies in each play of certain features of Shakespeare's versification, and notably the percentages of rhymes, double endings, and overflowing lines. I do not undervalue these features as elements in determining the chronology of the plays. No doubt there was a period— —not, I think, his earliest period—in which Shakespeare made free use of rhyme; and thereafter even occasional rhymes dwindle. Even more important is an increasing tendency to escape from the tyranny of the 'drumming decasyllabon', and to emphasize the verse paragraph rather than the individual line, by the help of such devices as the double ending and a varied and subtle distribution of pauses. The tables need to be used with great discretion. Fleay's methods, in particular, were never 'inexorable'. His earliest tables were grossly inaccurate. He published a revised set, obscurely, in the book of another man.[1] I have spent much time, which might, perhaps, have been

[1] C. M. Ingleby, *Shakespeare, the Man and the Book*, Part II (1881).

better employed, in checking some of these.[1] They are still inaccurate, but less so. It is disquieting to find that little handbooks of facts about Shakespeare, compiled by distinguished scholars, still reproduce the unrevised tables as authoritative. Other tables, due to Goswin König, give only ratios and not the counts upon which they are based. This does not inspire confidence. If statistical precision were material, the calculations would probably have to be done afresh. I do not think that it is material. The tests cannot give an exact chronology; in fact, different tests do not give the same chronology. They can only indicate a trend of development, and the trend may be diverted in any play by accidents of subject-matter, such as refractory personal names which have to be coerced into the metre; by the appropriateness of particular rhythms to scenes of particular temper; above all, by Shakespeare's experimentalism, which certainly extends to rhythm. It does not therefore trouble me to find a rather high percentage of double endings in such early plays as *Comedy of Errors* and *Two Gentlemen of Verona*, and then to find the curve dropping through *Midsummer-Night's Dream*, *King John*, and *1 Henry IV*, and then rising again with *2 Henry IV* and other plays. But it does trouble Mr. Robertson, and, as he is debarred from putting *Comedy of Errors* and *Two Gentlemen* later in the chronological order, because that would throw out the overflow curve, he falls back upon a theory that they are mainly the work of other writers with metrical habits different from Shakespeare's. This longing for a smoothly progressive curve is only one aspect of a general tendency to seek an unimpeded development in Shakespeare's art. There is a philosophical predisposition behind. Mr. Robertson dislikes the idea of what he calls a 'cerebral cataclysm'. To suppose that Shakespeare passed suddenly from the merely average and imitative merit of *Two Gentlemen* to the 'supreme poetic competence' of *Midsummer-Night's Dream* is contrary to a doctrine which sees in 'artistic growth as in other organic phenomena a

1 Cf. my *William Shakespeare* (1930), ii. 397.

process of evolution'. I do not know whether the latest theories of organic evolution have solved that old *crux* of the emergence of variations. But in any case biological analogies do not help us very directly in analysing the development of the creative impulse in human consciousness. And when Mr. Robertson expresses himself as taken aback by the notion of 'a literary miracle of genius elicited by some sudden supernatural troubling of the waters', I can only reply that he has given an admirable description of the way in which genius does in fact often appear to effloresce.

I have not quite done with the percentages. Obviously they have no value, unless they are worked upon a sufficient number of lines to allow a fair average to establish itself. This is common to all statistics. The ratio of blue eyes to black ones throughout England has a statistical meaning; the ratio in your house or mine may have a meaning, but it is not statistical. Possibly the two or three thousand lines of a play leave room for the averaging of double endings. But to work the percentage of double endings in a single speech or scene leads to nothing. Or rather, it should lead to nothing. It does sometimes lead Mr. Robertson to infer that scenes in a play which give very different percentages cannot have been written by the same hand, or at least by the same hand at the same date. Surely this is an illegitimate inference. If a play has 25 per cent. of double endings, they are not spread evenly at the rate of one double ending in every four lines.[1] They come in nuggets here; there are considerable spaces without them. Largely this is mere accident; they just fall so. But clearly that adaptation of rhythm to subject-matter, which may qualify the general trend of metric development in a whole play, is even more potent in single passages. Here are two examples. The first scene of *King John* is

---

[1] I am told that the term 'double endings' puzzled some of my hearers. They are also called 'feminine endings', and are those in which the stressed second syllable of the last foot of a line is followed by an additional unstressed syllable.

largely a discussion of the paternity of the Bastard Faul-conbridge. And the rhetoric requires the emphatic use of the words 'father', 'mother', 'brother', at the ends of lines. These words account for about half the double endings in the scene, and the percentage, which for the play as a whole is 6, goes up in this scene to 16. Take again *Coriolanus*, a play which Mr. Robertson has not yet assailed, or expressed an intention of assailing. The double ending percentage is 28. But in v. iii is a passage of twenty-four lines without one double ending and another of thirty-five lines with only three. One contains the stately inter-change of courtesies between Coriolanus and his wife and mother on their entry to Corioli; the other the more solemn part of Volumnia's appeal to her son. Are these, therefore, un-Shakespearian or debris of early Shakespearian work?

My third cautionary note is on the final stage of Mr. Robertson's process, the quest for alien hands, with the clues of vocabulary and phraseology. Here I will be brief, for the land is unmapped and the footing treacherous. Are we really able to ascribe a distinctive diction to each of Shakespeare's predecessors? Do they not largely, together with the young Shakespeare himself, use a com-mon poetic diction, much of it ultimately traceable to Spenser and to Sidney? We could tell better, if we knew more clearly what each of them wrote and did not write. The problem seems to me one which calls for exploration upon a general and disinterested method, rather than along the casual lines of advance opened up by the pursuit of an author for this or that suspected or anonymous play. The relation of Shakespeare's maturer diction to Chap-man's is a problem of a somewhat different kind. There is not much point in a controversy as to which was the greater neologist. They both innovate freely, and apparently in much the same manner; and, as far as I know, Shakespeare at least was not likely to have had any scruple about using neologisms not of his own mintage. If he borrowed his plots, why should he not borrow his words? Nobody would suppose that he could not mint them fast enough, if he wanted to. It certainly does not move me to be told that Chapman must have worked over a scene, because it contains words not found elsewhere in Shakespeare, but found half a dozen times in Chapman. The oftener Chapman used a word, the more likely it was to stick in Shakespeare's memory. But Chapman is the recurrent *deus ex machina* of Mr. Robertson's speculations upon half a dozen plays of the canon. Writing about *Hamlet*, he formulates a theory of

'A frequent employment of Chapman by Shakespeare's company either as a draftsman or as an adapter of plays, and as a "repairer" or patcher of some; and the corollary that Shakespeare, often revising Chapman's work, which he must frequently have found trying, might very well let pass, as appealing to sections of the audience, *genre* and other work which he for his own part would never have thought of penning.'

It all seems to have begun with *Timon*, and here a more intimate relation between the poets is revealed. *Timon* is a play 'imperfectly drafted' by Chapman and 'imperfectly revised' by Shakespeare. Mr. Robertson, like some others, thinks that Chapman was the 'rival poet' of the *Sonnets* and the Holophernes of *Love's Labour's Lost*. But this was merely a 'humorous quarrel with his testy rival', and after all the two men 'had a common patron', and 'there is no difficulty in conceiving that, with or without the patron's intervention, Shakespeare's company may have bought a play of Chapman's for Shakespeare to adapt'. We are bidden to remember that Chapman was poor and that Shakespeare must have seen that he was 'worth helping'. The greater poet had 'no artistic jealousy', and knew that 'the quality of mercy is not strained', and 'even if Chapman had ruffled him somewhat by his pedantic asperities, he of all men best knew the human struggle behind the "paste-board portico", the weakness under the shining armour of literary bravado'. Mr. Robertson is an austere rationalist, but I think that this little fantasy would have evoked comment even in the pages of Shakespeare's more sentimental biographers. However this may be, I find it difficult to fit this employment of Chapman by Shakespeare's company into the probabilities of literary history. We know a good deal about Chapman, at any rate from about 1596, when he begins to appear in Henslowe's diary. He wrote, or began to write, seven plays for the Admiral's men during the next three years, of which two were published, and one was a considerable financial success. And he is conspicuous in Henslowe's motley crew as the one who held most aloof from anything in the way of collaboration. The only exception is a play which he undertook, but quite possibly never finished, on a plot by Ben Jonson. About 1599 he drops out of Henslowe's record, and the next decade is covered by a long series of nine plays, all of which were published, for the boy companies. One of these was written in collaboration with Jonson and Marston. Thereafter, so far as we know, Chapman abandoned stage-writing, and devoted himself to his translation of Homer and to other non-dramatic work. In 1613, however, he did a mask for the Princess Elizabeth's wedding. He lived to 1634, and it is conceivable that in Caroline days he touched up some of his early plays, or lent a hand to the younger playwright, Shirley. The only trace of any external evidence for a connexion of Chapman with the Chamberlain's or King's men is the ascription to him by the publisher Moseley, in 1654, of *Alphonsus Emperor of Germany*. Hardly any one now believes that he wrote *Alphonsus*, which was produced at the Blackfriars in 1636, two years after his death, and twenty after Shakespeare's. The Stationers' Register names the author as John Poole.[1] All this is, of course, no proof that Chapman did not write for Shakespeare's company, concurrently with the Admiral's or the boys. A dramatist, who was not himself an actor, was not tied to a single paymaster. But Chapman was evidently a successful writer from 1596 onwards. He is one of the seven

[1] An error, due to the printed *Stationers' Register*. Dr. Greg tells me that the manuscript has, quite clearly, 'John Peele'.

lauded by Webster in 1612. And it does not seem to me likely, on *a priori* grounds, that he would have needed Shakespeare's patronage for an introduction to the company; that no work done by him for them would have reached publication; that his temper would have submitted to constant revision by Shakespeare; or that, if his work proved unsatisfactory, the company would have continued the experiment over half a dozen plays.

I have slipped from the internal to the external evidence on the canon. Mr. Robertson is rather cavalier with the external evidence. Of the Folio editors he says:

'We may pardon the players for obstinately specifying as Shakespeare's works—in order to maintain their hold on the copyrights about which they are so obviously and so naturally anxious—a collection of plays as to which they knew and we know that much of the writing is not Shakespeare's at all.'

I am not concerned to argue for the literal inspiration of the Folio. It is quite conceivable that in some cases a substantial Shakespearian contribution, short of full authorship, may have been held to justify the inclusion of a play. But it was certainly not an undiscriminating collection, since it left out, for one reason or another, no less than nine plays which had already been printed under Shakespeare's name or initials. And what has copyright to do with the matter? I do not know what copyright Mr. Robertson thinks that the players claimed in published plays; but, so far as our knowledge goes, no kind of printing copyright existed, which could be strengthened by ascribing a play to a particular author. As for Francis Meres, he, we are told, 'simply stated the claim of the theatre company, which the Folio enforces'. Meres was a schoolmaster and divine, with an interest in literature, but not, as far as we know, in any relations with the players, such as might lead him to act as their catspaw in a commercial fraud. Even if he went to the players for his list, there is no reason to suppose that they told him anything but the truth. The facts must have been well enough known in the London of 1598, and any false claim for Shakespeare would have been open to the challenge of Chapman or another. The testimony of Meres, even if it stood alone, would be at least as good evidence for Shakespeare's authorship of the early plays of the canon as we have for Peele's authorship of *The Arraignment of Paris* in a casual reference by Nashe, or for Kyd's authorship of *The Spanish Tragedy* in a casual reference by Heywood, or for Marlowe's authorship of *Tamburlaine*, of which there is no contemporary record at all. Yet take away these, and Mr. Robertson's whole elaborate edifice of conjectural ascriptions falls to the ground.

I will now leave Mr. Robertson and his Marlowe and Chapman complexes. I turn to the parallel speculations started by Professor Pollard and pursued by Mr. Dover Wilson in his new edition of the plays. Here the problem of the canon is approached from another angle. The emphasis is less upon versification and diction than upon critical bibliography; the study of printing-house usage in handling copy, of the relation which the copy for the plays may have borne to Shakespeare's autograph, of the changes which that copy may have undergone before and after it reached his hands. The methods of critical bibliography are a notable addition to the equipment of scholarship. But scepticism may be permitted as to whether they really carry the superstructure of theory about the revision of the canonical plays, which Mr. Wilson is piling upon them. His work is, of course, only beginning. It has now covered seven of the comedies, and not one of them is allowed to be an integral and untouched product of Shakespeare's creative energy, in the form in which he first conceived and wrought it. Inevitably I throw Mr. Wilson's cautious and modestly expressed hypotheses into more categorical statements. *Comedy of Errors* is 'of Shakespeare's writing in the main', but it is a revision of an older play, perhaps the *Historie of Error* given by a boy company at court in 1577; and of this parts have been retained, including the doggerel, none of which is Shakespeare's. Moreover, the extant text is an abridgement made in the playhouse by two distinct scribes. *Two*

Gentlemen is also an abridgement, with passages added by the adapter, who contributed the whole character of Speed. *Love's Labour's Lost* was based by Shakespeare upon a play by a writer of the 'eighties. He himself gave it a revision, and may then have eliminated bits of the original which he at first let stand. Traces of the first Shakespearian version are left, owing to imperfect cancellation in the copy. The Folio text shows some further playhouse alteration. *Much Ado* contains two strata of Shakespearian work, and has therefore also been revised. There is no obvious indication of a second hand, although an earlier play may have served as a source. Here again there are playhouse alterations in the Folio text. *Merry Wives* is a transformation by Shakespeare, 'perhaps, with help from others', of an earlier play, *The Jealous Comedy*, of which parts remain. There may have been an intermediate version. I do not understand Mr. Wilson to regard *The Jealous Comedy* as Shakespeare's own. In *Measure for Measure*, Shakespeare may only have recast an old play, with a history going back to Whetstone's *Promos and Cassandra*. But the text, as we have it, has undergone a double adaptation by later hands; firstly an abridgement, secondly an expansion, accompanied by the re-writing of Shakespearian verse-scenes as prose. Finally, *The Tempest* has had a pre-history and a post-history. Substantially, it is a late recast by Shakespeare of an earlier play, perhaps his own, and at this recast, matter originally played in scenes before the wreck has been put into narrative form. Then the recast has itself been abridged, mainly by Shakespeare, and into the abridgement has been inserted the mask, the authorship of which is left undetermined. Mr. Wilson does not, it will be seen, extrude Shakespeare from any of the seven comedies in as wholesale a fashion as that in which Mr. Robertson extrudes him from *Richard II* or *Henry V*. But he finds much alloy due to earlier versions and much alloy due to later adaptations; and these, together with the habit ascribed to Shakespeare of revising his own work, produce sufficiently ambiguous results.

Implicit in it all is the doctrine of continuous copy. The foundation of this doctrine has, I think, four corner-stones. The first is a notion of theatrical precaution and economy; precaution in not having too many copies of a play about, lest one should fall into the hands of a rival company; economy, in avoiding unnecessary expenditure upon copyist's charges. The second is the actual condition of a particular manuscript which has been preserved, that of *Sir Thomas More*. This has been plausibly shown by Dr. Greg to have been originally written out in a single hand; then altered in several other hands, partly by cancellations and marginal insertions on the original pages, and partly by tearing off some of the original pages and substituting separate slips; then submitted to a censor and marked by him with directions for the modification of disallowed passages; and finally, or at an earlier stage, gone through by a stage-manager, who added some technical notes for the production. Thirdly, there is the obvious re-writing, scene for scene, of the *Contention of York and Lancaster* as 2 and 3 *Henry VI*.[1] And, fourthly, there is the courageous attempt of Professor Pollard and Mr. Wilson themselves to explain the relation of the 'bad' to the 'good' quartos of certain Shakespearian plays by a theory which entails the progressive revision of lost versions. And so we arrive at the notion of the long-lived manuscript in the tiring-house wardrobe, periodically taken out for a revival and as often worked upon by fresh hands, abridged and expanded, recast to fit the capabilities of new performers, brightened with current topical allusions, written up to date to suit new tastes in poetic diction. Additional scenes may be inserted. If the old pages will no longer hold the new matter, they may be mutilated and replaced by partial transcripts. In the end hardly a single line may remain as it was in the beginning. Yet, in a sense, it is the same play, even as our human bodies, the cellular matter of which is continuously

[1] I now (1932) take a different view of this; cf. my *William Shakespeare*, i. 281.

renewed, remain our bodies from the cradle to the grave. A perpetual form; an evanescent ὕλη! Who is the author of such a play? We cannot tell. The soul gets a 'dusty answer', when hot on that particular certainty.

Again I will attempt one or two general propositions bearing upon the issue. I feel some doubt whether the case of *Sir Thomas More* is altogether typical; whether, that is to say, the Master of the Revels would as a rule have been willing to accept for reading a play in the state of picturesque confusion which characterizes that famous document. Professor Pollard, I gather, thinks that he would, and explains it by a reference to 'the easy temper of English officialdom at all periods'. Well, Mr. Pollard is an English official, and so am I, and that is the kind of compliment we bandy between ourselves. Comments in a different tone sometimes drift in to us from the outside world. I am sure, however, that if the Master of the Revels had to tackle many manuscripts like *Sir Thomas More*, that progressive increase in his emoluments, which is a feature in the history of the office during the seventeenth century, was well justified. And personally I feel that his instinct would have been to call for clean transcripts. Clean transcripts would, of course, be fatal to the doctrine of continuous copy in its extreme form, and in the preparation of them most of the bibliographical evidence, upon which Mr. Wilson relies to prove the revision of plays, would disappear. That any substantial revision, as distinct perhaps from a mere abridgement, would entail a fresh application for the Master's allowance must, I think, be taken for granted. The rule was that his hand must be 'at the latter end of the booke they doe play'; and in London, at least, any company seriously departing from the allowed book would run a considerable risk.[1]

---

[1] This raises a further question. Did the Master himself keep copies of allowed books for purposes of control? Certainly Herbert laid down in 1633 that such copies must be furnished to him by the book-keepers, but it is not clear whether he was establishing a new, or asserting an old, practice. A reference to the burning of Sir George Buck's books

Whether the manuscript of *Sir Thomas More* is typical or not, Mr. Wilson has, of course, no such direct evidence for any play of the canon. He supplies its place by pointing to indications of what he calls 'bibliographical disturbance' in the early editions, departures from typographical uniformity, such as the use for printer's copy of an analogous revised manuscript might explain. There are passages written as blank verse, but set up by the printer as prose. There are incomplete lines of verse, taken by Mr. Wilson as signs of 'cuts'. There are passages which duplicate one another and suggest the accidental survival of alternative versions. There are variations of nomenclature in speech-headings and stage-directions, which may betray composition by different hands or at different dates. It may be observed that, while bibliography can constitute the existence of these phenomena, and can sometimes contribute to an explanation of them from a knowledge of printing-house methods, it can by no means always give a full explanation. And then the bibliographer, like the rest of us, has to fall back upon what he can learn or guess of the methods of the tiring-house, or upon his own insight into literary psychology. Thus the setting up of verse as prose is explained, prettily enough, as due to the failure of compositors to appreciate the metrical character of insertions written continuously in cramped margins. But if you ask why any particular insertion was made, bibliography is dumb. Mr. Wilson tends to guess that it was made as part of a general revision. I find myself often guessing that it was only an after-thought at the time of original writing. Similarly, a broken line may be, and I dare say often is, due to a 'cut', but it may also be a mere rhythmical variation and it may often indicate a dramatic pause, for reflection or the insertion of stage business. And it is not bibliographical knowledge, but a feeling for rhythm and dramatic values, that must determine the

suggests the latter. But this also is obscure; it is possible that these were not books kept by Buck, but licensed by him, and burnt at the Fortune in 1621.

most likely explanation in each case. Mr. Wilson is, of course, just as well qualified to apply the literary as the bibliographical criteria. But the doctrine of continuous copy seems to have a great fascination for him.

I will draw to a close with some 'external' reasons for thinking that the amount of revision in the canon is not likely to be very great. The 'revival' of old plays was familiar to the Elizabethan stage. I first note the technical phase in a letter of 1605, which states that the King's men had 'revived' *Love's Labour's Lost*. 'Revived' is printed 'revised' by a contributor to Mr. Wilson's edition; that is a mere slip, but revival and revision are not synonymous. The distinction between a new and a revived play has financial implications in Sir Henry Herbert's office notes of 1622–42. In 1628 he secured from the King's men a 'benefit' during each summer and winter, 'to be taken out of the second daye of a revived play'. In 1633 he laid down that 'ould revived playes', as well as 'new' ones, must be brought for allowance, and fixed or confirmed fees of £2 for reading a new play and £1 for an old one. He has a significant entry of the £1 on one occasion, as being for allowance 'to add scenes to an ould play and to give it out for a new one'. After the Restoration, a dispute, of which we have not the conclusion, arose as to whether the Master's fee 'for supervising reviv'd plaies' was of ancient custom, and as to 'how long plaies may be laid asyde, ere he shall judge them to be reviv'd'. All this is late evidence and complicated by Herbert's bureaucratic tendency to magnify his office and multiply his emoluments. But the notions involved were clearly ancient, and even at the Rose a measure of revision probably entitled a 'revived' play to rank as 'new'. When Henslowe marks *Longshanks* in his diary as n.e. we need not suppose that we have to do with anything but a recast of Peele's *Edward I*. There was money in it. Even if the entrance charges for a new play were not higher, novelty had its appeal to the Elizabethan temperament. Dekker and Jonson have their laugh at the poets employed as 'play-patchers' and 'play-dressers'.

I dare say the process was often only colourable. 'New titles warrant not a play for new,' says a seventeenth-century prologue. On the other hand, a popular stock play, a 'get-penny', might draw well enough at a revival, without revision. Revision then, as well as revival, is a *vera causa* on the Elizabethan stage. It is more difficult to give a quantitative estimate of its frequency. But something can be collected from Henslowe's dealings with the Admiral's men, and something at a later date from Herbert's notes. During the six years from 1597 to 1602 the Admiral's men acquired about 100 new plays, paying fees to the poets which exclude any probability that we have only to do with 'new titles'. Of these we can trace the actual production of about 50, from the purchase for them of new garments and properties; others may, of course, have been furnished from the existing tiring-house stock. As against the 50 new plays, we can trace on similar evidence about 23 revivals. These had probably been exceptionally successful old plays, since 13 of them have come down to us in print, a quite disproportionate number, in view of the oblivion which has overtaken most of the 300 or so plays named by Henslowe. But most of these revivals do not seem to have been accompanied by any substantial payments to poets for carrying out the work. There are ten payments. Three are small sums for 'altering' or 'mending' plays, in one case a new and not a revived one, for the court, presumably as a result of the special scrutiny which plays selected for court performance underwent from the Revels officers. Three others are only for the provision of prologues and epilogues, in one case also for the court. There are, therefore, during these six years and for these 23 revivals, only four cases of substantial revision, carrying substantial fees to the poets.'[1] We have three of the four revised plays, and two of them we have

---

[1] The normal payment for a new play was £6. The revision of *Dr. Faustus* and *Tasso's Melancholy* cost in each case £4; that of *The Spanish Tragedy* £2 and an unspecified part of £10; that of *Old Fortunatus* £9, including some further alterations for the court.

both in the revised and the unrevised forms, so that we can see exactly what took place. They are *Doctor Faustus* and *The Spanish Tragedy*; in each case the revision amounted to the insertion of new scenes into an otherwise substantially unaltered text. The third play is *Old Fortunatus*. Here we have only the revised text; the original was probably written in two parts, and the revision compressed them into one. Henslowe's record, therefore, bears very little testimony to any widespread practice of revising plays upon revival. It bears still less to any literary recasting of the whole substance of revived plays, such as the theories which I have sketched envisage. I do not overlook the possible difference in methods between Shakespeare's company and the Admiral's. Two plays belonging to the former, outside the canon, have undergone alteration of known character. One is *The Malcontent*, the other *Mucedorus*; in both the revision took the form of inserting scenes, not of stylistic rehandling. Jonson, no doubt, re-wrote *Every Man in his Humour*, before the folio of 1616, and replaced the work of a collaborator by his own in *Sejanus*, before publication. But Jonson's literary attitude to his 'Works' is too personal to be taken as representative.

I come now to Sir Henry Herbert's notes. Such extracts from these as have been preserved record 130 licences for the production of plays between 1622 and 1642. Only fifteen were old plays, and in only seven is there any record of revision. One is a play of Fletcher's 'corrected' by Shirley; one had undergone 'renewing' and one 'alterations'; four had had one or more scenes added. We cannot be sure that the eighteenth-century scholars took all such notices out of Herbert's office-book, while it was available. And we cannot be sure that the Elizabethans and Jacobeans were not fonder of re-writing plays than the Carolines. But, for what it is worth, Herbert's evidence tends to confirm Henslowe's.

We ought to be very grateful to Mr. Robertson and Mr. Dover Wilson. We had come to think that all the critical

questions about Shakespeare were disposed of; the biographical facts and even a little more than the facts
chronicled, the canon and the apocrypha fixed, the chronological order determined, the text established; that there
was not much left to be done with Shakespeare, except
perhaps to read him. They have shown us that it is not so;
and we must now go over the ground again, and turn our
notional assents, with whatever modifications may prove
justified, into real assents. We have all the spring joy of
re-digging a well-tilled garden.

FROM 'HENRY V' TO 'HAMLET'[1]

By HARLEY GRANVILLE-BARKER

I WANT to speak of what seems to me to have been the crucial period of Shakespeare's development as a dramatist, and to glance at what prompted the crisis and what resulted from it. And if I must seem dogmatic, it is not that I am in love with my dogma, or feel dogmatic at all, but merely that in spending an hour upon a controversial subject one must save time. I shall speak of him simply as a dramatist, and primarily as an Elizabethan dramatist; a view too long ignored, though now returning to favour. In fact for an ideal standpoint I would throw myself and you back, if I could, by not quite three hundred years, to be listeners to such a talk as I imagine might have had place —let us say about 1635, at the Pegasus Inn in Cheapside, and at supper time, between three playgoers returned from some performance at the Blackfriars; not of one of Shakespeare's plays, but of the latest Massinger or Shirley.

The chill shadow of Puritanism was already falling, and within seven years the theatres were to be closed. It was the time of the decadence of Elizabethan drama; though that, no doubt, was a question of contemporary dispute. I will imagine our three playgoers disputing it. Let one of them be elderly, and the two others young; one of these two an enthusiast, and the other—as common a type—a great frequenter of theatres and a greater despiser of them. After a while the elder might drift—if the supper and the wine and the company were generous I feel sure he *would* drift—into reminiscence of the better time 'when you young blades were in your cradles', when Shakespeare and Burbage were the men. It is to such a point of view of

---

[1] First published 1925. Now published with considerable correction.

Shakespeare's art that I wish I could lead you this afternoon. For from it we could still see him as the topical wit,
and he was that; as the successor to Kyd and Marlowe, in
a perspective which would give us the contemporary value
of that heritage; as the popular playwright and the pro-
vider of effective parts for Burbage, Heminge, Phillips,
Field, Pope, and the rest; for he was this too, and upon this
must have hung much of his contemporary reputation.
Finally, I suspect, we should have to consider him as the
dramatist who—his head turned by too much success,
maybe—tried to do more with the theatre than the
theatre's nature allowed, and, for all his reputation, failed.
The youngest of the trio, our contemptuous playgoer
would, I feel sure, urge this very smartly. (Had he lately
spent 20s., perhaps, upon a nice new copy of the second
folio ? A second-hand copy of the first would have been a
better investment for the future.)

'*Hamlet* ? Yes, interesting; but I'd sooner read than see
it. Can it be a good play then ? *Macbeth*, with its elliptical
obscurities of language—do you call that poetry ? *King
Lear*, with its verbal thundering and lightning, and the
whole thing as inchoate as the thunder-storm—is this sort
of stuff suitable to a theatre ?'

In which last objection, of course, most modern critics
join; but they are apt to blame the theatre and not
Shakespeare for it. We should perhaps have heard his
earlier work preferred to his later. Did he, after all, ever
do anything more delightful than *Love's Labour's Lost* and
Richard II ? Or his latest liked better than all; the pastoral
scenes in *The Winter's Tale* and *The Tempest*. And our
young and contemptuous playgoer—who had in prospect,
shall we suppose, a career of acrid success in the Long
Parliament till Cromwell should grow sick of his sophistries
—would finally protest that the only play he unreservedly
admired was *Troilus and Cressida*. At last the elder man,
capturing the talk, would tell them what he thought really
happened to Shakespeare, the popular playwright, at the
crux of his career.

'Let me remember. When was it I first saw *Julius Caesar*? About 1600. Yes, thirty-five years ago . . .'

It is his discourse which, with unavoidable differences, I will try to make mine.

In 1599 Shakespeare produced *Henry V*. He was at a height of success and popularity. He had never looked back since Marlowe died and left him, so to speak, the sceptre of heroic blank verse as a legacy. In *Henry V* he is wielding that sceptre—incomparably and with a difference —but it is that same sceptre still. The play was, no doubt, a contemporary success. But it bears signs, like many successes, of having brought its writer to a 'dead end'. And, standing at Shakespeare's side at that moment (I do not suggest he did anything of the sort himself), one might pertinently have asked: 'In what has the vitality of your work really lain?'

The answer must involve a glance at the development of the whole Elizabethan theatre up to this time. Roughly speaking this is what has been happening. Within the rather more than twenty years since the building of James Burbage's famous theatre—*The* Theatre—these stage-players' pranks have become in some opinions a pleasing and an almost respectable calling, out of which, that is to say, people are beginning to make reputation and money. There has developed a school—several schools—of play-wrights. There has necessarily developed also a school of actors. This last phenomenon was possibly the more noticeable one to the Elizabethans, though it is in retrospect, of course, the less obvious to us. But let us look into it a little. What players did the earlier dramatists find to draw upon? Foremost in popularity with the public were the clowns. But from the dramatist's point of view they were not very satisfactory actors. Their skill lay in dancing and singing and improvisation; the shackles of set dialogue, as we know, they as often broke as wore. More important recruits for the poetic need of the plays would be the boys —now growing and grown to be men—the child actors trained by Farrant and his like in such choir schools as

Paul's. Delicate, charming, scholarly speakers, we may be sure. Translate their acting at Court or the Blackfriars into the terms of the singing in a good Cathedral choir to-day, and you have approximately the aesthetic effect they made. But they would find a very different audience in the open public theatres, to which the whole unruly town might come. Put this in political terms; it would be the difference between a debate in the House of Lords and an 'Irish' night in Parnell's day in the Commons. Then there would be the barn-stormers, the actors of all work, who had, with one qualification or another, found a place in this or that company of 'Lords' men'.

We must consider, then, the development of the drama from 1580 to 1600 from the point of view (among others) of its interpretation; and this in the light of the combination of skilled youth and glorified barn-storming—glorified by the gifts and demands of the young poet-dramatists, of Marlowe and Shakespeare in particular. It was surely this new art of emotional acting which gave the drama its sudden hold on the people. The older plays had not provided for anything like this. If we ask what sort of acting it was that people found so stirring, there are parallels to-day, though the nearest are not in the theatre. Go to a revivalist meeting in Wales—or, if you prefer, go to the Opera. Elizabethan music did not attempt the frontal assault on our emotions that much modern music does; modern opera, in particular. But orotund drama was a rough equivalent. And if any one recollects, some twenty-five years ago at Covent Garden, Caruso's finish to the first act of *Pagliacci*, I think they can estimate the sort of effect created by Alleyn and (while he emulated him) Burbage on the Elizabethan stage. Much else, however, had gone to the making of the complete art of the theatre as it existed in 1600. Skill in high comedy and the development out of clowning of what we now call 'character' acting. Externally, richer resources for properties and costume; a fair touch of pageantry. But the heroes of the public as of the plays were Burbage and Alleyn and

their peers, for they gave their audience music and poetry
and popular oratory in one.[1]

Now let us see what Shakespeare's characteristic contri-
butions to the theatre had been. There were the obvious
ones; and some not yet perhaps quite so obvious. For there
were two sides to Shakespeare the playwright, as there are
to most artists, and to most men brought into relations
with the public and its appetite (which flatterers call its
taste). There was the complaisant side and the daemonic
side. His audience demanded exciting stories. He was no
great hand at inventing a story, but he borrowed the best.
They asked for heroic verse. He could do this with any
one, and he did. I always fancy that the immoderate
length of *Richard III* is due to the sheer exuberance of the
young man put on his mettle to claim the inheritance of
the dead Marlowe's mighty line. Euphuism had its vogue
still. He could play upon that pipe too very prettily; and
Love's Labour's Lost is as much homage as satire. But from
the very beginning, signs of the daemonic Shakespeare
can be seen, the genius bent on having his own way; of the
Shakespeare to whom the idea is more than the thing,
who cares much for character and little for plot, who
cannot indeed touch the stagiest figure of fun without
treating it as a human being and giving it life, whether it
suits Shakespeare the popular play-provider to do so or
not. And sometimes it doesn't. Life in the theatre will
play the devil with artifice.

Look into *Love's Labour's Lost*. We laugh the play
through at the ridiculous Armado; no mockery, not the
crudest sort of banter is spared him. But at the end, with
one touch of queer, pathetic, dignity, Shakespeare and he
make the fine gentlemen of the play, who are mirrors of

[1] It is likely, I think, that Alleyn, conquering the town with Tamburlaine, set a high standard of rhetorical acting, and more than possible that
he never did anything better, or very different. Burbage, on the other
hand, though he may have begun on these lines, must have developed his
art out of all knowledge in subtlety and resource by the time he came to
play Hamlet, Othello, and Lear.—H. G.-B. 1932.

the fine gentlemen in the audience, look pretty small. Consider Sir Nathaniel the country curate. The late Mr. W. S. Penley in the *Private Secretary* was no greater scandal to the dignity of the Church (though Mr. Penley also knew too much about comedy not always to keep a little dignity in hand) than is Sir Nathaniel attempting to enact Alexander the Great. But, when he has been laughed off the mimic stage, hear Costard's apology for him to the smart London ladies and gentlemen, his mimic audience:

'There, an't shall please you; a foolish mild man; an honest man look you, and soon dashed! He is a marvellous good neighbour, faith, and a very good bowler; but for Alisander—alas, you see how 'tis, a little o'erparted.

That does not belong to the plot or the mere fun-making scheme. Nor is it a thing you learn to do by following any fashion or going to any school of play-writing, to-day's or yesterday's. But here already, in 1591, his age twenty-five, is the true Shakespeare having his way. Fifty words (not so many) turn Sir Nathaniel the Curate (and Costard too) from a stage puppet to a human being, and send you away from the theatre, not only knowing the man, having, as we say, 'an idea' of the man, but liking him even while you laugh at him, and feeling, moreover, a little kindlier towards the next man you meet in the street who reminds you of him. *This* is the Shakespeare who was finally to people, not his little theatre only, but the whole intellectual world for the next three hundred years with figures of his imagining.

This is the Shakespeare that turns the Romeo of Act I into the Romeo of Act V, and the Mercutio of the Queen Mab speech (charming stuff though it be) into the Mercutio of

'No! 'tis not so deep as a well, nor so wide as a church door; but 'tis enough, 'twill serve . . .

It is the Shakespeare who recklessly lodged that dynamic human figure of Shylock within the preposterous fairy tale of *The Merchant of Venice*, the Shakespeare who trium-

phantly made the Falstaff of the speech on Honour and of
the scenes of *Henry IV, Part II* out of the old pickpurse
of Gadshill (strange that a later inhabitant of Gadshill
should have done much the same sort of thing two and a
half centuries later with his *Pickwick*). If in fact we are
to look for the informing thing, the vital quality in
Shakespeare's developing art, it will lie not in the weaving
and unravelling of plots, but in some spirit behind the
plot, by which it seems to move of itself; and not so much
in the writing of great dramatic poetry even, as in this
growing power to project character in action.

Now if emotional rhetoric was a new thing to the
Elizabethan theatre, this last thing—done as he was doing
it—was yet a newer. To-day we can distinguish him in the
first stage of his career passing from sketches to full length
figures, from the play and the part that is half convention
and half a living thing (read the entire Juliet; not the
Juliet as commonly cut for performance) to the thing that
abounds in its own life from first to last. It was not such an
easy journey to make; for Shakespeare the daemonic genius
had always to strike some sort of a bargain with Shakespeare
the popular playwright, who would be content with the
finish of *The Taming of the Shrew* or the last Act of *The
Two Gentlemen of Verona*. But truly the bolder spirit was
justified by success, and went from success to success,
from Richard III to Richard II, from Shylock to Falstaff,
from Mercutio to Hotspur, from Romeo to Prince Hal.

This, you may protest, is merely to say that he was learning how to write good plays. For is not the chief test of a
good play that its characters will come vividly to life when
it is acted? It is easier, as we shall see, to call this a truism
than to admit all that its truth must imply. Make such
a comparison, however, between Shakespeare and his contemporaries; set, for instance, Marlowe's Edward II by his
Richard II's side, and see if here is not the essential difference between them. Then look closer to where the actual
detailed differences lie. How does this vitality manifest
itself? Did we not mark it rightly in that little speech of

Costard's in *Love's Labour's Lost*? Is not Shakespeare's
progress as a playwright very much to be measured by the
increase of those suddenly illuminating things that seem to
light up not merely the one dramatic moment, but the
whole nature of a man, sometimes even the very background of his life? By such things as Prince Hal's famous
apostrophe to Falstaff, shamming dead:

> Poor Jack, farewell,
> I could have better spared a better man.

—As Mr. Justice Shallow's

> 'Barren, barren, barren; beggars all, beggars all, Sir John.
> Marry, good air!'

—such as the hostess's tale of Falstaff's death:

> '. . . I knew there was but one way; for his nose was as sharp as
> a pen, and a' babbled of green fields.'

—and old drink-sodden Bardolph's

> 'Would I were with him, wheresome'er he is, either in heaven
> or in hell.'

Are such things trifles? They are immortal trifles. They
should not be torn from their context, and their true
context is the acted scene. But are they not the things
that give this peculiar quality of life to the plays? And is
it not the ever greater abundance of this quality which
marks his approach to the mastery of his art?

Shakespeare was learning too, in these years, to adapt
the chief convention of his medium—the convention of
rhetorical verse—to his own needs. He had also, it is true,
the directer one of prose; and he could make a magnificent
music of that when he chose. Falstaff certainly lacks
nothing of force or fire by being freed from the bonds
of metre.

> 'If sack and sugar be a fault, God help the wicked. If to be
> old and merry be a sin, then many an old host that I know is
> damned; if to be fat is to be hated, then Pharaoh's lean kine are
> to be loved. No, my good lord, banish Peto, banish Bardolph,

banish Poins; but for sweet Jack Falstaff, kind Jack Falstaff, true
Jack Falstaff, valiant Jack Falstaff, and therefore more valiant being
as he is, old Jack Falstaff, banish not him thy Harry's company:
banish not him thy Harry's company: banish plump Jack, and banish
all the world.'

But compare Romeo and Richard II with Hotspur and
Prince Hal. Hotspur is set almost entirely within the convention of verse; but how little conventionalized phrasing
there is in it. And Prince Hal's turns from prose to verse,
with the turns of his character, are made with excellent
ease. And the caricature of the convention in Pistol is
worth remark.

Shakespeare is working, as most artists will, towards
making his medium perfectly malleable, and is developing
technical resource which defeats mere technical criticism.
He was ever a forthright worker; he would precipitate
himself into tight places, and then with extraordinary
daring and agility be out of them (think of the time-
problem in *Othello*, and of the manœuvring of the sub-
plot in *King Lear*). He came to possess, indeed, that combination of judgement and instinct which, serving another
end, made the deeds of our young airmen in the War a
marvel that their elders by reason alone could neither rival
nor explain. And, to further the comparison, Shakespeare
was working in the youth of an art, to which such freedom
is more allowable. Let us not suppose, though, that, for
all their seemingly slap-dash ways, these Elizabethan
dramatists would not be concerned with the technique of
their craft. They had not developed its vocabulary. They
did not write books, or have to listen to lectures on the
subject; though one may suspect that rare Ben Jonson
thumped the tables of the Mermaid pretty hard to this
purpose. But by an older and better dispensation the little
group of comrades and rivals would bandy sharp personal
criticism upon work in the doing with the religious fervour
which properly belongs to a living art.

Somewhat thus, then, Shakespeare stood towards the
theatre when he set out upon the writing of *Henry V*.

What is it, in this play, which disappoints us—which, as I believe, disappointed him—and marks it as the danger-point of his career?

From now on I will but assemble before you, as a counsel might, the facts that I think sustain my view of this artistic crisis through which Shakespeare passed. I do not, of course, attach equal importance to them all. Nor do I pretend that, the truth of one admitted, the truth of another must follow. For, however else Shakespeare's genius worked, it was not upon logical lines, and to put anything about it to that test is almost certainly to be misled.

Well, here he is, an acknowledged master of his craft and in the full flush of success, setting out to write a fine play, a spacious play, with England as its subject, no less a thing. He is now to crown the achievement of the earlier histories and, above all, of the last two, in which he had so 'found himself'. He is to bring that popular favourite Prince Hal to a worthy completion; and to this obligation—though against his formal promise to the public—he sacrifices Falstaff. It is easy to see why. Could Falstaff reform and be brought back into the company of the reformed Henry? No. Once before Shakespeare has hinted to us that the fat knight, if he grow great shall grow less, purge, leave sack, and live cleanly. But not a bit of it. *Henry IV, Part II*, when it came, found him more incorrigible than ever. On the other hand, had Falstaff made his un-authorized way to France, how could Henry's new dignity suffer the old ruffian's ironic comments on it? He had run away with his creator once: better not risk it. So to his now unimpeachable hero Shakespeare has to sacrifice his greatest, his liveliest creation so far. Does the hero reward him? No one could say that Henry is ill-drawn or uninteresting. But, when it comes to the point, there seems to be very little that is dramatically interesting for him to do. Here is a play of action, and here is the perfect man of action. Yet all the while Shakespeare is apologizing—and directly apologizing—for not being able to make the action effective. Will the audience, for heaven's sake, help him out? One need not attach too much importance to the formal modesty of the prologue.

> O pardon! Since a crooked figure may
> Attest in little place a million,
> And let us, ciphers to this great accompt,
> On your imaginary forces work.

This might be merely the plea of privilege that every playwright, ancient or modern, must tacitly make. But when we find the apology repeated and repeated again, and before Act V most emphatically of all; when we find there the prayer to his audience

> . . . to admit the excuse
> Of time, of numbers, and due course of things
> Which cannot in their huge and proper life
> Be here presented—

does it not sound a more than formal confession, and as if Shakespeare had distressfully realized that he had asked his theatre—mistakenly; because it must be mistakenly— for what it could not accomplish?

Turn now to Henry himself. When do we come closest to him? Not surely in the typical moments of the man of action, in

> Once more unto the breach, dear friends, once more . . .

and upon like occasions. But in the night before Agincourt, when, on the edge of likely disaster, he goes out solitary into the dark and searches his own soul. This is, of course, no new turn to the character. Prince Hal at his wildest has never been a figure of mere fun and bombast. Remember the scenes with his father and with Hotspur. Still, soul-searching is—if one may use such a phrase of Majesty—not his long suit; and the passage, fine as it is, has the sound of a set piece. It is rhetoric rather than revelation.

In the later speech to Westmoreland:

> We few, we happy few, we band of brothers . . .

Henry, set among his fellows, is more himself. But
Shakespeare makes practically no further attempt to show
us the inner mind of the man. The Henry of the rest of
Act IV is the Henry of the play's beginning. While, since
for Act V some new aspect of the hero really must be
found, we are landed with a jerk (nothing in the character
has prepared us for it) into a rollicking love scene. And
this well-carpentered piece of work is finished. I daresay it
was a success, and the Shakespeare who lived to please and
had to please to live, may have been content with it. But
the other, the daring, the creative Shakespeare, who had
now known what it was to have Shylock, Mercutio, Hotspur, and Falstaff come to life, and abound in unruly life,
under his hands—was he satisfied? No doubt he could
have put up as good a defence as many of his editors have
obliged him with both for hero and play, for its epic
quality and patriotic purpose. Though had he read in the
preface to the admirable Arden edition that—

> Conscientious, brave, just, capable and tenacious, Henry stands
> before us the embodiment of worldly success, and as such he is
> entitled to our unreserved admiration . . .

I think he would have smiled wryly. For he was not the
poet to find patriotism an excuse for the making of fine
phrases. And he knew well enough that neither in the
theatre nor in real life is it these 'embodiments of worldly
success' that we carry closest in our hearts, or even care
to spend an evening with.

No, he had set himself this task, and he carried it through
conscientiously and with the credit which is sound work-
manship's due. But I detect disappointment with his
hero, and—not quite fancifully, I believe—a deeper disillusion with his art. The 'daemonic' Shakespeare, then,
was only a lesson to the good. But it was a valuable lesson.
He had learnt that for presenting the external pageantry
of great events his theatre was no better than a puppet-
show; and that though the art of drama might be the art
of presenting men in action, your successful man of action

did not necessarily make the most interesting of heroes. For behind the action, be the play farce or tragedy, there must be some spiritually significant idea, or it will hang lifeless. And this is what is lacking in *Henry V*.

What follows? We next find him writing three comedies the three mature comedies as they are called: *As You Like It, Much Ado About Nothing, Twelfth Night*. Let us note one or two things about them.

The dominant characters are women, not men; that is one thing.

For another, in *As You Like It* and in *Much Ado About Nothing* it is almost as if he set out to write the plays in prose, as if he were sick of rhetoric, meant somehow to have an intimate, if a commonplace, medium to work in. But poets write poetry as ducks swim, and, at the first excuse, he drops back into it. And in *Twelfth Night*, the latest of the three, he has returned to his accustomed usage of both prose and verse, while his verse is still finding new freedom.

As usual, he borrows his stories, but his treatment of them is now really outrageous. In *As You Like It* it is a mere excuse for him to amuse himself and us in the Forest of Arden; and, when he must wind it up somehow, he does so with a perfunctoriness which makes the part of Jaques de Bois, introduced to that end, one of the laughing-stocks of the theatre. In *Much Ado* he lets it turn to ridicule; the end of the Claudio-Hero theme is cynically silly. In *Twelfth Night* he is a little more conscientious. Malvolio and his tormentors carry it away to the utter despite of Orsino and his high romance; but Viola holds her own. The value of *Much Ado* lies in the characters of Benedick and Beatrice and Dogberry, which are Shakespeare's arbitrary additions to the story. And in *As You Like It*, if Orlando and Rosalind are the story's protagonists (which Jaques and Touchstone certainly are not) yet the story itself may stand still while he develops them; and thankful we are that it should.

We need not insist upon the peculiarity of the three

titles, though one is tempted to. *As You Like It, Much Ado About Nothing, What You Will!* As if they and the things they ostensibly stood for were bones thrown to the dogs of the audience, that wanted their plot and their ear-tickling jokes. Well, let them have it. Shakespeare meanwhile is doing what *he* will, and what he can do as no one else can, creating character, revealing character.

Then he finds his manly subject again in *Julius Caesar*, in that great theme of Rome and the old Roman world, which makes the matter of the English Histories seem parochial. How significant it must have been to any imaginative Englishman of that age, with a new world of discovery, its chances and rivalries, its matter for thought and dreams opening up to him! Shakespeare was to return to Rome and the thought of Rome again and yet again; and he was never to return in thought—if he did in subject —to the narrower horizons. But note two things about *Julius Caesar.* We have no complaints of the inadequacy of his stage to the representing of the Senate or the battlefield of Philippi. On the contrary, he trusts in his fourth and fifth Acts to one of the oldest and simplest of Elizabethan conventions, the confronting upon the stage of two whole armies, symbolized by Generals, their standard-bearers and drummers. And whom does he choose as hero? Not Caesar himself, the triumphant, though doomed, man of action; but Brutus the philosopher, and the man, who for all his wisdom, invariably does the wrong thing. Brutus proves a not quite satisfactory dramatic hero. He is too unemotional, not impulsive enough; and Shakespeare, taking much of him ready made from Plutarch, never quite fathoms his stoicism. So first Cassius runs away with the play and then Mark Antony. When a character springs to life now Shakespeare is not going to refuse him his chance. Still, he resolutely comes back to the developing of Brutus. And his care is not for what his hero does, which is merely disastrous, but for what he *is*; this is the dramatic thing, and the essential thing.

> Thou seest the world Volumnius, how it goes;
> Our enemies have beat us to the pit . . .
>   Countrymen,
> My heart doth joy that yet in all my life,
> I found no man but he was true to me.
> I shall have glory by this losing day,
> More than Octavius and Mark Antony
> By this vile conquest shall attain unto.

If *Henry V* was the danger-point, *Julius Caesar* is the turning-point of Shakespeare's career.

Further, he is now rapidly bringing his verse to its dramatic perfection, is finally forming it into the supple and subtle instrument he needed. He had seldom, in trying to give it conversational currency, fallen into the pit—from which some of his contemporaries hardly emerged—of making it ten-syllabled prose. Rarely, rarely does one find such a line. Rhetoric was to be preferred to that, for rhetoric at least lifted drama to the higher emotional plane, except upon which it was hard to hold his audience in illusion. But he now relegates rhetoric to its proper dramatic place. Cassius is rhetorical by disposition; Antony because it suits his purpose. Shakespeare will bring his verse to a greater—and to a stranger—perfection yet. From now on, however, it is ever a more ductile and transparent medium, no bar either to the easy progress of a scene or to intimacy with a character.

But as the study of Brutus draws to an end do not the accents change a little? He is brooding on the issue of the coming battle.

> O that a man might know
> The end of this day's business ere it come;
> But it sufficeth that the day will end
> And then the end is known.

Does not that echo to us a more familiar voice?

'If it be now, tis not to come; if it be not to come it will be now; if it be not now, yet it will come: the readiness is all; since no man has aught of what he leaves, what is't to leave betimes? Let be.'

It is indeed the voice of Hamlet. And here was to be his

next task. And here, not with *Henry V*, his crowning achievement.

It has been often enough remarked that Shakespeare had been making attempts at *Hamlet* all his playwright's life. We find a young euphuistic Hamlet in the first Act of Romeo, we find him in Richard II, and an impatient touch of him in Jaques. But now at last the daring, the inspired, the 'daemonic' partner in this dramatic firm once and fully and for all has his way with the amenable, politic play-provider. Yet, looking at it in the light of its success, do we realize what a breaking of bounds it was? By foot-rule criticism the thing has every fault. A play should be founded upon significant action; and this is about a man who never can make up his mind what to do, who, when he does do anything, does it by mistake. The story is interesting enough, and the device of the play within a play is a well-seasoned one. But the plot, as a plot, is worked out with scandalous ineptitude. At the play's most critical period the hero is absent from the stage for forty minutes, and the final tragedy is brought about by a precipitate and inartistic holocaust. And not only does Hamlet moralize about everything under the sun, but the rest of the characters—even the wretched Rosencrantz—follow his example upon the least excuse; and the whole thing is spun out to an intolerable length.

But the play was a success. Shakespeare the poet could have a good laugh at Shakespeare the popular playwright about that. And it has been the world's most consistently successful play ever since. And I think we can hear Shakespeare, the poet, saying, 'Yes, I know now what my theatre can do and what it can't. I know at least what *I* can do. Agincourt and its heroic swashbuckling—no! The stoic Brutus with his intellectual struggles? That was better, though it made hard going. But the passionate, suffering inner consciousness of man, his spiritual struggles and triumphs and defeats in his impact with an uncomprehending world—this may seem the most utterly unfit subject for such a crowded, noisy, vulgar place as the theatre; yet this is what I can make comprehensible, here is what I can do with my art'. And where now is that fine upstanding gentleman, Henry V ? He is still at hand, and still commands our unreserved admiration. But his name is Fortinbras, and he is often (though he shouldn't be) cut out of the play altogether.

Hamlet is the triumph of dramatic idea over dramatic action and of character over plot. Shakespeare—grant him the conventions of his stage, with the intimate value they give to the soliloquy and to the emotional privileges and demands of poetry—has now found the perfectly expressive character. The play in every circumstance, and Hamlet himself in every quality and defect, seem to answer the dramatist's need. He has found, moreover, perfect ease of expression. Verse, as he has now released it from its strictness, losing nothing of its rhythm, cannot, one would think, fall more aptly to the uses of dialogue than, say, in the scenes with Horatio and Marcellus, or to the direct expression of intimate emotion than in the soliloquy beginning

> O, what a rogue and peasant slave am I!
> Is it not monstrous that this player here ... ?

And we may note in passing that if in *Henry V* he was concerned with the disabilities of his stage, he now takes a chance of commenting on the art of acting, the more important matter of the two, by far. Further, that while the effect of the play within a play is greatly strengthened by letting the mimic play be of an older fashion (for thus there is less disturbance of the illusion created by the play of *Hamlet* which we are watching), he, in the very midst of his new-fashioned triumph, makes opportunity for a tribute to such men as were masters when he was but a prentice to his work. He has Hamlet speak of the play which was 'caviare to the general', but of

'. . . an honest method, as wholesome as sweet, and by very much more handsome than fine.'

How gracious a thing to do!

Shakespeare has written his masterpiece. What is to happen next ? Will he try to repeat his success, or will he fall back upon amusing himself with pettier work ? His restless genius lets him do neither. As becomes a great piece of dramatic art, *Hamlet* is too vital to be perfect; and he knows this, and it is evident that he submitted himself to criticism, his own, or other people's, or both. It was certainly much too long (I think it must always have been cut for ordinary performances). It does lack form; the knotting of its plot is cut rather than unravelled; and the other characters do many of them suffer from being written too much from Hamlet's point of view. Is this why in *Measure for Measure*, which probably was his next play, we find Shakespeare confining himself within the bounds of a symmetrical story, done at normal length ? But we find too, I think, that for all the beauty and ruthless wisdom of the play, he is not working happily. And in doing his duty by the plot, truth to character has to suffer violence at the end. Next comes *Othello*. Dr. Bradley calls it the most masterly of the tragedies in the point of construction. Shakespeare is now obviously determined not to let himself be cramped by plot in the working out of character. There is no introspective hero to outbalance the play. He has another device—Iago's quite inhuman cunning—for letting us learn the inwardness of *Othello*. But he had, we see, to make a heroic effort to keep it a normal length. If he were not so successful one would take leave to call it an impudent effort; for as critic after critic has noted, and as one would think anybody of common sense among the audience could see for themselves, the compressions of the middle of the action make the whole plot impossible; there never *was* any moment when Desdemona could have been guilty of adultery with Cassio, and Othello must have known it. Shakespeare knew though, that common sense was the last faculty to be exercised in the theatre; or, to put it more advisedly, he knew that, once away from watches and clocks, we appreciate the relation of events rather by

the intensity of the experiences which unite or divide
them in our minds than by any arithmetical process.
'Short time' and 'long time' is less a definite dramatic
device than a psychological commonplace—as most good
dramatic devices are.

But he was now thinking of more than constructional
compression and time-saving. He had opened up for himself a very complex artistic issue. Drama was to lie only
formally in the external action, was to consist of the
revelation of character and of the inevitable clashes
between the natures of men. And besides, behind these
there would be the struggle within a man's own nature;
and the combatant powers there must be dramatized.
(A living play is like life itself in this: each part of it is of
the same nature as the whole, and partakes of the power
of the whole.)

> Between the acting of a dreadful thing
> And the first motion, all the interim is
> Like a phantasma, or a hideous dream:
> The genius and the mortal instruments
> Are then in council; and the state of man,
> Like to a little kingdom, suffers then
> The nature of an insurrection.

This is a recipe for tragedy. Brutus is speaking, but it
might well be Macbeth. With Brutus the problem of
dramatizing this insurrection had been mainly avoided.
In *Hamlet* it almost solved itself, for this was the very
subject of the play; but one would not always happen upon
so apt a story or so naturally histrionic a character. In
Othello the problem is solved, as we have seen, by per-
sonifying the power of evil—and Shakespeare was a good
Manichaean—in Iago. And in *Macbeth* he finds himself
on the track of the same solution, with Lady Macbeth for
an Iago. But he turns aside from the danger of self-
imitation, somewhat to the truncating of her character.

Now, I think, the issue can be defined. These people of
his imagining had to be made to show us their innermost
selves, and to show us things in themselves of which they

were not themselves wholly conscious. Further, the physical and moral atmosphere in which they move, and its effect on them, will be of importance. All this apart from the telling of the story and the outward contest! Yet in this complex task he can look for no help worth speaking of but from interpretative acting. To what else could he look? Scenery, in the illusionary sense, he had none. Pageantry may be very well on occasion, but it is apt to leave your drama precisely where it found it. He had the spoken word. But he could not let his characters dissipate the audience's interest in themselves with long descriptions of outward things. While, if for intimate revelation the soliloquy has been till now, and must always be, a great resource, too many soliloquies do undoubtedly relax the tension and weaken the structure of a play. And I think we may notice that from *Othello* onwards they are either shorter or more sparingly used. No; he has to fall back on dialogue, and on a fair proportion of short-range hard-hitting dialogue, if his characters are to seem to hold each other's attention or are to hold the audience's upon these not very simple questions. He has done with passages of rocket-like rhetoric, which so obviously soar over the person they are addressed to for a landing in the back of the gallery (though Shakespeare the popular playwright must still be allowed one or two, that a scene may be rounded off in the recognized way). In fine, then, the physical conditions of his theatre, combined with the needs of his art as he now perceives them, drive him to depend for story-telling, character-building, and scene-painting upon what can be made of the art of the actor alone. Moreover—here is the point—for brevity's sake and for the sake of the tenseness, by which alone an audience can be held in the bonds of illusion, he must find some formula of dramatic speech into which these three things can be wrought, all three together.

It is in *Macbeth* that he seems most directly to face this problem; how he solves it remains his secret. Maeterlinck, in a preface to his own translation of the play, gives a masterly analysis of the effect created. I wish I could quote it at length. But this is his summing up:

A sa surface flotte le dialogue nécessaire à l'action. Il semble le seul qu'entendent les oreilles; mais en réalité c'est l'autre parole qu'écoute notre instinct, notre sensibilité inconsciente, notre âme si l'on veut; et si les mots extérieurs nous atteignent plus profondément qu'en nul autre poète, c'est qu'une plus grande foule de puissances cachées les supporte.

And he remarks that throughout the play we find practically no 'expressions mortes'.

But that is not to explain, of course, how lines are written which—in their place—will have the magic of

> Light thickens,
> And the crow makes wing to the rooky wood.

or the power—though it seems, and is, a line a child might write—of

> It will have blood: they say blood will have blood.

Or that can give the effect—really one cannot remove this from its place—of Macduff's.

> He has no children.

There is, finally, no explaining the marvel of the sleep-walking scene (if only actors would not try to make it more of a marvel and so make it less!), in which Lady Macbeth speaks but sixteen sentences, of which the most distinctive are merely such simplicities as

> Hell is murky.

as

> The Thane of Fife had a wife; where is she now?

as

> All the perfumes of Arabia will not sweeten this little hand.

('Little' hand! Mark its placing in the sentence and its significance. One may divine touches like that.)

Here then is a secret that Shakespeare mastered and never lost, and that no one else has ever found. It is during the period of his work, which covers *Macbeth*, *King Lear*, and *Antony and Cleopatra*, that he wields the magic

of it most potently. But the spell is not fully operative—
this we must always remember—unless we are within the
charmed circle of the play itself. And when Bradley says,
and surely says rightly, that Lear's last speech—

> And my poor fool is hang'd! No, no; no life!
> Why should a dog, a horse, a rat, have life,
> And thou no breath at all? Thou'lt come no more,
> Never, never, never, never, never!
> Pray you, undo this button; thank you, sir,
> Do you see this? Look on her, look, her lips,
> Look there, look there!

—leaves us upon the topmost pinnacles of poetry, people
who cannot transport themselves into the magic world
of the living play must wonder what on earth he means.
Whatever *is* there in Antony's

> I am dying, Egypt, dying; only
> I here importune death a while, until
> Of many thousand kisses the poor last
> I lay upon thy lips.

Or—as she holds the aspic to her—in Cleopatra's failing

> Peace, peace!
> Dost thou not see my baby at my breast,
> That sucks the nurse asleep?

And, returning to *Macbeth*, can we even account for the
full effect of such passages as the familiar

> I have liv'd long enough: my way of life
> Is fall'n into the sear, the yellow leaf . . .

or

> To-morrow and to-morrow and to-morrow . . .

Shakespeare keeps his secret.

Macbeth is the shortest of the tragedies: even could we
restore the probable mutilations I expect it would still be
the shortest. It is the most concentrated, the most stripped
and stark. In spite of all the circumstances of its form, it
comes, as has been said, the nearest to Greek tragedy. A
last look at it gives us the figures of Macbeth and his wife
carved, monumental and aloof, as if Sophocles had been

at them. Was it a success? It was given one or more Court
performances. James I, with all his faults, had a taste for
good drama; or if he only pretended to one, it would, for
me, be a pardonable piece of snobbery. Still, it is significant that the folio editors found nothing but a text which
Middleton had been called in to enliven with song and
dance.

But now note that for his next task our reckless genius
flings off to the very opposite extreme.[1] In *King Lear* he
provides himself with a doubled plot, whose working out
would leave him with a longer play than *Hamlet*; and from
this mischance he saves himself only by the most heroic
measures. Moreover, in Lear himself he finds a character
who runs away with him as no other has done yet. It is
the play of his widest outlook. In *Julius Caesar* he thought
he was taking a world view. But he stood at Plutarch's
side and perhaps did not understand all he saw. This is
his own vision; and from this mountain top what we should
now call his social conscience searches widest. Anatole
France, speaking of great men, has another word for it.

'La pitié, voyez-vous, M. le Professeur, c'est le fond même du
génie.'

And if Shakespeare had looked into his new edition of the
Bible he would have found in a pertinent passage yet
another word freshly restored there, the word 'charity'.
By this test, here is his greatest play.

How does he marshal his resources?

The play starts off disciplined and conventional, pro-
mising to be as 'Greek' as *Macbeth* has been. But in the
development of Lear himself—and to this for a time
everything gives way and everything contributes—Shakespeare soon breaks all bounds. He rallies every stage device
he can think of: even the now old-fashioned figure of the
Fool is turned to account—and to what account! But
above all, his theme requires that he shall relate Lear to

[1] I am, it seems, in error in placing *Macbeth* before *King Lear*. I must
accept, to that extent, the vitiation of my argument.—H. G-B. 1932.

the crude world we live in, and to the rigours of that
world as it may fall on rich and poor alike—as it must fall,
crushingly for his purpose, upon the proud old tyrant
himself. He needs that storm, as he needed the mob in
Caesar, the ghost in *Hamlet*, or the personified evil of Iago.
How does he create it? We are far from the Chorus'
apologetics of *Henry V* for what the stage could *not*
provide. We are far even from the technique of *Julius
Caesar*, where Cicero, Cassius, and Casca are set to
describe at length, though little to the advancement of
the play, the tempest that heralded the great murder.
Shakespeare is for bolder methods now. He turns one
character, Edgar, in his disguise as a wandering, naked,
half-witted beggar, into a veritable piece of scene-painting
of the barren, inhospitable heath. And for the storm
itself, he shows it us in its full play as a reflection of that
greater storm which rages in the mind of Lear—of anger,
terror, pity, remorse—lightening and darkening it as a
storm does the sky, and finally blasting it altogether. For
that storm, as Shakespeare knows now, is the really dramatic
thing; and it is the only thing that his art can directly
and satisfactorily present. To say no more of it than this,
here is a marvellous piece of stagecraft, the finest and
most significant single thing he ever did—and some of the
best critics have decided that in itself it makes the play
impossible for the stage!

At which stumbling-block of a paradox we may end
this journey. We need not glance on towards *Antony and
Cleopatra*, which is in some ways the most perfect, and
altogether, I think, the most finely spacious piece of play-
making he ever did; nor to *Coriolanus*, where he managed
at last to make his 'man of action' dramatically effective;
nor to the latest romances, fruits of a well-earned and
tolerant repose.

But *is* 'King Lear' unfitted for the stage and so a failure?
We cannot turn the question by contemning the theatre
itself. A play written to be acted, which cannot be
effectively acted, is a failure. What should we say of a

symphony which no orchestra could play? And the answer to this question will, as I contend, involve, though with a difference, all these greater plays that we have been considering. The question will indeed become: did Shakespeare, when with *Henry V* he came to the end of all he could find to his purpose in the technique of the drama as his contemporaries and masters understood it, when, passing over that bridge which is *Julius Caesar*, he found in the working out of *Hamlet* the technique best suited to his genius, did he then and thereafter take the wrong road? One had better not be too ready with a straight Yes or No. Frankly, I am for Shakespeare the playwright and No. It is a hard road, but not a blind one; it leads us ahead. If you are for Shakespeare the playwright, what other answer can there be? But much critical authority—though it will not quite say Yes—is still apt to imply it. Through all the important appreciation of his greater work there flows an undercurrent of something very like resentment that he should have been so ill-advised, so inconsiderate as to write it for the theatre at all. And if some of those ingenious contrivers on his behalf of 'short time' and 'long time' could bring that useful system into a sort of retrospective operation in real life that would abolish the three hundred odd years which separates them from him, could they meet him for a talk during that crisis in his career, happen on him, for instance, just when he was discerning what the working out of the theme of *Hamlet* was to involve, I fancy they would advise him in all friendliness that the subject really was not suitable for a play. Had he asked in return what form, then, he had better cast it in (and it would be a fair question): well, there is the Platonic dialogue; there is the example of Milton turning deliberately from drama to the epic; and Goethe could be held up to him as an awful warning. Beethoven was the luckier man. He could write symphonies in which to enshrine such tremendous emotions; from him descend the great dramatic poets we choose rather to listen to to-day, and music is their language. To which Shakespeare might answer that his Elizabethans felt the need and responded to the art of personal expression more than we do, whose minds are full of science and machinery and of all sorts of things, actual and speculative, that cannot be reduced to terms of human emotion. 'Though can they not be ?' he might add, 'and must they not be at any rate brought within the range of it, if you are really to comprehend them ?' He might even be able to refer to a remark which that sympathetic Frenchman, Monsieur André Maurois, has let fall lately in a current book of his—in no way about the theatre, and truly it is written in particular about the French—concerning the universal 'besoin de mimer'. Monsieur Maurois sees this need of physical expression as the sign of a well-balanced being. A mind isolated from the body, which should be its reflection and its picturing, will be no more effective, he says, than a bird trying to fly in the ether instead of in the air. And after all, Shakespeare might argue, the final test to which everything in the world, great or small, good or evil, must be brought is its effect upon man himself; not upon your economic man, your democratic man, your man-in-the-street, nor any other of the abstractions which Governments and able editors are now concerned with, but upon that strange mixture of thought, appetite and immortal soul —'a poor forked animal he may be, but I make my king own to brotherhood with him. And the claim of this drama of mine', he would say, 'as I have now evolved it, is to bring you into immediate and intimate contact with that man as he essentially *is*, in an *ever present tense*. What other art can do this as mine can ?'

That is a fine claim, no doubt; but the practical question remains whether, considering the limits of time and all the other limits and imperfections of the theatre itself, considering its motley mixture of an audience of poor forked animals and kings, considering not least the limitations and imperfections of the actors themselves—does the dramatist seriously expect a company of these actors, decked in borrowed clothes and borrowed passions, strutting the bare boards for an hour or so, to compass these tasks he had set them?

To which Mr. Shakespeare, for all his famed gentleness, might reply rather tartly: 'My dear sir, I was an actor myself. I may not have been a very good one; that was partly because I could not give my whole mind to it, for the writing of even such a trifle as *The Merry Wives of Windsor* takes it out of a man. But I know a good deal more of the possibilities of the art of acting than you do; and am I likely to have been so inconsiderate and so foolish as to risk the success of any play by setting its actors tasks that they could *not* perform?'

Excellent repartee; but it still does not settle the question. It is absurd to suppose that such a restless and daring genius would check himself in full career to ask whether Burbage and his fellows could do well with this and that sort of scene or not. Without doubt Shakespeare imagined effects, which never were fully achieved in his theatre. But there is a great gulf fixed between this admission and saying that he imagined effects that never *could* be achieved, saying, in fact, that he ceased altogether to write in the terms of the art he had mastered. Genius is often a destructive force, and the question is a fair one, and we may press it: did Shakespeare in his greatest work, trying to enlarge, only shatter his medium? Yet before we credit this last accusation, think of the masters of other arts—of music especially—whose most mature work was received at best with the respect to which earlier success had entitled them, but with the protest that really these Ninth Symphonies and these music dramas were but negations of music. Yet what difficulty do we find in appreciating them now?

Posterity's answer, as given to the great revolutionary masters of music, has been, by one chance and another denied to Shakespeare; for these greater plays have never yet been put to full theatrical proof. To begin with, the theatre for which he wrote was itself undergoing one revolutionary change even before he ceased writing for it; it was shifting from outdoors in. To compare the effect of this upon his plays to the bringing of the *Agamemnon* into the back drawing-room would be an exaggeration, but with a strong spice of truth in it. Then came suppression of the theatres; tradition was broken, its thread lost, and more was lost than this. Contemporary evidence points to it, even if study of Restoration drama did not. We must always question very closely the testimony of people who mourn the 'good old times', especially the good old times of the drama. No performances are better than those of our earliest recollection; and I suppose it follows that the best of all must be those we never saw. (These, however, are the actor's means to immortality; so let us not grudge them to him.) But when the speakers in the dialogue *Historia Histrionica* in 1699, looking back sixty years, refer to the actors of the King's Company, which was Shakespeare's, as having been 'grave and sober men, living in reputation', it is likely to be the truth; for there is confirmation of it. Heminge and Condell were two of them. Does not the introduction to the first folio reflect as much gravity and sobriety as you like? Consider, too, that for fifty years here was a guild (that best describes it) of great renown, with many privileges, for long attached to the Court. No women were admitted; and this, at the time (and even now perhaps) would make for its greater gravity. Its younger recruits were the boy apprentices, thoroughly and severely trained from their childhood. It was a body made to perpetuate tradition. This first chance to come abreast with the greater Shakespeare passed. It passed with the deaths of Shakespeare and Burbage. The theatre had its daily bread to earn and fashion to follow. A re-creative interpretative genius would have been needed. And with the Puritan revolution it vanished. Then followed the demoralization of the Restoration period. Betterton did much to rescue the theatre, but he developed a more Augustan tradition, which dominated the eighteenth and much of the nineteenth century. This was a time, too, of the mutilation of texts in the theatre, though scholars were restoring them in the study; also of Shakespeare by flashes of lightning, those flashes of lightning that are apt to leave us in deeper darkness between times. Nineteenth-century scholarship suffered from a surfeit of Shakespeare as philosopher, Shakespeare as mystic, as cryptogrammatic historian, as this and that, and as somebody else altogether. And the nineteenth-century theatre suffered from the nineteenth century; it was commercialized. Till at last it has seemed but common sense to return to Shakespeare as playwright, and even, for a fresh start, to Shakespeare as Elizabethan playwright. Upon which basis we have within these last five-and-twenty years largely relaid the foundations of our study of him. For this latter-day pioneering we have to thank scholars and men of the theatre both, men of diverse, not to say antagonistic, minds, methods, and standpoints. Mr. William Poel, with a fine fanaticism, set himself to show us the Elizabethan stage as it was. Dr. Pollard put us on the track of prompt-books. Dr. Chambers, Sir Israel Gollancz (if in his presence I may name him), Mr. Lawrence, Mr. Dover Wilson—we are in debt to many. And one I will more particularly name; William Archer, whose death five months ago was a bitter blow to his friends and a heavy loss to the causes he loved and served. He loved the theatre of the past—though at times he might dissemble his love—not less because he felt the theatre of the present needed his watchful praise and criticism more. To this present question he brought industry and knowledge, and to his writings on it a generosity of judgement, which was only to be chilled by his intolerance of slovenliness and humbug; in fact, to this, as to all his work, he brought the standards by which he lived, of constancy and truth.

We have set ourselves, then, for a fresh start, to see Shakespeare the playwright as his contemporaries—as my old playgoer of 1635, whom I fear I have been forgetting, whom I will now finally forget—saw him. But even so we must not narrow our view. More is involved than the mere staging of his plays, than the question whether they must be acted in a reproduction of the Globe Theatre or may be decked out in all the latest trimmings. We know well enough what the Elizabethan stage was like. We do not know fully all the effects that could be gained on it, for only experiment will show us. Such experimenting, therefore, will always be valuable. But surely this principle can be agreed upon; that, whether or no one can ever successfully place a work of art in surroundings for which it was not intended, at least one must not submit it to conditions which are positively antagonistic to its technique and its spirit. Such an agreement involves, in practice, for the staging of Shakespeare—first, from the audience, as much historical sense as they can cultivate without it choking the spring of their spontaneous enjoyment; next, that the producer distinguish between the essentials and the incidentals of the play's art. Many even of its essentials may be closely knit to the Elizabethan stage of its origin. But whether it is to be played upon a platform or behind footlights, whether with curtains or scenery for a background (and scenery which is more than a background sins even against its own nature) this at least is clear, if my contention of to-day be allowed: Shakespeare's progress in his art involved an ever greater reliance upon that other art which *is* irrevocably wedded to the playwright's—the art of interpretative acting.

And it is in this aspect—of the demands which his greatest work makes upon acting according to the privilege which the technique he evolved bestows upon it—that his art has not yet, I think, been either very fruitfully studied or illustrated. Nor, for the historical reasons I have given, do I see how it well could have been. Nor is the path to its studying very easy even now. There are gleams of light along it, but only gleams. From the scholar's side we had, a generation ago, Moulton's *Shakespeare as a Dramatic Artist*; the work of a powerful mind, a little apt in the excess of its power to break its subject in pieces

and remould it as stern logic requires, but a book nevertheless which does elucidate some of the fundamental
things in which Shakespeare's art abides. When Dr.
Bradley's masterly *Shakespearean Tragedy* was given us—
this was a bright gleam, though it still surprised some
people a little to find an Oxford professor treating not
only poetry as poetry, but plays as plays. Nowadays,
however, Sir Arthur Quiller-Couch takes lucky Cambridge
men for delightful picnics (may one so call them ?) in the
sunny meads of literature, dramatic and other. And we
even find him publicly confessing that he stage-managed
a performance of *The Merchant of Venice* a few years ago
and learned a lot about the play in the process. And if
this is the first the Chancellor of that dignified University
hears of such a shameful fact, I hope that he hears it
unmoved.[1]

There is always a danger, however, that the scholar,
approaching a play from its histrionic standpoint, may trip
himself up over some simple snag. This is unfortunate and
unfair; for after all it is a very proper way of approach.
But the drama is an old art; it cannot be wholly reduced
to the terms of the printed page. To printer and publisher
and editor it bows with gratitude. Where would Shakespeare be to-day without them ? Much of its practice,
however, particularly on its histrionic side, can only be
handed down from master to pupil in the traditional way,
as other arts and mysteries are. But in this present case
and at the present time the artists fail us too, I fear. Their
individual excellence is not in question, but that opportunity for constant collaboration which is the theatre's
peculiar need, by which tradition is formed and preserved.
We have no care for the traditions of our theatre.[2] Within

[1] The late Lord Balfour was in the chair.
[2] Something is, I believe, being done to preserve the beauty of English
speech; gramophone records of it are now kept at the British Museum.
How like the time! Have they a record, I wonder, of the most beautiful
piece of speaking I ever heard, Sir Johnston Forbes Robertson's 'Buckingham's Farewell' in *Henry VIII* ? I have been waiting for thirty years and

my own day one school of Shakespearian acting has perished; it was not a very good one, but it had its own virtues. The present attempts at a new one are being made under conditions that cannot at any rate make it fit for the task we are discussing now. I would not say one word in discouragement of the efforts of the hard-worked young men and women who gallantly fly the flag and have the trumpet blown for them at Stratford-on-Avon and the Old Vic, and elsewhere. Theirs is a very necessary task. But it is conditioned by the fact that they must be constantly providing a three-hours' entertainment for their audience. To that overriding necessity everything else must give way. Now there are many plays—plays of Shakespeare's too—that fulfil such conditions very well. Act them, if not a little better, then a little worse, and no great harm is done. But the five great tragedies do not come into that category. Viewed as an evening's entertainment 'King Lear' *is* a foredoomed failure, even as Beethoven's great Mass and Bach's Matthew Passion would be. For it comes, as they come, into another category of art altogether; it is not the art that by perfect and pretty performance will charm and soothe us, but that which, in the classic phrase, purges by pity and terror. We don't expect to enjoy the Mass as we do *The Mikado*, or even as we may enjoy a Mozart sonata. There is as much enjoyment of the common sort in *King Lear* as there is in a shattering spiritual experience of our own; though we may come to look back on both with gratitude for the wisdom they have brought us. Incidentally, the due interpretation of such art will purge the interpreters with mental and emotional and physical exhaustion too. It demands from them an extraordinary self-devotion. Its greatest effects may be within their reach, but will always

more to hear it again. But he has never played the part again, has never had the chance. Were we so rich in such talent that we could afford to let it be spent at large? And we are to tell our students of to-day that they can hear it on the gramophone! It is not by such creaking methods that artistic tradition is handed on.

be a little beyond their grasp. Actors and singers are brought to the point where they forget themselves and we forget them. And beyond that boundary—it may happen to some of us a dozen times in a lifetime to cross it—we are for a crowning moment or so in a realm of absolute music and of a drama that Shakespeare's genius will seem to have released from all bonds. I say that we must not look for perfect performances of such plays, for there is nothing so finite as perfection about them. They have not the beauty of form and clarity of expression which distinguish Racine and his great Greek exemplars. But, in virtue of a strange dynamic force that resides in them, they seem to surpass such perfection and to take on something of the quality of life itself. And they do this the more fitly, surely, in that they demand to be interpreted, less conventionally, in terms of life itself, through this medium of living men and women. Therefore, while we arrive at no perfection in their performance, there need be practically no limit to, nor any monotony in the inspiration actors can draw from them. And their essential technique is likely to lie in the fruit-fulness and variety of the means by which the significance of human relations—of men towards each other, of man to the invisible—is revealed. A later theatre has made for us an illusion by which we see men as beings of another world. But Shakespeare worked for an intimacy which should break the boundaries between mimic and real, and identify actor and audience upon the plane of his poetic vision. Is there another art in which the world of the imagination can be made so real to us and the immaterial so actual, in which, not to speak it profanely, the word can be made flesh, as in these few boldest flights of his genius?

I do not pretend that I have fathomed Shakespeare's secret; my contention is that it has not been fathomed yet, and that it cannot be given to the world by such means as we have now at hand. The scholar, at best, will be in the case of a man reading the score of a symphony, hum-ming the themes. He may study and re-study a play, and

M

ever find something new. I have seen and read *Julius Caesar* times enough, and now at the moment I am flattering myself with the discovery—though doubtless it is *not* a new one—that the decried last Act is a masterpiece. Again, who will not confess with me that at any performance some quite unsuspected effect (unsuspected often by the interpreters themselves) may suddenly glow into life before him ? For instances: the fullness of tragic irony that resides in the very meeting of the jovial sensualist Gloucester, deprived of his eyes, with Lear, the man of intellectual pride, robbed of his wits; the edge given to the tragedy in Othello, when he and Desdemona, on the brink of the abyss, must yet concern themselves with entertaining the Venetian envoy to dinner. These are little things; but as we saw, the great plan of the plays apart, it is the wealth of such touches, many of which can hardly be expressed in other terms than the art's own, that endow them with their abundant life.

Can the full virtue of any art be enjoyed except in its own terms ? This is the crucial question. To transport Shakespeare from the world of the theatre into a vacuum of scholarship is folly. Must we say (I will not admit it) that in the theatre scholarship cannot find a place ? But the conditions under which the theatre works to-day—and always has worked in England—are no more compatible with the stricter obligations of scholarship than is any other form of journalism. The theatre to-day does much that is effective, even as many journalists write exceedingly well. But if the higher tasks of literature had all to be essayed with the printer's devil as call-boy at the door, heaven help us!

So here is a high task and a hard task, and a task, as I contend, never fully attempted yet. For Shakespeare *did* in these greater imaginings break through the boundaries of the material theatre he knew, and none that we have yet known has been able to compass them. Can such a theatre be brought to being ? How can we say till we have tried? But as he never ceased to be the practical playwright and man of the theatre the chances are, perhaps, that it can. Only, however, I believe, by providing for some continuance of that guild of grave and sober men of reputation to whom the work was first a gift. A gift too great for them, perhaps; is it still too great a one for us? Or can we, after three centuries, amid the never-ceasing chatter of tribute to Shakespeare as the marvel of our race, also contrive to make his art at its noblest a living thing?

No need to discuss here how such a guild could be formed. There are fifty ways of doing it if we had the will. But a first clause in its charter would need to secure the privilege which all good scholars claim—for its members would be scholars in their kind—that the work should be done for its own sake. It would involve hard discipline, in the retracing and re-treading of the road upon which Shakespeare as playwright passed and beckoned. The foundations of poetic drama, this most national of our arts, would need to be retrodden firm. It is not, even in its genesis, the art of slinging fine blank-verse lines together upon a printed page, but—and here the first thing to restore—the art of speech made eloquent by rhythm and memorable by harmony of sense and sound. For here was Shakespeare's first strength; from this he advanced. And if we cared to follow him faithfully for the hard length of his pilgrimage, scholars of the printed page side by side with scholars of the spoken word, it might be that we could enter into and enjoy that still mysterious country of his highest art. An inheritance, one would suppose, well worth the effort and the journey!

THE BACCHIC ELEMENT IN
SHAKESPEARE'S PLAYS[1]

By PROFESSOR EMILE LEGOUIS

I HOPE I shall not be accused of disrespect to the greatest of English poets by inviting you to examine for an hour's time what place he made on his stage to drinking and drinkers. There are so many loftier aspects by which his works appeal to the world that it may well seem unpardonable to call the attention of such a distinguished audience to that which appears to be the mere scum and froth of his genius. But it so happens that in the innumerable studies inspired by his person and his plays, none has yet been, to my knowledge, specially devoted to this seemingly humble question, so that I was first allured by its comparative novelty.[2] Moreover, owing to the hypnotic effect of the fixed idea, by considering the problem for some length of time, I have seen it loom larger and larger, grow transcendent and paramount. This is the wonted result of monomania: it imparts to the man of science or the scholar a blissful conviction that the universe is contained in the atom under his magnifying glass. Not Shakespeare only but the whole Renaissance seemed to me after due concentration of thought to be illumined by the sparkle of ruby or amber in the wine-cup.

But, to be in the proper mood for such an inquiry, we must momentarily, at least for the first half of this lecture, doff our present habits of thought regarding alcohol, as

---

[1] First delivered 1926. Save for a few slight changes this lecture is here reprinted as originally published in 1926.

[2] When I wrote this I had not yet read a most interesting article on 'Shakespeare and Wine', published by Dr. F. H. Hayward in *The National Temperance Quarterly* of spring 1925. Written from the temperance side of the question, Dr. Hayward's article may well serve as an antidote to the present lecture.

we now say, keep away the dismal ideas put into us all by the statistics of learned physicians, the constant association of drink with disease, crime, and degradation, the eloquent denunciations of its misdeeds by philanthropic societies—and consent to look at it in its freshness and glory, and it was in the sixteenth century, a thing of joy, akin to poetry and love.

Was it not the current belief of the Renaissance that poetry was enthusiasm, a sort of divine fury distinct from the slow and cold processes of deliberate logic? Enthusiasm was a form of intoxication and described in the same manner as the effects of wine on the brains. Drayton calls it 'a fine madness' or 'a clear rage', and expects the poet to see 'brave translunary things'. Shakespeare himself will have it that the poet's eye is 'in a fine frenzy rolling'. A temperate head is looked down upon as unfit for the loftier flights. Poor Samuel Daniel is somewhat contemptuously dismissed from the number of great poets as being too self-possessed, too cold-headed. Prose is the region for the water-drinker.

The literary paganism of the age added to these notions the consecration and the dream. Had not the Greeks ascribed a common origin, and a divine one, to verse and wine? Had they not made Dionysus or Bacchus the springhead of both? Besides, had not one of their most popular, most imitated poets, Anacreon, the Omar Kayyàm or Fitzgerald of pre-Christian times, placed liquor on the same level as love as the source of his inspiration?

The Renaissance rings with the echoes of the Bacchanals, and repeats to satiety the themes of Anacreon, in Italy, in France, in England. A diffused platonism, hovering like a nimbus over all the deliriums of the mind, still helped to exalt the praise of ebriety.

We French may proudly lay claim to the writer who then carried to the highest pitch the eulogy of drink and made wine, as it were, the hero of his strange epic: the famous 'curé de Meudon', François Rabelais.

Rabelais is the great priest of Bacchus. His book is the

Bible of drinkers. Wine is for him the promoter of good fellowship, the prick of wit and wisdom. His characters, whether men or giants, Panurge and Frère Jean des Entommeures, Gargantua and Pantagruel, are eternally thirsty and, according to their size, pour into their throats whole mugs or whole tuns of liquor.

The central episode of the epic, the hesitations of Panurge as to whether he ought to marry or remain a bachelor, finally results, after due consultation of all oracles human or sacred, in an appeal to the 'dive bouteille' or divine bottle, as the supreme source of light in this incomprehensible world of ours. The last word of wisdom is inscribed on the sides of the prophetic flask:

'O bottle—full all—of mysteries,—with one ear—I hearken to thee;—delay not—and utter the word—to which my heart is suspended;—in the celestial liquor—enclosed within thy sides,—Bacchus, who was the conqueror of India,—holds all truth confined; —divine wine, from thee is excluded—all lie and all treachery . . . '

> Vin tant divin, loing de toy est forclose
> Toute mensonge et toute tromperie . . .

And, as you know, the word that comes out of the divine bottle is *trinc*; whereupon Bacbuc, the priestess, applying the flask to Panurge's lips, pronounces these words:

'Not to laugh but to drink is the propriety of man; I don't mean simply and merely to drink, for so do all brutes, but to drink good fresh wine. Note this, friend, that from wine one grows divine; there is no argument so certain, no divination less deceiving . . . For it hath power to fill the soul with all truth, all knowledge and philosophy . . . In wine is truth hidden.'

After which Panurge and his friends begin to rime out of prophetic fury.

Our poet Ronsard was not long after Rabelais to celebrate Bacchus, with scarcely less rapture, and with much more solemnity. His *Hymn to Bacchus* does not only contain some of his most graphic verse, but adopts the ancient idea of the civilizing God from whom all good accrued to the earth and to the human race:

> Toy grand, toy sainct, toy dieu . . .

Man owes him music, owes him liberty, owes him truth.
Through Bacchus man attains valiance, reason, prophetic
power:

> Par toy les Devineurs troublés en leurs poitrines
> Frémissent sous le joug de tes fureurs divines . . .

Bacchus refines man's morals, raises his imagination to
heaven, and makes him feast with the gods:

> Through thee, Father, full of thy sweet ambrosia,
> We lift up our human fancy to the skies;
> Rapt in thy chariot, and purg'd from all vice
> By thy liquor, we dare climb to heaven
> And sit at great Jove's own table.

That this was not mere official praise, nor a mere copy
of an antique theme, is shown by other passages of the
same poet in familiar epistles, where he perhaps even
better shows his proneness to identify the workings of
wine with the spirit of youth and poetry. Such are the
superb lines in his Epistle to his friend l'Huillier, a few of
which I beg leave to quote in the French:

> Comme on voit en septembre ès tonneaux angevins
> Bouillir en escumant la jeunesse des vins,
> Qui, chaude en son berceau, à toute force gronde,
> Et voudroit tout d'un coup sortir hors de sa bonde,
> Ardente, impatiente, et n'a point de repos
> De s'enfler, d'escumer, de jaillir à gros flots . . .
> Ainsi la poésie en sa jeune saison
> Bouillonne dans nos cœurs, peu subjecte à raison . . .

The same idea of the incomparable inspiriting power of
wine prevails in England, and in the very poets who have
won renown as the champions of temperance or even of
puritanism—one at the entrance, the other towards the
end of the great Renaissance epoch—Spenser and Milton.
Spenser who was soon after to sing the praises of Sire
Guyon, the type of all moral restraint, had first declared
that the poet was utterly unable to write great verse unless
he was heated by copious cups. Instead of humble
pastorals, would not he himself be fit to compose a warlike

epic or some heroic tragedy, if provided for by rich patrons that would soak his Muse in liquor ?

> Who ever casts to compasse weighty prise,
> And thinkes to throwe out thondring words of threate,
> Let powre in lavish cups and thriftie bitts of meate,
> For Bacchus fruit is frend to Phoebus wise,
> And when with wine the braine begins to sweate,
> The nombers flowe as fast as spring doth ryse.
>
> Thou kenst not, Percie, howe the ryme should rage,
> O, if my temples were distained with wine,
> And girt in girlonds of wild yvie twine,
> How I could reare the Muse on stately stage
> And teache her tread aloft in buskin fine,
> With quaint Bellona in her equipage.

And much later in life, when he had become a grave teacher of morality, we have proofs that he had by no means sworn off his early allegiance to Bacchus. He would have every guest, every neighbour, drunk on the day when he married his Elizabeth:

> Poure out the wine without restraint or stay,
> Poure not by cups, but by the belly full.
>   Pour out to all that wull,
> And sprinkle all the posts and walls with wine,
> That they may sweat, and drunken be withall.
> Crowne ye god Bacchus with a coronall,
> And Hymen also crowne with wreathes of vine . . .

Young Milton, 'the lady of Christ's', was not behind-hand with Spenser or Ronsard in his trust in the verse-inspiring power of the grape-juice. True to say he confided his faith not to the English but to the Latin Muse. As his friend Diodati had complained to him that the Christmas festivities in the country hindered him from writing poetry, Milton would admit no such reflection on the gifts of Bacchus. He answered:

Why dost thou say that poetry hath been put to flight by meat and wine?
Poetry loves Bacchus, Bacchus loves poetry;

Phoebus was not ashamed to wear green corymbs
And to prefer the ivy to his own laurel.

He reminds his friend of the intimacy between Bacchus and the Nine Sisters; he also reminds him of Ovid, Anacreon, and Pindar, in whose poems, he says:

Every page is redolent of the wine they have absorbed . . .

It was after having drunk a four-your-old wine that Horace

Sweetly sang Glycera and fair-haired Chloe.

It will be the same with Diodati if he drinks deep enough. A rich meal 'nourishes the mind's strength and fosters genius'. 'Cups of Massique wine make the veins teem and foam; verse is poured from the amphora wherein it is concealed.' Diodati will then be moved to take his lyre and make the maidens dance; whereupon 'he will feel silent Phoebus creep through his breast, a sudden heat enter into his bones'. Bacchus is indeed the inspirer of all love poetry, together with Erato, Ceres, and Venus:

Therefore are large meals allow'd to love-poets
And to be often drench'd in old wine.

Thus sang young Milton in Latin verse. It is true that, unlike Spenser, he recommends in the same Elegy a frugal life and the use of pure water to the more ambitious bards who, like himself, aim at writing epic or religious poetry. Yet his belief in the enkindling effect of wine is beyond contest.

Was all this mere theoretical Bacchism, mere literary carousing? By no means. In fact the poets' hymns to Bacchus were only the crown and crest over a broad popular epicurism. One of the best drinking-songs in the world, the one in *Gammer Gurton's Needle* whose burden is

Backe and syde, go bare, go bare;
Both foot and hande, go cold:
But bellye, God sende thee good ale ynoughe,
Whether it be newe or olde,

3932 N

has nothing to do with Bacchus and mythology. It is the sheer expression of an elementary appetite; though comical in intent, it is almost appalling in its thirstiness—a true British beggar's song as Robert Burns alone was able to match in after years.

Now, in the comparisons often made between the different nations of Europe as regards their drinking capacities, England then had one of the foremost ranks. Rabelais himself modestly withdrew all claim to the palm for his own country, and described a man overcome with drink as 'drunk as an Englishman'. Yet England's supremacy did not pass quite unchallenged if we take Shakespeare as an umpire. When his Portia portrays the several European pretenders to her hand, she makes the young German, the duke of Saxony's nephew, the type of the absolute drunkard. On the other hand, Hamlet attributes to the Danes what seems to him a shameful superiority in this respect. It 'makes us traduc'd and tax'd of other nations', says he, 'they clepe us drunkards and with swinish phrase soil our addition'.

It is well known that these lines of the second quarto of 1604 were suppressed in the folio of 1623 for fear they should reflect on the habits of Ann of Denmark, James's consort. But still it is an open question whether the poet aimed at Denmark or England when he wrote them. He never was very particular about local colour. Denmark might as well mean Great Britain to him as Rome usually meant London. Three years later, at any rate, Iago gave the palm to the English without hesitation. They were according to him 'most potent in potting'. 'Your Danes, your Germans, and your swag-bellied Hollanders are nothing to your English . . . Your Englishman drinks you with facility your Dane dead drunk, he sweats not to overthrow your Almain, to give your Hollander a vomit, ere the next pottle can be filled.'

But though it is hard to decide the question from the international point of view, there is but little doubt of the extremely convivial habits of England under the Tudors and the Stuarts—chiefly of those that prevailed in the theatrical world of the time. Intemperance had played sad havoc among Shakespeare's early companions or rivals, Greene, Peele, and Marlowe, and it does not appear that much greater sobriety had been induced by the example of their premature deaths.

Surely the most representative poet between Spenser and Milton, if we except Shakespeare, is Ben Jonson. He, too, like his Justice Clement, had an unshaken faith in the virtue of sack. Of Spenser's verses he liked best those to the praise of wine I have just quoted. His creed was not abstract but practical. He astonished a hard-drinking society by the depth and breadth of his potations. Aubrey says of him: 'He would many times exceed in drink: canarie was his beloved liquor, then he would tumble home to bed; and when he had thoroughly perspired, then to studie.'

His host in Scotland, Drummond of Hawthornden (whose notes, in spite of a recent attack of scepticism, are still held genuine by most), after enjoying his company for some days, said of him that 'drink was one of the elements in which he liveth'. Jonson himself told without shame how he had been made dead drunk by Sir Walter Raleigh's son, whose tutor he was, then laid on a cart and drawn through the streets of a continental city. He also bragged that 'after he was reconciled with the Church, i.e. the Church of England, and left off to be a recusant, at his first communion, in token of his reconciliation, he drank out all the full cup of wine'. He kept a vivid remembrance of one of his gouty fits (surely after some drinking-bout), when he had 'consumed a whole night in lying looking to his great toe, about which he hath seen Tartars and Turks, Romans and Carthaginians, fight in his imagination'.

He used to preside in his old age over the merry nights at The Old Devil Tavern, in the room of Apollo, for which he wrote his *Leges conviviales* and had these truly Rabelaisian lines inscribed over the entrance door:

Welcome all who lead or follow
To the oracle of Apollo.

> Here he speaks out of the pottle,
> Or the tripos, his tower-bottle.
> All his answers are divine,
> Truth itself doth flow in wine . . .
> Wine is the milk of Venus . . .
> Tis the true Phoebian liquor,
> Cheers the brains, makes wit the quicker . . ., &c.

A little earlier in life he used to lead the revels at The Sun, The Dog, or The Triple Tun, commemorated by Robert Herrick. Earlier still it was at The Mermaid, universally known by his friend Francis Beaumont's Epistle. Beaumont complained of the wretched liquor he had to put up with in the country instead of 'the full Mermaid wine' quaffed with Ben Jonson. Without such wine he had no hope of writing good verse:

> What things have we seen
> Done at the Mermaid! heard words that have been
> So nimble, and so full of subtle flame,
> As if that ev'ry one from whence they came
> Had meant to put his whole wit in a jest,
> And had resolv'd to live a fool the rest
> Of his dull life . . .

Among the guests present on such occasions there often was Shakespeare himself. We might guess it from Beaumont's allusion to the 'words so nimble and so full of subtle flame'. But we have moreover the later testimony of Thomas Fuller with his famous description of the wit-combats between bulky Jonson and brisker, quicker-witted Shakespeare, which we are irresistibly drawn to locate in the historic tavern. I have only arrived at him after a long preamble and many circuits. But they may not seem superfluous if I have by this means somewhat recreated the atmosphere, shown the wide place filled by drink in the minds of men of letters under Elizabeth and James, and in their lives. These were the soothing poetical fictions as well as the daily realities among which Shakespeare lived.

Of his personal habits we know very little, much less

than of Ben Jonson's. Recent criticism has become so sceptical regarding the early Shakespearian traditions that many reject them in the lump nowadays as idle gossip or mere forgery. I confess I remain one of the few that still believe there may be something in them, that smoke is best accounted for by fire. Now, however inaccurate in its details, however distorted by distance and hearsay, the tradition, after depicting his father as a 'merry-cheeked' good fellow, conveys the idea of a rather wild youth associating with the Stratford poachers, a kind of people who seldom go dry; of a London actor haunting the taverns like all his compeers; of a middle-aged man retired in his native town whose death was hastened by a visit of his London comrade Jonson and of his fellow Warwickshire man Drayton, in which more wine was drunk than was good for him.

These are among the least disputed records—the nearest also to his own time. We may discard with a smile the local legend only recorded in 1762 which credits him with engaging in a prolonged and violent drinking-bout at Bidford, a neighbouring village, as the Stratford champion; after which he went to sleep under a certain memorable crab-tree. Against those hints of unequal value but all congruent, there can only be invoked an obscure manuscript note on a fly-leaf in Aubrey's papers wherein it is said of some one, who, according to the context, may be either Shakespeare, or John Fletcher, or the dancer Ogilby, that he was 'the more to be admired *quia* he was not a company-keeper, and would not be debauched'. Yet as it is added concerning the same person that 'if invited to writ, he was in paine', the attribution to Shakespeare seems impossible.

Upon the whole, the old traditions better account for the marvellous drinking-scenes in his plays than would stories representing him as a propagandist against wine and revelry. They better agree with his lifelike portraiture of boon companions, his delight in describing them, his enjoyment of their fun, at least during the first half of his dramatic career. Who can doubt he had excellent opportunities for observation, and fully, heartily, shared in the merry-makings of his day ?

Yet, there is this difference between him and Spenser or Milton, that he never confessed his own feelings or tastes directly, in his own person, but through imaginary characters. What he himself thought is always hidden from us, and can only be guessed from the sympathy or antipathy projected by him over the creatures of his fancy. He also differed from them in another way: his genius was far more deeply rooted in the English soil than that of either Milton or Spenser. He was not only the interpreter of the Bacchic or anacreontic traditions. He also voiced the instincts and beliefs of the common people, of his London surroundings, or of his countryside. The two streams flow together, mixed or separate, through his plays. At times the convention, literary or theatrical, is more apparent; at other times, realism is uppermost.

Perhaps least realistic of all is his most famous creation, the character whose name comes first to every one's mind in connexion with drink. Falstaff is bigger than nature and to a certain extent out of it. Though in a way more substantial than ordinary man, with 'a whole merchant's venture of Bordeaux stuff' in his belly, he is fantastical, he is a symbol. In this one character, Shakespeare has summed up the spirit of the Rabelaisian epic. Both Panurge and Frère Jean des Entommeures revive in him. He personifies the bacchanalian creed of the Renaissance, its belief in the genial virtues of wine. Even as Biron, in *Love's Labour's Lost*, had been the mouthpiece of Plato's doctrine of love, from which all wisdom and all poetry proceed, asserting that women's eyes are

> the ground, the books, the academes,
> From whence doth spring the true Promethian fire;

even as Biron had endeavoured to give a sort of physiological explanation of the process:

> Other slow arts entirely keep the brain,
> And therefore, finding barren practisers,

Scarce show a harvest of their heavy toil;
But love, first learnéd in a lady's eyes,
Lives not alone immuréd in the brain,
But, with the motion of the elements,
Courses as swift as thought in every power
And gives to every power a double power
Above their functions and their offices . . .
Never durst poet touch a pen to write
Until his ink was temper'd with Love's sighs. . . .

even so does Falstaff interpret the other side of anacre-
ontism. He can tell the 'two-fold operation' of a good
sherris-sack and follow it from its entrance into a man's
throat to its bright metamorphosis into imaginative power
or eloquence:

'It ascends me into the brain; dries me there all the foolish, and
dull, and crudy vapours which environ it; makes it apprehensive,
quick, forgetive, full of nimble, fiery, and delectable shapes; which,
deliver'd o'er to the voice, the tongue, which is the birth, becomes
excellent wit . . . Learning is a mere hoard of gold kept by a devil,
till sack commences it, and sets it in act and use.'

It is true that with still more eloquence Falstaff will
demonstrate that sherris is the source of all valiance, while
he is a living proof that infinite drinking may result in
infinite cowardice. His creator here betrays him to our
laughter, but surely he does not give him the lie for what
regards wit and glibness of tongue. Falstaff justifies half
his own boasting. His genius springs fresher and livelier
from every new draught.

This shows that after all he is no real drunkard. His sack
is a stage-property, fictitious and harmless. We never see
him the worse for it. He may empty cup after cup, none
of the usual effects are perceptible in him. He is indeed
said to have drunk whole hogs-heads; he is even showed us
once asleep and snoring behind the arras, but he never
opens his lips without giving proof that his tongue is
nimbler, his brains more alert, his head cooler than those
of the more temperate mortals. He is not once caught
tripping, or hiccupping, or dull, or heated so as to lose his

self-control. From one end to the other he remains in-
tellectually triumphant. He never lapses into absurdity
and nonsense. The more he is said to swallow, the
brighter and shrewder he becomes. Shakespeare has
spared him the keen realistic probing he has applied to his
other topers. For all that Falstaff is a coward, a liar, and
a buffoon, there is an aureole round his grey-haired pate.
His supposed potations are the best of him, the redeeming
feature in his otherwise contemptible nature. A dry
Falstaff would be a monster.

There is at least a part of his philosophy that is not con-
tradicted by Shakespeare, rather approved by him. Falstaff,
to celebrate the virtue of sack, contrasts his young tavern
companion, Prince Hal, with his brother, Prince John, the
pattern of goodness and temperance. Of the latter he says:

'Good faith, this same young sober-blooded boy doth not love
me, nor a man cannot make him laugh, but that's no marvel, he
drinks no wine.'

Falstaff will, on the contrary, ascribe Prince Henry's
excellence to his potations:

'Hereof comes it that Prince Henry is valiant, for the cold blood
he did naturally inherit of his father, he hath, like lean, sterile, and
barren land, manured, husbanded, and tilled, with excellent endeavour of drinking good, and good store, of fertile sherris, that he
is become very hot and valiant.'

Shakespeare has no wish to gainsay Falstaff here. After
all Falstaff in this monologue is not departing from the
truth for fun or interest. He is merely stating a fact. Now
Prince Hal as heir to the throne and later as King Henry V
is the one indubitable hero on the Shakespearian stage.
We are inevitably led, not only by Falstaff's words, but by
the three plays in which he is conspicuous, to the conviction that Henry was by no means injured by his early
excesses—quite the reverse. His heroic qualities are distinctly shown to spring out of his youthful wildness.
Neither his temperate father nor his sober brother
appeal half so much to our sympathy or admiration. The

fact of having drunk with Falstaff and enjoyed his company is part of the halo with which the poet has surrounded
his glorious head. We are invited to admit that a goodly
quantity of sack should enter into the composition of the
complete man, of the full-blooded warrior, of the perfect
king.

That Shakespeare was towards that time full of indulgence for the Bacchic spirit is again shown in *Twelfth
Night*. Sir Toby Belch is the not unworthy successor of
Sir John, though with a difference. He has a zest for
fighting which the other had not. But there is more than
that: he is no longer half-mythic but thoroughly real.
Drinking in Olivia's rooms below stairs is not nominal as
it was at the Boar's Head. The cups served by Maria are
full of blood-red wine, not of stage-stuff. Here realism,
which had been kept in check by the creation of a super
drunkard, comes into play. Sir Toby is a very convincing
tippler. The effects of drink are obvious in his sayings
and doings. They affect, turn, and twist his natural wit
and shrewdness. The impudent rollicking devil of wine
rules over him, carries him away to acts of folly and
extravagance. His talk is an uncertain succession of
lightnings of good sense and of mere senseless vociferation,
while his companion and dupe, poor foolish Sir Andrew
Aguecheek, descends from one draught to another into
deeper and deeper abysms of stupidity.

Yet here again Shakespeare keeps a tender corner in his
heart for Sir Toby. He likes him for his fearless love of
fun, for his innate jollity. He allows him to have the better
of sober, conceited Malvolio with his sullen abhorrence of
merry drinking-bouts. He puts into his lips the fittest of
retorts to puritanical strictness and interference: 'Dost
thou think, because thou art virtuous, there shall be no
more cakes and ale?' And though he lets him be soundly
cudgelled by Sebastian, he will permit him to have his
joke and wine to the end, with Maria's hand to boot,
whatever happiness there may be in that.

Sir Toby is the last of the first series of Shakespeare's bibbers. He is as amusing as he is full of amusement, and therefore, upon the whole, sympathetic. The spirit of enjoyment goes out with him from Shakespeare's plays for several years. Up to this time, i.e. till the year 1601, when he was thirty-seven years old, Shakespeare has only been alive, so it seems, to the comedy of drink. His essential, inevitable rectitude of mind has indeed kept him from turning habitual topers into patterns of wisdom and virtue. He has never allowed us to lose sight of the lower side of their epicurism. But he has let them cheerfully follow the bent of their humour and has made them the occasion of abundant merriment to us. Whatever relates to drink is hearty and inviting. Some of Falstaff's own glory falls on the faces of his acolytes: Bardolph with the flaming nose, Nym with the inexhaustible 'humours', Pistol with his bombastic quotations from old extravagant tragedies. The devil in the bottle has nothing really wicked in him: his worst freaks are 'quips and cranks and wanton wiles'. He causes his devotees to muddle words and stutter; he will make Mrs. Quickly's arguments spring hurried, halting, and pell-mell out of her lips; he will induce Justice Shallow's cousin, Silence, forgetting his muteness and his name, to break out into scraps of incoherent songs till he is finally carried to bed. He will totally upset the never very steady head of Slender and make him swear: 'If I be drunk, I'll be drunk with those that have the fear of God, and not with drunken knaves.' The tragedy of drink is unknown or hidden in Shakespeare's first period.[1]

Ever since the chronology of Shakespeare's plays has

[1] I owe to the kindness of Professor Moore Smith a precious correction here. One or two years before *Hamlet*, in *As you Like It*, Shakespeare had given a serious warning to inveterate drinkers. Old Adam has kept hale and strong because in his youth, says he,

... I never did apply
Hot and rebellious liquors in my blood. II. iii. 47–53.

The admitted date of the play being 1600, this passage may be taken as the first indication of a change in the poet's attitude.

been established with a high degree of probability and has won almost universal assent, no critic of the poet has failed to notice a strange break in his career from *Henry V* to *Hamlet*', as Mr. Granville-Barker put it last year in his memorable lecture. The sudden beginning of a dark period about 1601 or 1602 is perhaps the best ascertained fact in his biography. Many explanations have been offered: domestic grief, the death of his father, the treason of the dark lady he loved and of whom he was robbed by his dearest friend; political disappointment, the execution of Essex to whose party he belonged as closely attached to Essex's friend, Southampton. On the other hand, the darkening of his stage has been accounted for by the public craving for melodrama to which, as the playwright of his company, Shakespeare thought it opportune to give the required food. There may of course be some parcel of truth in every one of these reasons, but no one, I believe, has ever held any of them quite decisive, nor them all put together quite sufficient.

Without rejecting these conjectures, I should be false to my subject if I did not endeavour to examine whether drink affords a better clue to the problem. That it is somehow related to the change is manifest, and Professor Bradley, best of guides, commenting on *Hamlet* and *Othello* wrote that 'possibly the subject (i.e. drunkenness) may for some reason have been prominent in Shakespeare's mind about this time'.

Let us first of all consider the large room he made for it in his great tragedies. It might very well have been otherwise. It was a theme for Thalia, not for Melpomene. You scarcely find a trace of it in the solemnity of ancient or modern tragedy. Yet Shakespeare will assign it one of the foremost places in his gloomy masterpieces. The scenes he now offers us show no less keen observation, no less insight into the workings of wine than the former ones. But instead of setting off the jollity of bacchanals, he now insists on their danger or their shame. Their results are no longer jests and jokes but catastrophes.

His comments on drunkenness are now therefore bitter and moral.

Young Hamlet speaks with disgust of the Danish habit of keeping wassail: 'It's a custom more honour'd in the breach than the observance ... It takes from our achievements, though perform'd at height, the pith and marrow of our attribute.'

Cassio distrusts the entirements of wine: 'I have very poor and unhappy brains for drinking: I could well wish courtesy would invent some other custom of entertainment.'

When he has wounded Montano, he is full of shame and remorse: 'Drunk? and speak parrot? and squabble? swagger? swear? and discourse fustian with one's own shadow?—O thou invisible spirit of wine! If thou hast no name to be known by, let us call thee devil ... O God! that men should put an enemy in their mouths to steal away their brains! that we should, with joy, pleasure, revel, and applause, transform ourselves into beasts! ... To be now a sensible man, by and by a fool, and presently a beast! O strange! every inordinate cup is unblessed, and the ingredient is a devil.'

No better mottoes could be found for Temperance societies than Cassio's exclamations. And in fact I hear that they have been more than once used by them, in wise preference to Sir John's or Sir Toby's utterances. It is still more to the discredit of wine that its defence should be assumed by treacherous Iago, who, after leading Cassio into temptation for his evil ends, calls him 'a too severe moraler', protests that 'good wine is a good familiar creature if it be well used', that 'any man living may be drunk at some time'.

In the drinking scene between the triumvirs, on Pompey's galley, after poor fuddled Lepidus, 'the third part of the world', has been carried out on the back of a strong slave, and the remaining guests have been madly dancing hand in hand round the table, invoking 'Plumpy Bacchus with pink eyne', Augustus Caesar who has himself, though more sparingly, shared in the potations, utters the protest of a reasonable man against more carousing:

> Gentle lords, let's part;
> You see, we have burnt our cheeks. Strong Enobarb
> Is weaker than the wine, and mine own tongue
> Splits what it speaks; the wild disguise hath almost
> Antick'd us all . . .

In all these passages, instead of the rosy nymphs bearing Anacreon's cup, breathing love and poetry, wit and laughter, we have a view of the dishevelled, shameless, frantic Maenads. There is still a genius in the amphora, but an evil one, inciting men to madness, crime, and ruin.

The drunken king Claudius is his brother's murderer. Poor Cassio leads to tragic issues by once yielding to the demon of wine. Heavy drinking precedes and facilitates the assassination of Duncan by Macbeth. Lady Macbeth has asked of strong spirits the boldness she wanted for the fearful deed:

> That which hath made them drunk hath made me bold:
> What hath quench'd them hath given me fire.

The revels of debauched Antony, the orgies of the assembled triumvirs end in a cataclysm that shakes the whole world.

But there is a problem of still greater import suggested by the series of tragedies we are now dealing with. Are not all the heroes or rather protagonists in them affected and stirred by a strange alcohol that 'works like madness in their brains'?—the whole line of them, Hamlet, Othello, Lear, Macbeth, Timon of Athens, Antony, Coriolanus?

That excess of drink is responsible for their wild behaviour is surely not meant by Shakespeare, except to a certain degree as regards Antony. A case might perhaps be made against Hamlet who, while he expresses his contempt for Danish intemperance, admits that he is 'native here and to the manner born'; or against Lear whose hundred knights among whom he lives are acrimoniously, but perhaps not wrongly, described by Goneril as:

> Men so disorder'd, so debosh'd and bold,
> That this our court, infected with their manners,
> Shows like a riotous inn: epicurism and lust
> Make it more like a tavern, or a brothel,
> Than a grac'd palace . . .

And it is quite possible that the old king was only blind to that rioting because such had been the manners of the rough generation to which he himself belonged.

There also appears to have been much heavy revelling in Macbeth's country, time, and surroundings (does not in a way the whole tragedy reek of strong spirits?), and a great deal of refined banqueting in Timon's prodigal and princely hospitality.

But we have no hint of the sort in reference to Coriolanus, save that, after a terrible day of hand-to-hand fighting, he very naturally asks for a drink: 'Have we no wine here?' As to Othello, for all that his life was spent in the camps, he seems to have the innate sobriety of the southerner. His advice to his officers on the night set for the celebrations of his nuptials shows him temperate:

> Let 's teach ourselves that honourable stop
> Not to out-sport discretion.

Yet in all those great tragic characters, in spite of the deep differences in age, situation, country, race, colour, passion, we cannot help noticing the workings of a similar temperament—a disorder of which there was but small intimation in the earlier plays. First of all Shakespeare now generally calls our attention to some physical derangement, which he scarcely ever did before. He will insist on some mysterious correspondence between body and soul. He was formerly like men in perfect health who remain unconscious of their bodily organs, till their existence is revealed to them by pain and disease. The root of his heroes' unsoundness is fixed in the ill-defined region between the physical and mental or moral worlds. Hamlet

and Macbeth are a prey to hallucinations; Lady Macbeth
to somnambulism. Othello has a trance plausibly called by
Iago an epileptic fit. Lear feels the rising of hysteria and
names it as men of art then did, while his hand explores
the sore place of his body:

> O, how this mother swells up toward my heart!
> *Hysterica passio!* down, thou climbing sorrow!
> Thy element is below . . .

In all these men physicians are invited to determine a
diathesis. And we pass on from medical symptoms to
psychology proper, there to be confronted by common
characteristics: impulsiveness, irrepressible vehemence,
want of self-possession and self-control in words and deeds,
lack of balance, sudden shiftings of determination, bitter
melancholy fits, a tendency to outrageous railing and curs-
ing;—such traits as have often been noted in men who
either bear the penalty of previous excesses of their own
or suffer from ancestral intemperance. Whether good or
bad, virtuously or viciously inclined, none of them are
wholly sound. Different explanations can of course be
offered for the wildness and desequilibrium apparent in all:
the shock of an atrocious domestic tragedy for neurasthenic
Hamlet, the tortures of jealousy for Othello, real madness
for Lear, the fury of remorse for Macbeth, the utter
disillusion of friendship for Timon, the exasperation of
pride for Coriolanus, self-abandonment to voluptuous love
for Antony. But still it remains to say why such contrary
passions should in all cases assume much the same form
of wild derangement. Those men truly are one family of
beings, different in soul but alike in temperament. At any
rate the fury in them all is almost identical in its manifestations.

When Marlowe's ranting heroes made their appearance
on the stage, his rival Nashe had at once denounced them
as the products of an imagination overcloyed 'with a more
than drunken resolution'. The clever satirist John Hall
had followed suit, accounting for the thundering threats

of a Tamburlaine by 'the drink-drownéd spright' of the author. This gross statement is much too one-sided to be accepted as a sufficient explanation of Marlowe's fiery genius or even of his Scythian shepherd's splendid bombast. How far less acceptable if applied to the infinitely more varied, subtle, and complex psychology of a Hamlet or a Lear or a Coriolanus! The latter are no longer the mere mouthpieces of a wild lyrical poet, but such acute studies of character as have taxed to the utmost the analysing faculties of the keenest critics. Yet the hint that wine had something to do with the stage-frenzy of the age should be kept in mind.

The temperamental resemblance between his tragic heroes induces us to admit that Shakespeare was for a time fascinated by the contemplation of a prevailing type whose pattern was before his eyes—either a single striking personality or a company of men all more or less off their hinges. Or shall we say that he may well have felt in himself in that period the workings of that disease resulting from many years of strenuous exertions, over-strained feelings, long sharing in tavern-life, a recourse to stimulants that surely was moderate in comparison of a Jonson's huge potations, but still had somehow exasperated to a degree the high-strung nerves of his sensitive nature, while his serene intellect left untouched could follow in his own self the steps of the disorder, and his imagination lashed to greater vividness than ever, turn it to supreme artistic realizations ?

It now remains for the man with a fixed idea to see whether the whole evolution of the Shakespearian drama might not be plausibly accounted for from the Bacchic point of view. Nothing would indeed be easier.

First come in the happy creatures of Shakespeare's fancy that some one of the fifty-six kinds of light wines enumerated by Harrison, sets talking and laughing: the Biron of *Love's Labour's Lost*, the Mercutio of *Romeo and Juliet*, or the lively youths of Venice who strive to drive away by their frothy chat Antonio's melancholy. To them are to be added the merry maidens made giddy—I was going to say by the least little sip of sparkling champagne, but I am afraid champagne is an anachronism and, in fact, Queen Elizabeth and her maids of honour had beer at breakfast—the most fascinating of voluble, flippant babblers, bridleless of tongue, exquisitely impudent, the Beatrices and Rosalinds, dancing and flirting in Leonato's drawing-room or picnicking in the forest of Arden. At respectful distance are discovered the stout bibbers with a preference for sack and high-spiced Spanish wines, Sir Toby ogling Maria over his bumper, incomparable Falstaff with his retinue of toss-pots, teased to more and more rollicking invention by an inabstinent Prince of Wales. All is jovial, frolicsome, jocose in the optimistic period when the cup is only a provocative of wit and fancy.

Then come the days of surfeit and penance. The halo round the cup has faded away, and brooding melancholy, anguish, and remorse are at the bottom of it. Man who formerly was a creature of reason and will is now upset, irascible, with nerves strained to the breaking-point, with fits of disproportionate anger. Hamlet's staccato notes alternate with paroxysms of ungovernable railing. Will he nill he, he 'must like a whore, unpack his heart with words, and fall a-cursing like a very drab, a scullion'. Lear, though not yet known to be insane, suddenly, with the mere shadow of a pretext, jumps from tender love to utter hate of his favourite daughter, from absolute trust in Kent to extravagant threats of death and a sentence of banishment. Coriolanus who has just promised to humour the people on whom his election to the consulate depends, at the first encounter loses all self-control and racks the language for the worst insults: 'Hence, old goat', 'Hence, rotten thing'. And once stirred, he cannot stop:

> You common cry of curs, whose breath I hate
> As reek o' the rotten fens, whose loves I prize
> As the dead carcasses of unburied men
> That do corrupt my air . . .

The fumes in Macbeth's head conjure up red-blood daggers or ghosts of murdered men. Is the end of all to be mere raving and delirium ?

But the poet finally recovers. He leaves more and more the London taverns and with a sure instinct for restoration, just as if he was obeying the prescriptions of a wise and friendly physician, gives as much of his time as he can to his native Stratford. A period of convalescence, relieved of the over-excitement of the preceding decade, though, it may be, still exposed to relapses on extra-ordinary occasions. Some of his earlier liveliness comes back to him. His denunciation of the poison in wine becomes less bitter as he purges it from his veins. He can give us again a lively sketch of the country truant Autoly-cus who declares that 'a quart of ale is a dish for a king'. But he will not desist, even in comic scenes, from setting off the beastliness of the drunkard. Only Caliban can now take fuddled Stephano for a god. And Caliban is half-man, half-beast. The drinking-bout between the two and the Fool Trinculo echoes the loud jollity in Olivia's house when Toby, Aguecheek, and Clown were carousing together, but this time the topers' aim is not a practical joke, it is sedition and murder. And the moral is empha-sized when undeceived Caliban exclaims:

> What a thrice double ass
> Was I, to take this drunkard for a god
> And worship this dull fool!

Thus is Bacchus contemptuously dismissed in the end by the poet who had first done him homage in the true Renaissance spirit.

The cycle is now complete and the demonstration will, I hope, appear to you incontrovertible for the hour being. Though I cannot help being partial to it, I do not expect it to obtain absolute and eternal recognition. Nothing in this ever-changing world of ours is more evanescent than the theories about Shakespeare's genius. One thing at any rate is certain: the matchless competence of the poet for all his drinking-scenes, whether painted in bright or dark colours. No less than Falstaff and Sir Toby do Cassio and the Triumvirs prove his amazing knowledge of the subject. How he came to master it to that degree; how he was led to a diametrically opposite attitude from that of his youth when the mature years had thinned his once abundant hair, is a question that every one will decide according to his inner lights. But no reasonable doubt can be entertained as to the wonderful lifelikeness of his drunkards and their performances, not eclipsed in their artistic perfection by the nobler creatures of his fancy or the sublimer scenes in which he explored the heights of human nature.

SHAKESPEARE IN AMERICA [1]

By ASHLEY THORNDIKE

WHAT is the influence of a great poet upon the civilization of a particular country? What effect does he
have on its manners, its art, its thinking, its faith? What,
for example, are the meaning and value of Homer for the
English nation? or of Virgil? or of Dante? Is it possible
to come to any measure of the sway of a great writer
over men's minds, any estimate of his effect in moulding
the character and quality of a people? What part have the
writings of Shakespeare played in the making of the
United States?

These are large questions. The one to which I am inviting your attention for a few moments is manifestly of a
magnitude equal to that of the United States plus that of
Shakespeare plus that of a large space left free for speculation. Far from attempting to treat it exhaustively, I have
only a few scattering comments to offer. But perhaps our
question may be given a little more definiteness if we put
it in this form—How has Shakespeare's influence on the
United States differed from his influence on any other
great nation? And we may find a clue to a partial answer
in the history of this United States which differs from that
of all other great nations. Our three centuries of history
disclose a pioneer people, always in touch with the unknown wilderness, conquering a continent, and, in spite of
many differences of race, speech, and religion, creating in
the new world a powerful nation united in spirit and uniform in culture.

A few groups of colonists, representing nearly all the
nations of Europe, make their way across an almost untrav-
ersed ocean and establish settlements scattered here and

[1] First delivered 1927, this lecture is reprinted as originally published in
1927.

there along a thousand miles of sea-coast. These become a
haven for those who, for reasons political, religious, economic, or personal, find their old homes no longer hospitable
or comfortable. The settlements grow, and become pre-
vailingly English in language, law, and government; and
then after a century and more the majority unite to form
an independent nation. No sooner do the seaport towns
become sizable than pioneers are pushing up the streams,
beyond the tidal waters to the hills, from the hills over the
mountains to the great prairies of the middle-west, and
then from the prairies across the deserts and mountains to
another ocean. Ships are ever moving back and forth
across the Atlantic, renewing and enlarging those bonds
that unite the new world with the old; but to the west
men are ever pushing on to a new frontier, away from
Europe, away from the Atlantic cities, away from old
associations and habits, into a region where no civilization
exists.

The United States has always had a frontier, has always
been subduing wild land, establishing civilization anew.
Even now our country is very unsettled compared with the
lands of western Europe whence we came. For a long time
yet our economic surplus must be spent largely in material
improvements. Bridges are still to be built, swamps
drained, forests felled, deserts irrigated. Our energies have
gone into the work of to-day, in preparation for to-
morrow. Why should we care for the literature of yesterday? I suppose it is difficult for an English audience to
understand how this pioneer spirit still separates us from
Europe. Consider a prospector of to-day hunting minerals
or oil, or the home-steader building his shack, or any one
of the thousands seeking new homes in new conditions,
like the many thousands before them, any one whose stake
is wholly in the future and who finds the distant east as
remote as the unrecorded past. Is it not strange that he
should think at all of what a man, Shakespeare living
thousands of miles away, wrote hundreds of years ago
about other persons—Caesar, Cleopatra, Hamlet—who

whether in fable or history lived still longer ago and farther away?

Of the great American migration of his race Shakespeare knew only the tiny beginnings, and he had little to say about them. He dreamed and wrote of the old world, of battles long ago, of an ancient story-land already splendid in its braveries and devotions. He uses the word America only once in the plays and then casually. He has left no sign of any interest in those daring voyagers and pirates who were making the western ocean the scene of such displays of human intrepidity as ancient story could scarcely match. He may have known Raleigh and Gilbert; he certainly knew Southampton, who was a leader in colonization companies, but he has given no hint of his feelings as he saw little ships dropping down the Thames loaded with adventurers to Virginia. But late in his career reports of the unexpected security found in the 'still-vext Bermoothes' by Sir George Somers's expedition to Virginia aided his imagination in the creation of a tale of an enchanted island that carries a parable of the future contact of civilized man with the powers of nature and with his savage brothers. The island of *The Tempest*, the home of Caliban and Ariel, is as near as Shakespeare's imagination came to America in his lifetime.

Within a few years after his death, however, his plays were to join in the migration and to become a part of men's thought and fancy throughout the colonies. It is often said that these colonists took with them from the mother country law and religion, language and literature. This is broadly true, but these Lares and Penates are too extensive to be carried in the first ship or to be fixed firmly in a new land until after long years of colonization. During the seventeenth century there were churches and clergymen a-plenty in America but very little law, few lawyers, no journals, and few books except of a theological sort. The scattered colonies had increased until the population was half a million. Virginia with its tobacco plantations and Massachusetts with its commerce were thriving and maintaining considerable intercourse with England; but these new communities seem as yet to have known little about Shakespeare.

In England itself the poet's reputation, though growing, can scarcely be said to be established until near the close of the seventeenth century. When the theatres were reopened at the Restoration, the genius of Betterton found its best expression in the great tragic roles, and henceforth Shakespeare's supremacy on the stage remained unquestioned, although many of the plays, particularly the romantic comedies, were discarded until well into the next century. The criticism of Dryden led in the discussion of Shakespeare's merits and defects and toward a full recognition of his dramatic and poetic greatness. Yet his readers still remained comparatively few. His collected works had appeared in four folio editions, the last in 1685; but I suppose that at the close of the century not over two thousand copies of these existed in all England.

It is doubtful if any copy had yet made its way to America. The copy of the first folio that has been longest resident in the United States is reported to have belonged originally to no other than the arch-Puritan and witch-baiter the Rev. Cotton Mather. A folio of Shakespeare was to be found alongside of folios of Ben Jonson and Beaumont and Fletcher in the fine library of Colonel William Byrd of Westover, Virginia, where it was inventoried for sale in 1777.[1] It may have been purchased at any time between 1696 and his death in 1744. Unfortunately, no one has attempted a thorough search for references to Shakespeare in the early Colonial books and records, but my own slight study has discovered nothing certain before 1700.

The edition prepared by the poet-laureate Nicholas Rowe and published in 1709 may be said to mark the beginning of a rapid and continued growth in the readers of Shakespeare. That edition promptly made its way to America. A copy was purchased for the library of Harvard

[1] *The Writings of Colonel William Byrd*, ed. J. S. Bassett, New York, 1901.

University as appears from the first catalogue of 1723, and in 1722 it is advertised for sale by a bookseller. In 1719 Benjamin Franklin was apprenticed to his brother James, who was beginning as a printer in Boston and who two years later was to start one of the earliest newspapers, *The New England Courant*, and Shakespeare's Works were in the printing house library by 1723. Yale University in 1714 received gifts of various books from England, including Milton, Spenser, and Ben Jonson, but its first Shakespeare was a later gift of Bishop Berkeley.[1] During the mid-century, references to Shakespeare become common, and he seems to have been read by all those who read anything in poetry and drama. As soon as the new republic was fairly started, a sufficient demand existed to give success to an American edition of his works, that of 1795.

In the meantime the plays were becoming known through the theatre as well as by the printed book. Play-acting was strictly forbidden in Puritan Boston, barely tolerated in Quaker Philadelphia, and not much encouraged anywhere, but occasional performances are recorded here and there during the first half of the century. The first specific mention of a Shakespearian performance is on 3 March 1750, in New York, when *Richard III* was given 'by a company that had already acted in Philadelphia'. Nine years earlier Garrick's performance of the same play at Goodman's Fields had inaugurated a new theatrical era and a new popularity for Shakespeare on the London stage. New York had still a long way to go to overtake the older city as a theatrical centre. In 1751 a performance of *Othello* is recorded, and in the following year a company of professionals, under the leadership of Lewis and Mrs. Hallam, made their way from England to America and opened at Williamsburg, then the capital of Virginia, with *The Merchant of Venice* on 15 September 1752. This company, though with many changes in its

[1] Thomas Goddard Wright, *Literary Culture in Early New England*, 1620–1730, New Haven, 1920.

membership, continued to act until the Revolution, travelling up and down the coast and presenting a repertory that came to include *The Merchant of Venice*, *Richard III*, *Hamlet*, *Othello*, *Lear*, *Henry IV*, *Macbeth*, *Romeo and Juliet*, *King John*, *Cymbeline*, and *The Tempest*.[1]

Some of their experiences in disseminating Shakespeare were novel. Within two months of their arrival they played *Othello* before 'The Emperor of the Cherokee Indians with his Empress and their son, the young prince, attended by several of his warriors and Great Men and their Ladies'. Everywhere their service to 'the works of the immortal Shakespeare' was urged as a reason against the prohibition of authorities and statutes, but Shakespeare's name was not always sufficient to overcome the hostility to the theatre. In Newport, Rhode Island, it was necessary to present *Othello* as 'a moral dialogue' with the morals fully expounded upon the programmes; and when in Providence a theatre was forbidden, the actors built a schoolhouse where they inculcated their moral lessons. In spite of many difficulties, however, the theatre was by the time of the Revolution fairly well established in the larger towns outside of New England. After the War, the Hallam company returned to Philadelphia and New York, the theatres were reopened, and even Boston finally succumbed to the drama.

What influence did Shakespeare exert on the fathers of the country? It can scarcely be argued that he directed their efforts or that he had any more effect upon them than upon leading Englishmen of their time—Chatham, Burke, Fox, and Lord North. But he did respond to what was an astonishingly wide and active intellectual interest, represented not only by such outstanding examples as Franklin and Jefferson, but in the tone of the societies of Boston, Philadelphia, and Williamsburg. Franklin must have read him as a boy, John Adams quotes him, James Otis is enthusiastic in praise, and Thomas Jefferson, who certainly read him as a college student, late in life exempts him

[1] G. C. D. Odell, *Annals of the New York Stage*, New York, 1927, vol. i.

from the warning that 'too much poetry should not be indulged'. Washington was not much of a reader but he was very fond of the theatre. He may possibly have attended the first performance of the Hallams; in March 1761 his diary records that he spent £2 7s. 6d. on theatre tickets at Williamsburg, and nearly every subsequent year has a similar expenditure. In 1773 when he brought his stepson to New York to enter him in King's College he took the boy to see *Hamlet*. When he was president he went frequently to the play, often invited guests, and was conducted to his box with due ceremony. He may very possibly have seen every Shakespearian play that was acted in the country.[1]

The dawn of the nineteenth century found the new nation largely confined to the Atlantic coast but already beginning its westward march. The seaboard cities continually adopting the fashions and customs of Europe, maintaining a culture essentially European, were becoming more and more separated from the frontier of scattered farms where there were no centres of cultivation and few towns large enough to support a church, a printing press, or a school But the course of the century was not to increase the division, rather it was to create a civilization strikingly uniform over the vast expanses of the continent. In spite of the differences of climate, occupation, and race, in spite of the dividing and almost disruptive force of negro slavery, in spite of the constant clash between frontier and older communities, the end of the century saw a nation united politically and so uniform in ideas, customs, recreations, and reading that to some critics it presents a deadly sameness. But a certain irritation at the uniformity of our schools, text-books, costumes, social gatherings, hotels, churches, orations, and manners must not detract from the astounding nature of this great achievement, the rapidity and thoroughness with which men have built a united civilization. In this process Shakespeare has

[1] Paul Leicester Ford, *Washington and the Theater*, New York, The Dunlap Society, 1899.

been a symbol of unity, a moving force, almost a directing deity. He was worshipped in the libraries and theatres of the Eastern cities in much the same way that he was being worshipped in England, but in the West the travelling elocutionist, the lecturer, the company of actors on a Mississippi show-boat became his emissaries and evangels. The frontier would not leave him to Europe and the East; no other writer was so quickly assimilated in the wilderness. Reverence for him became the symbol, the mark of culture, which united the frontiersman with Lowell and Emerson.

In the growth of this tradition, so unifying an element in our culture, I shall ask you to glance at a few of the more peculiar aspects in the records of our theatres, our schools, and our scholarship.

From the beginning of the nineteenth century the theatres in the Eastern cities were kept in close touch with those of London and Paris. A piece successful in Europe was shortly produced in New York, and soon an interchange of actors, plays, and even of dramatists was taking place. The pronunciation of London was to be heard on the stage if nowhere else in the United States, and Shakespeare was interpreted by the greatest actors of different nations. The chief American actors, Edwin Forrest, Charlotte Cushman, and Edwin Booth, were heard abroad, and an American playwright wrote 'Home, Sweet Home' to be sung on the London stage. As time goes on, the chronicles of Shakespeare in the theatre disclose less and less difference between London and New York.

One important consideration, however, should be kept in mind. While the theatre in England was flourishing under the processes of democratization and commercialization that were influencing everything Victorian, the drama was being given over to farces, melodramas, and adaptations from the French. Few new plays were being produced that had any lasting value or literary merit. During this lamentable break in the great tradition that had long linked literature to the theatre, the plays of Shakespeare were about the only dramas that brought poetry, imagination, and humanity to the stage. In the United States they performed a similar but more difficult and distinctive service. In a new country, where prejudice against the stage was still more general than in England, and where the absence of standards of art or of a large polite society tended to render the theatre more vulgar and meretricious than even in Victorian London, the plays of Shakespeare were almost the only pillar that supported the dignity of the drama, the only survivor of its tradition as a great form of imaginative art. Irving, Cooper, Hawthorne, Thoreau, Emerson, and others were creating a new literature, and the response of the public showed that it was eager for the joy that beauty ever incites. This literary movement which, until checked by the devastating influence of our Civil War, was so impressive and so creditable to the aesthetic and spiritual aspirations of the new nation, found little companionship in music or painting or any other of the fine arts, but in the theatre it had Shakespeare.

Away from the Atlantic coast the stage took on strange methods and forms, but it was never without Shakespeare. Amateur performances were given in Kentucky even before the beginning of the century, and in 1801 a theatre was opened in Cincinnati with a prologue prophesying the great days to come, when

> 'Twill be remember'd that in the days of yore
> Between a ragged roof and sorry floor,
> The laughing muse here for the first time sate
> And kindly deign'd to cheer our infant state.[1]

By the beginning of the second decade companies of professionals were making their way from Montreal up the St. Lawrence and the Great Lakes or over the Allegheny Mountains and down the Ohio, to Lexington, Louisville, and Cincinnati, and then by keel boat in slow and perilous fashion along the rivers on an eighteen-day journey to St. Louis. By the third decade of the century star actors

[1] R. L. Rusk, *The Literature of the Middle West*, 2 vols., New York, 1925.

from the Eastern theatres were being heard along the Ohio and Mississippi on the river route from New York to New Orleans, and in 1831 came Charles Kean from England, and in 1838–9 Ellen Tree. During the forty years of pioneering in the Middle West before the railroads, Professor Rusk has recorded over 7,500 theatrical performances, and out of fewer than 1,800 that were of the legitimate drama, 433 or one-fourth were of Shakespeare's plays.[1] Seventeen at least were acted, and of these *Othello* and *Hamlet* were the favourites. They had no rivals except the pieces of Kotzebue, then enjoying a world-wide popularity.

As soon as Shakespeare was established with some degree of dignity in the growing towns, theatrical enterprise carried him on into more remote and less accessible places. By 1833 a 'Floating Theatre' had been devised on a flat boat to visit the little towns along the Ohio, the first of the 'show-boats' that were soon making Shakespeare familiar in the hamlets along the 'father of waters'. No actors were too ignorant not to desire to perform the great roles of the stage, and no audience was too rude not to delight in the great dramas of the race. An extraordinary chronicle might be gathered of the various and peculiar conditions under which Othello has wooed and Hamlet soliloquized upon the American scene. I recall the story of a lady who was coaching a group of eager amateurs in our Far West for *The Merchant of Venice*. Appropriate costumes being entirely lacking, she advised each actor to dress his part as seemed fitting. She was, however, a bit startled when Portia appeared disguised as a learned judge in overalls, khaki shirt, and sombrero—these being the articles of dress of the only judge she knew—the local justice of the peace. Hamlet in modern clothes is by no means a novelty. Shakespeare has been acted everywhere and in every way, and is now being broadcast over the radio to the delight of many. I suppose you already have that in England, but you can scarcely have—as do we in

[1] R. L. Rusk, *The Literature of the Middle West*, 2 vols., New York, 1925.

New York—theatres where negro actors play *Othello* to negro audiences.

I have not touched upon the chief glories of our Shakespearian theatre, of the famous performances of the past, or of the actors and managers of the present who have produced the plays with distinction and beauty, because, after all, these achievements are not unlike your own. I have preferred to stress Shakespeare's service in giving the drama significance and impressiveness, in preserving it as one of the fine arts while a new country was establishing itself in material prosperity and security, and, on the other hand, the service of the theatre in carrying Shakespeare's art in the very vanguard of the march of civilization across a continent.

Shakespeare began to be a factor in popular education at about the same time in England as in the United States. When, shortly after Waterloo, Brougham announced that the schoolmaster was abroad in the land, that meant the appearance of text-books and lectures on English literature as well as on the natural sciences, and a diffusion of useful knowledge that included an acquaintance with Shakespeare. In the United States it was admitted, even by those who found the theatre a place of abomination, that wise maxims and irreproachable sentiments were embedded in the works of the great dramatist. Moreover, these were useful not only for inculcating morality but as samples of grammatical difficulties and as tests for elocutionary powers. Aphorisms were there which could grace an oration or even adorn a sermon. One of the main approaches to literature and one of the chief humanistic disciplines of our frontier was oratory. Demosthenes and Cicero might serve as guides for the learned, but Shakespeare could be found in the grammars, readers, and books on elocution which flooded the country or could be heard from some itinerant elocutionist or lecturer. Schools of oratory were established where the main test of eloquence was furnished by passages from Shakespeare. Reciters and lecturers made the platform scarcely less entertaining than the stage. Perhaps the mightiest of these was Robert Ingersoll, whose lecture on Shakespeare, consisting largely of quotations, was delivered countless times with unfailing eloquence. One must not be tempted to scoff at such educational processes; a worse aesthetic practice can be imagined than this of constantly reciting or hearing recited passages from Shakespeare.

But education was not long content without a severer poetic discipline. Free public schools spread throughout the land; universal education became accepted as a necessary corollary of democratic government; and the nation set itself to the tremendous task of making sure that every one had a certain amount of instruction. In the face of a huge and increasing immigration of people of foreign speech, and in face of differences of religion, race, geography, and heredity, we were also determined that so far as he went each should be educated in just the same way as all the others. We have a genius for compulsory legislation, and we decided to compel every child to get an education, and this soon included the study of Shakespeare.

The story of this great enterprise in schools and colleges, even in so far as it relates to Shakespeare, can scarcely be touched upon here. But two elements are significant for our purpose. In the first place, the education did become surprisingly uniform throughout the country. Though there have always been backward places and progressive places, and all varieties of schools and colleges and new experiments, still the boys and girls have in general studied the same text-books and been taught by the same methods through the length and breadth of the land for a hundred years, and the schools are more nearly uniform to-day than ever before. Whatever one young American learns about Shakespeare is just about the same as is taught to all the others. In the second place, in our vast system, the Greek and Latin classics proved an impossible basis for popular education. In their place was substituted somewhat slowly but inevitably the study of English language and literature. The sciences, and especially the applied sciences, naturally secured an enlarging place in our curriculum; but of the humanities, of all the studies dealing with men and their activities rather than with the physical world, the study of English has been easily first, and its pre-eminence seems to be rapidly increasing. Of this study of the mother tongue, Shakespeare is the head and front. The infants learn to lisp his songs, the children read him in selections, the high school boys and girls must con three or four of his plays. He is the basis for the study of metrics, grammar, and much else. I suppose that he is taught in every one of the many hundred colleges and universities that grace our land. There is no escaping him.

Miss Ellen Terry in her Reminiscences relates that when she and Irving were playing Shakespeare, Lord Randolph Churchill was so interested that he was led to read the poet, of whose plays, he confessed that he had not up to that time read a single one. This could not happen with us. No such delayed discovery, no such postponed pleasure, is possible. You can't be president of the United States unless you have read Shakespeare. The most indifferent schoolboy carries into adult life the recollections of having taken an examination upon his life and works.

No one will imagine that all this teaching and examining has been free from serious defects. One method after another has been adopted—and worked to death. The elocutionary discipline was followed by the analysis of dramatic technique, and that by the writing of essays, interpreting the characters, and that by the study of the text of a play, explaining Elizabethan meanings and labouring over difficulties that have long puzzled scholars.[1] *Macbeth* in particular has served nicely for a drill in vocabulary, metrics, and syntax, and I fear it is remembered by many American citizens chiefly as a most perplexing puzzle.

[1] F. T. Baker, *Shakespeare in the Schools*, Columbia Studies in Shakespeare, 1916.

Of late years, I believe we have improved upon the elementary teaching of Shakespeare chiefly by regarding each play not as a collection of quotations, difficult phrases, or enigmatical characters, but as something which can be read and enjoyed as a whole and can be acted by the pupils. Whatever remains that is undesirable or ridiculous in the old methods is at least supplemented by the practice of acting the plays which has now become general in schools as well as colleges, and by the unphysiological but aesthetic belief that a play or a poem is something which can first be swallowed whole and digested later.

But what is gained by this teaching? What benefits accrue from this compulsory culture? What is the effect of this enormous propaganda for Shakespeare? I prefer to answer these questions indirectly by a few quite disconnected observations. First, an educational system must have some basis. The Athenians had Homer. At Oxford Aristotle's Ethics once served. Matthew Arnold urged that an age of science should make the basis of its education Greek literature. In a mechanical age, for an enormous democracy, we have made the basis of our education English literature—and Shakespeare. How could we have done better? Second, I beg to suggest that this practice is one of the main forces that ensure comity and friendship between England and the United States. In the years of the Great War some excited protests were heard against passages in our school histories which spoke none too sweetly of England's conduct during our long distant wars. I believe some milder excitement now exists because the offensive passages were deleted in favour of others that are now regarded as too complimentary to the mother country. But how trivial would be the influence of any such passages, fair or unfair, favourable or unfavourable, in comparison with the great tribute of admiration and reverence which is paid by our schools to English literature. Your poets and teachers are our poets and teachers. It is our schools that have elected Shakespeare the perennial ambassador between the two nations. In the third place, as to all this teaching, I would suggest that Shakespeare stands the test. After all, it is a hard test to submit a poet to the tender mercies of schoolboys. I think no other author—certainly not Virgil or Milton—comes through the test so unscathed—still the object of worship by those who have been driven to his service by task-masters.

In looking at the theatre we found Shakespeare tried in the privations and crudities of a pioneer people forming the outposts of civilization. In treating of the schools we have found him used by a great democracy as an instrument for securing a certain basis of culture and ideas in its variegated population. In turning now to scholarship we are considering a nation that is past the pioneer stage that is no longer in need of unification, that is rich and powerful and able to determine the values and satisfactions which it desires.

The first scholarly edition was that of 1844-7 under the editorship of Gulian Verplanck, an author and lawyer of some note. This was followed by the first edition of the Rev. H. W. Hudson in 1851-6, and by that of Richard Grant White, 1867-8. In 1871 H. Howard Furness began the great labour of a new Variorum edition, of which he completed fifteen plays before his death in 1912, and the edition is now being carried on by his son. Since the beginning of this monumental work, Shakespearian scholarship has rapidly expanded and multiplied. Indeed the astonishing thing about it to-day is its quantity.

Within less than a generation the number of students in our colleges is said to have increased tenfold; and the number of graduate students in English literature must have multiplied many times more rapidly. No nation before ever had such a large proportion of college teachers in its population, and no nation ever had such a large proportion of its professors teaching the literature of the mother tongue. As a consequence of these conditions, a large and increasing number of persons are well versed in the course of Shakespearian scholarship up to the present

time and are eager to extend it through their individual
ministrations.

Though it is true that some of our most eminent
specialists both of the past and the present have worked
outside of the universities, still our universities now possess
an organized and trained body of students of Shakespeare
that is unprecedented in numbers and in promise. Several
of our larger institutions have issued volumes of Shakespearian studies by members of their respective faculties;
an American edition of Shakespeare presents each play
edited by a scholar of some distinction; and other evidences
might be cited of the possibility of co-operative enter-
prises far more extensive than any which have been yet
undertaken. I may not praise the work of my fellow-
countrymen before this audience, where there are so
many Sir Hubert Stanleys; but our scholars are at least
imposing in numbers and solidarity.

It cannot be said that the universities as yet afford large
endowments for scholarships. In view of the ever-in-
creasing number of students, the problems of organization
and of teaching are likely to continue to engage the resources of the endowments and the energies of the faculties.
But the professor, though kept busy writing text-books,
teaching large classes, and attending committees, may still
find opportunity and encouragement for scholarly work.
The pressure brought upon the younger men to publish is
indeed continuous and not altogether wholesome. Their
prospects for promotion, their standing among their
colleagues, even the reputation of the institution to which
they belong, are supposed to be enhanced by the appearance of articles from their pens in the learned publications.
The average merit of such writing is not likely to be in-
ordinately high, and some of it is quite superfluous, but
at the worst it represents a trained familiarity with the
researches of others. I suppose it is true that a first-class
book on Shakespeare will find more critical students in the
United States than in all the rest of the world together.
An English, a German, or a French scholar will look to us

for the bulk of approval or criticism. In offering here my homage to the imposing and enduring work of English Shakespearian scholars and critics, I am voicing the admiration of a body of fellow-workers that I am sure you will not disdain.

With the improvement of our libraries, with the transference across the Atlantic of many rare books and manuscripts, with the increased wealth of educational endowments, with the ready means for co-operation and division of labour, the opportunities in our country for the further advance and extension of scholarship are enormous. But I do not think that its importance lies chiefly in what may be accomplished in the usual paths of literary research, whether as to Shakespeare or another. The great importance of our literary scholarship lies rather in its influence upon our criticism, not only of literature but of life. This is a matter on which I must not enlarge here. To do that would lead us into a consideration of the values of a literary as a complement to a scientific discipline, and of the service of scholarship in supplying a basis for a criticism as broad as that which Matthew Arnold liked to proclaim as 'a disinterested endeavour to learn and to propagate the best that has been known and thought'. But this much is, I think, evident without any far-flung discussion. Our teachers and scholars have the position and opportunity for an intellectual leadership that has never been exercised in such a large reading population. What will come of this leadership I shall not venture to predict. But this is true, the minds of both leaders and public have fed upon Shakespeare. Into whatever criticism of life the American nation may be making its way, into whatever synthesis of ideas, into whatever moral and aesthetic beliefs or hopes, no small direction towards these goals has been furnished by the study of the greatest of poets.

Many ways in which he has influenced America must go unnoticed in my hasty talk. I shall not touch on his effect on music or on painting, and I can give only a single word to the host of readers who not only buy the many editions of his plays but read them and—as did Lincoln—read them over and over. Countless clubs, in great cities and in small towns, where no theatres and no colleges exist, meet regularly year after year and study the plays that they love. In this era of radio and newspapers and moving pictures, the fear is sometimes expressed that books will cease to be read. But it is the simple truth that books are read more than ever before and old authors as well as new. Shakespeare still brings his amazing world of the imagination to many a quiet fireside.

But I have said enough to suggest to you how great and varied and growing is the dominion that he holds over that brave new world which he did not know. He is indeed the god of our idolatry. Washington, Lincoln, Shakespeare, they are the three whom Americans universally worship, and you will not find a fourth of ours or any other nation to add to this trinity. The pleasant town of Stratford has become a national shrine second only in our love and awe to Westminster Abbey. No Greek colony ever looked back with more reverence to the altars of the gods of their home whence they brought the sacred fire than we to these relics and monuments of the greatness of our common ancestry.

But I would not dwell over much on the pride of ancestry, on the filial admiration, on the affection for this island that Shakespeare arouses in America. Because, after all, it is not the unity of the English peoples that his plays proclaim but the unity of humanity. It is not for Stratford merely, nor for this land, nor for its people that he asks sympathy and affection but for the human race. He voices to Americans and to all, tolerance, magnanimity, greatness of mind and heart.

Has he carried any special message to the American people? After accompanying them on their pioneering, and in establishing a nation, after being accepted as essential in their education and scholarship, has he taught them anything more clearly than to other peoples? This is a question difficult if not impossible to answer, partly because of his comprehensiveness of soul, his power to expand and change to meet the needs of time or person, and partly because men are prone to seek in Shakespeare whatever they wish to find. He is not a sermonizer and he does not contain everything, and often gives no answer to the candid inquirer. The eighteenth century sought in literature and elsewhere for some plan of the dealings of Providence with man. Dr. Johnson wanted a poetic justice, a clearly indicated reward of goodness and a punishment for evil, and he complained because he could not find it in Shakespeare. The nineteenth century desired revelation, a disclosure of divinity, a vision of the infinite owning kinship to man. You will remember how, in the lonely hours at Craigenputtock, Carlyle brooded over his Shakespeare, seeking in vain for that sure guidance or that mystic communion by which the poet should approve of Thomas Carlyle's ways on earth. He may disappoint those to-day who seek for an analysis of the complications, depressions, infirmities, and epidemics of the present, and they may prefer the literature of the moment. Different ages and peoples seek different talismans, and I doubt that the Americans have found any sure key with which to unlock Shakespeare's heart.

They have sought, perhaps even more eagerly than others, for what all have found, a revelation of humanity, beautiful in remote places and distant times yet strangely like their own. They have sought too for what others have not always found, a faith in the greatness of human effort. I like to fancy that the American temper has a close kinship with the Elizabethan joy in experience, the venturesomeness in deeds, the heedlessness as to dogmas. I do not think that we have shown ourselves profoundly depressed by the riddle of existence; we are not much interested in philosophical doubt, or in regrets for the past. We have healed the wounds made by our Lost Cause, and we are inattentive to the laments over others— we are not greatly moved by the Decline and Fall of the Roman Empire or even by Paradise Lost. We have sought in literature for buoyancy and optimism, for an uplifting beauty, for an enlarged and fortified courage. In Shakespeare, whether in the tortures of Hamlet and Lear or in the triumphs of Rosalind and Prospero, we have found what we have sought, a renewing of our faith in man and his works.

PRINCIPLES OF EMENDATION IN SHAKESPEARE*

By w. w. greg

THE Professor of Latin in the University of Cambridge
has said what is perhaps the last word on the subject of
emendation, in a passage that runs as follows: 'A textual
critic engaged upon his business is not at all like Newton
investigating the motions of the planets: he is much more
like a dog hunting for fleas. If a dog hunted for fleas on
mathematical principles, basing his researches on statistics
of area and population, he would never catch a flea except
by accident.'[1] I do not believe that this is a fair account of
textual criticism in general, but so far as emendation is
concerned it comes extraordinarily near the truth. The
fact is that there is only one general principle of emendation, which is that emendation is in its essence devoid of
principle. At its finest it is an inspiration, a stirring of the
spirit, which obeys no laws and cannot be produced to
order. In other words, emendation is an art. Yet even
as such there should be some conditions which by its
very nature it must obey, for it is surely no idle dream of
scholars to be 'learned in searching principles of art'. And
if we can do nothing to help great critics in making
brilliant emendations, we may at least hope to discover
some rules that should prevent little critics from making
foolish ones.

As a starting-point for our search let us consider one or
two famous emendations, not necessarily in Shakespeare,
that have won general acceptance. There is one that may
be called Theobald's emendation *par excellence*, though it

* Delivered 23 May 1928. Save for a few slight changes this lecture is
here reprinted as originally published the same year.

was not entirely his own.[2] Mistress Quickly (that was) describes Falstaff's death:

after I saw him fumble with the Sheets, and play with Flowers, and smile vpon his fingers end, I knew there was but one way: for his Nose was as sharpe as a Pen, and a Table of greene fields.

So the folio, which is our only relevant authority. To-day all editions of Shakespeare read: 'for his nose was as sharp as a pen, and a' babbled of green fields'. When we remember that 'babbled' would very likely be written 'babld',[3] and that in the hands of the time 'b' and 't', and final 'd' and 'e' are often difficult to distinguish, there need be no hesitation in accepting what many readers feel to be a particularly Shakespearian turn of phrase.

My next instance is linked no less closely with the name of that great and modest scholar Arthur Bullen. Marlowe's Faustus in his study tosses the unprofitable Aristotle aside with the words:[4]

> Bid *Oncaymæon* farewell, *Galen* come:

according to the earliest edition. The second substitutes 'Oeconomy'. That this is wrong is clear from the metre (which was first doctored in the fourth edition) but it was the guess of some one with enough learning to know that one of Aristotle's works was the *Oeconomica*; hardly, one would suppose, a compositor. Bullen, pondering the passage, perceived that there was really no error at all, but only a rather misleading spelling of the Aristotelian phrase ὂν καὶ μὴ ὄν, 'being and not being'.

Lest the glamour of great names and famous lines should sway your judgement to an over-ready acceptance of what I would make the basis of my argument, I will add by way of challenge an emendation of my own. It is one of which I am rather proud, for it is in Latin, and my classical attainments are thoroughly Shakespearian. In an appallingly bad text of a very inferior play of Greene's there are some lines which have been printed by editors, after minor emendation, thus:

O vos qui colitis lacusque locosque profundos,
Infernasque domus et nigra palatia Ditis!

On which one editor remarked that no emendation could
relieve the verses of the false quantity in 'lacus'—which
shows that Classical Greats is not always a sufficient train-
ing for textual criticism. For it is evident that in this
passage 'locos profundos' has no meaning: what we want
is 'lucos' for the sense, and for the metre the inversion
'lucosque lacusque'. The line is based on a phrase of
Cicero, 'lacus lucosque colitis'. The change from 'lucos'
to 'locos' is a mere printer's error, but the inversion must
be laid to the charge of the author, for it is due to too close
a following of the prose original.[5]

I think that a careful consideration of these three examples will teach us something in respect to the principles—
or shall I say the limiting conditions?—of emendation,
and I propose to use them as illustrations in seeking answers
to certain questions. In the first place: What makes an
emendation acceptable? I do not, of course, mean the
appeal to sentiment or commonplace that pleases by
removing a phrase jarring to the feelings or calling for
mental effort at comprehension. One critic would have
Hamlet 'hot' instead of 'fat', another 'faint', another 'fey';
and when Collier forged in the Perkins folio the emendation 'blankness', for the line,

Nor heaven peep through the blanket of the dark,

an eminent actor, so I have heard, declared that he had
happily removed what had always been a stumbling-block
in *Macbeth*. Such things are mere folly. By an acceptable
emendation I mean, of course, one that strikes a trained
intelligence as supplying exactly the sense required by the
context, and which at the same time reveals to the critic
the manner in which the corruption arose. Most readers
of *Henry V* feel instinctively the justness of Theobald's
emendation, and few would question the appropriateness
of Bullen's; the third is supported by the detection of the
source. That this source at once explains the harder part

of the corruption is my excuse for thrusting the trifle on
your consideration; ὂν καὶ μὴ ὂν is rather a brilliant interpretation than a strict emendation; the change from
'babld' to 'table' is perhaps more obvious to us than it
was to Theobald.

The criterion of acceptance is high, and it is necessary
that criticism should insist rigorously upon the conditions,
for unless they are fulfilled there can be no certainty about
the emendation, and there may be half a dozen, or half
a hundred, with claims upon our attention. But of course
comparatively few emendations really satisfy the test.
This is a point I wish to stress, because I do not think that
criticism has always faced the implications of its own
methods. It is apt to forget two facts which it would
nevertheless not dispute. One is that even the most careful authors do sometimes write sentences which it is impossible to regard as affording a perfectly satisfactory
sense: the other is that corruption must sometimes occur
through agencies that by their nature it is impossible to
trace. Even Milton has 'Hermione' where he should have
had 'Harmonia', but no one now follows Bentley in therefore dismissing the passage as spurious.[5a] And if we were to
cast out of Shakespeare's text all phrases which we should
hesitate to admit into it as emendations, I think that we
should leave some considerable gaps in the canon. On the
other hand, who shall say what chance words overheard in
the printing-house may have found their way into a compositor's brain and so out at his fingers. In all likelihood
there are on record more—perhaps many more—actually
correct emendations that fail to pass the test, than there
are that emerge successful: they are correct but we can
never know that they are. This comes out clearly, I think,
in a textual study of Massinger. We are so fortunate as to
possess several hundred corrections made with his own
hand in the original editions of his plays, but among those
of any consequence I think there are not very many that
an editor would feel bound to accept on strictly critical principles. And it is significant that several correct

emendations proposed by Massinger's early editors were subsequently rejected in what remains the standard edition. Meanwhile, if we demand that a true emendation shall explain the corruption, we are left wondering how in one place the word 'Constantinople' came to be substituted for the word 'Court'.[6]

A second consideration suggested by the emendations with which I started brings me to what is really the substance of my thesis. It is this. When we have satisfied ourselves that an emendation is acceptable, the next question we ought to ask is what it implies with respect to the history and origin of the text. We may find that it implies something that is contrary to known fact, or at least something that conflicts with the implications of other emendations, or with evidence from some different source. Thus Theobald's emendation, though he may not have realized it, implies that the folio text of *Henry V* was set up from a manuscript written in the ordinary English hand of the period. In the circumstances this is, of course, what we should expect. But, had we reason to suppose that the copy supplied to the printer was prepared in modern spelling on a typewriter, the emendation would lose most of its plausibility. Again, if there were independent evidence that the second edition of *Doctor Faustus* was a naïve print from the same manuscript that served as copy for the first, we should have seriously to consider whether '*Oeconomy*' was not original, and '*Oncaymaeon*' but a freakish misreading. Lastly, the seemingly trivial emendation 'lucosque lacusque', or rather the whole reconstruction of the passage in which it occurs, bears quite a formidable weight of implication. It implies an illiterate compositor and a singular absence of proof correction; it implies, on the other hand, some scholarly revision of the copy, for below a superficial layer of printer's errors this Latin is in better order than, for instance, a corresponding passage of Italian in the same play; and lastly it implies an author whose composition was governed more by the *Gradus* than by an instinct for metre. In fact it implies, or at least suggests, something like a complete history of the text.

The central point at which I am aiming is this: that no emendation can or ought to be considered *in vacuo*, but that criticism must always proceed in relation to what we know, or what we surmise, respecting the history of the text. True, we surmise more often than we know, and a sufficient number of acceptable emendations would form good ground for the revision of any textual theory.[7] But we ought to realize clearly whither an emendation is leading us. It is no use proposing emendations in the hope that upon *some* theory they may prove possible. There are texts whose data are so simple, or whose history is so unknown, that a minimum of restraint is placed upon the invention of the critic. But where the available evidence is at all full, no one has a right to ask us to accept any emendation without attempting to show that its implications are not inconsistent with known facts or contrary to common sense. And if a critic is so bold as to propose several emendations in the same text, he may fairly be challenged to prove that they do not involve mutually contradictory theories of its origin.

I shall devote the remainder of the hour your kindness has placed at my disposal to grouping Shakespeare's plays in accordance with what is usually assumed to be their textual history, and to considering very briefly the limits which the conditions in each group impose upon the freedom of emendation, and what in fact the practice of editors has been.

In doing so I shall confine my attention to the canon of the first folio, leaving out of account *Pericles*, the textual history of which is anomalous without being very enlightening. We are left then with thirty-six plays, which I propose to divide into four groups. The first class consists of seventeen plays which were printed for the first time in the folio of 1623. They are, *The Tempest, The Two Gentlemen of Verona, Measure for Measure, The Comedy of Errors, As you Like it, All's Well that Ends Well, Twelfth*

Night, and *The Winter's Tale* among the comedies; *King John*, *1 Henry VI*, and *Henry VIII* among the histories; and *Coriolanus*, *Timon of Athens*, *Julius Caesar*, *Macbeth*, *Antony and Cleopatra*, and *Cymbeline* among the tragedies. In my second class each play had been previously issued in a separate edition and it was from this quarto that the folio text was printed. Nine plays belong here; I give them in the chronological order of their appearance: *Titus Andronicus*, *Richard II*, *Richard III*, *1 Henry IV*, *Love's Labour's Lost*, *The Merchant of Venice*, *Much Ado about Nothing*, *A Midsummer-Night's Dream*, and *King Lear*. The third class consists of three plays which the folio printed, not from the previous quarto text, but from an independent manuscript representing substantially the same version:[8] namely, *2 Henry IV*, *Troilus and Cressida*, and *Othello*. Lastly, we have a fourth class, each play of which survives in two different versions, one an authoritative text, whether quarto or folio, and the other a bad text, which, whatever its precise nature, may be fairly described in the famous phrase as 'stolen and surreptitious'. This class, which of course offers by far the best hunting to the textual detective, has seven members, to wit: *The Taming of the Shrew*, *2 and 3 Henry VI*, *Romeo and Juliet*, *Henry V*, *The Merry Wives of Windsor*, and finally *Hamlet*.

I wish to make it clear that in this classification I am not giving you results of my own investigations or even expressing my own views. I am merely gathering the best critical opinion on various points that I can find, in order to use it as a basis for certain further inquiries. It does not matter much, if at all, whether the assumptions are in every case correct: I think, however, that when a critic has had the opportunity of considering and comparing the views of investigators such as the Cambridge editors, P. A. Daniel, Mr. Pollard, and Mr. Dover Wilson, he should be in a fair position to form at least a provisional judgement. It is true that in respect to Class IV I have taken into consideration some comparatively recent speculation: I do not, however, ask you to accept this as certain, but only to consider what follows supposing it to be true.

Class I, in which we have but a single text of each play,[9] is the least interesting from our present point of view, for the textual data impose the minimum of restriction on conjecture. It is the happy hunting ground of the irresponsible editor, since his fancy can seldom be shown to conflict with textual logic. Yet even here there are some critical decencies to be observed. Emendation should be relative to the general nature and preservation of the text: a conjecture that was plausible in a corrupt text such as *Macbeth* might be inadmissible in a play like *The Tempest*, which may have been set up from Shakespeare's own manuscript. Of positive guides, beyond general suitability, there are perhaps only two: a knowledge of the errors a compositor is likely to make in setting the type, and a knowledge of those he is likely to make in reading his copy. There may be more to be discovered with respect to the first of these: our only appreciable advance of late has been the recognition of the fact that apparent errors of the ear are often due to the compositor trying to carry too many words in his mind at once. On the other hand much attention has recently been given to the problem of misreading, and though the study of manuscript forms may not have quite made good the promise held out by some enthusiasts, there can be no question as to its importance.[10] Every critic of Shakespeare's text ought in the first place to make himself thoroughly familiar with the various contemporary styles of writing, which is easy enough; with the type of hand which Shakespeare must have written, a matter not seriously in doubt; and, if possible, with the hand Shakespeare actually wrote, about which the less said on this occasion the better. But though excellent use has sometimes been made of the *ductus literarum*, I incline to think that, while the method should always be ready to the critic's hand, it cannot often be paraded with effect. Its value is greater as a hint than as a proof. Now and then, indeed, a consideration of manuscript forms may cast a sudden light upon the obscurities of type.[11] One of Heywood's printed plays has the startling peculiarity that in place of 'Actus 4' and '5' we have 'Actus 46' and '56'. If, however, we turn to his manuscript plays and observe the symbols he used for 'quartus' and 'quintus', we shall wonder, not that they were once misprinted '46' and '56', but that they were ever printed as anything else. But it is seldom that we meet such an illuminating example as this.[12]

I shall for the moment pass over Class II and consider Class III, consisting of those plays for which we have two basic texts printed from independent manuscripts but representing essentially the same version. Here then quarto and folio are independent witnesses to a common tradition, a fact that puts a fairly tight curb on emendation. As a rule one text may be expected to correct the other. In cases of failure the two may have a common error, or different errors. If the latter, emendation is specifically limited by the necessity of accounting for both corruptions. Common errors must be supposed to go back to the author's original or very near it. This is, of course, not unlikely, but it should make us scrutinize rather closely the evidence on which error is assumed.[13] And even when we are satisfied that corruption is present, it will be well to consider what interpretation was placed upon the text, as preserved, by the compositors and scribes who transmitted it, and by the actors who probably used it.

In 2 *Henry IV* there are a number of errors common to the two texts. Perhaps the most striking is where a speech that undoubtedly belongs to Bardolph is assigned to Poins. And since the quarto is clearly derived from a prompt copy and the folio represents a further stage-revision of the play, we cannot but wonder into what actor's part the speech was copied and who actually spoke it at the Globe. Not all the alleged errors are equally certain, but if editors have thought themselves obliged to resort to a considerable amount of conjecture, it has not been without some show of reason. Indeed, their practice appears to me less consistent with a belief in two independent witnesses, than with the assumption that the folio text is somehow based with revision upon that preserved in the quarto. And in this connexion it is possibly significant that I have been unable to find a good instance of divergent error in the two.[14]

In *Troilus and Cressida* there is at least one instance in which the quarto and the folio have different readings, both certainly wrong, and there may be others. And although I cannot think that editors have always been right in the common errors they have supposed, it is difficult to avoid the conclusion that these are by no means uncommon. This and certain curious agreements in spelling and punctuation seem to me to raise a difficulty in the way of supposing that the only relation between the texts is that of a common source to the manuscripts used as copy. Uncertainty on this point has important consequences. Take for example the wonderful speech of Cressida:

> Sweet, bid me hold my tongue;
> For in this rapture I shall surely speak
> The thing I shall repent. See, see, your silence,
> Cunning in dumbness, from my weakness draws
> My very soul of counsel! Stop my mouth.

'Cunning' is Pope's emendation for the original 'Comming', but the expression 'coming' was quite usual in the sense of forward, apt. The emendation does give a more perfect sense, and if the text rested upon a single witness we could be content to accept it; if however the reading has double authority it should I think be retained.[15]

Othello, the remaining play of this group, stands textually in sharp contrast to those we have just been considering. Among readings of any importance I think there are only four in which the Cambridge editors felt constrained to emend a reading supported by the two authorities, and in not one of these cases is it certain that they were right. A typical instance is seen in Iago's words:

> My wife must move for Cassio to her mistress;
> I'll set her on;

> Myself awhile to draw the Moor apart,
> And bring him jump when he may Cassio find
> Soliciting his wife: . . .

Instead of 'awhile' Theobald proposed to read 'the while'. This does, indeed, give a slightly better construction, and has I believe been generally accepted. Yet it is clearly impossible to say that Shakespeare cannot have written the text as it stands. In the case of *Othello*, therefore, there is every reason to suppose that quarto and folio are independent witnesses to the author's original, and conversely that the original came near to being textually perfect. It is useful to bear this fact in mind when considering such controverted lines as:

> A fellow almost damn'd in a fair wife;

and:

> Put out the light, and then put out the light . . .[16]

I must now revert to our second group of plays, which really forms a transition class between I and III. Its nine members agree in this, that a quarto and not an independent manuscript served as copy for the folio text, but they differ widely in the extent to which that copy was corrected and revised from some other source. At one end of the scale we have *1 Henry IV*, for which a quarto was reprinted almost without alteration, at the other end *King Lear*, the copy for which was so extensively revised and expanded that many critics have been led to believe that the folio text was printed from an independent manuscript. Between these extremes lie *Love's Labour's Lost*,[17] *Much Ado about Nothing*, *A Midsummer-Night's Dream*,[18] and *The Merchant of Venice*, in all of which the folio contains corrections and stage-directions derived from the playhouse; *Richard II* and *Richard III*, which have quite definitely been revised; and *Titus Andronicus*, in which a whole new scene has been added. In *1 Henry IV* the textual problem is essentially the same as in Class I. But even here, and progressively through the other members of the class, there is always the possibility that a folio variant may be a fragment of an independent textual tradition, and moreover one which an editor, working within a few years of the author's death and in close touch with his fellow actors, thought superior to that of the quarto. This is no ground why we should necessarily prefer the folio reading, but it is a ground for giving it respectful consideration. In *Lear* we reach a critical position almost analogous to that in *Othello*. Divergence between quarto and folio will imply divergence of textual tradition. On the other hand agreement between the two cannot (as in Class III) be assumed to mean fidelity to the original, since it is certain that not all the variants of the independent manuscript will have been transferred to the copy used for the folio.

Both the fact that the folio text of *Lear* was printed from the first quarto, and the fact that the revision of this quarto by comparison with the playhouse manuscript was not perfect, are rendered probable by an interesting bibliographical accident. For certain sheets of the first quarto exist both in a corrected and an uncorrected state, and some of these uncorrected readings survive in the folio, only partially assimilated to the corrected form. Thus the end of one line was originally set up in the quarto as 'come and tends seruise', but was later corrected to 'commands her seruice'. Here the folio prints 'commands, tends, seruice', suggesting that the compositor had before him an originally uncorrected copy which had been brought only partially into agreement with the corrected reading. Moreover, imperfect correction of the copy can be traced in a number of other passages. Since Theobald, Lear has said:

What, have his daughters brought him to this pass?

But the quarto reads 'What, his daughters', and the folio 'Ha's his Daughters'. Apparently the corrector, intending to insert 'has' after 'What', accidentally substituted it for that word. (Theobald's 'have' is a mere sophistication.)

But if these inferences are correct, it is extraordinary how seldom editors have agreed in rejecting readings of any consequence warranted by both texts. In one place

'*Historica passio*' is an obvious twin error for '*Hysterica passio*', and there are certainly some similar mistakes in punctuation, but the collection is a small one and even so includes some doubtful examples. A crucial instance is in Edmund's speech, which the more conservative editors print as follows:

> Well, my legitimate, if this letter speed
> And my invention thrive, Edmund the base
> Shall to the legitimate. I grow; I prosper:
> Now, gods, stand up for bastards!

For my own part I cannot quite reconcile myself to this, though at the same time I do not feel certain of the admirable emendation 'shall top the legitimate', first proposed by Edwards and adopted into the text by Capell and the Cambridge editors. Be this as it may, it seems to me that the text of *King Lear* is considerably better than on our textual theory it has any right to be, and I think there still remains a problem for investigation.[19]

We now come to our fourth class, that highly important group of plays that have reached us in two quite different versions. The view of the older critics, that one of these versions represented an early draft subsequently re-modelled, has gradually given place to the theory that it is a mangled text based somehow upon an actual representation and superseded by one published with authority. According to the former view the inferior version is chronologically antecedent to the other; according to the latter it is derivative, presupposing the other, though the possibility of subsequent revision is not excluded. This may be taken to represent in general the current opinion as regards *Romeo and Juliet*, *Henry V*, *The Merry Wives of Windsor*, and *Hamlet*.[20] It is only of late, and mainly through the investigations of Mr. Peter Alexander, that the theory has been extended to cover *The Taming of the Shrew* and the two later parts of *Henry VI*.[21] It has not yet passed into the mortmain of orthodoxy; and I do not ask you to accept it as more than a provisional hypothesis. Neither would I suggest that a single history applies, except perhaps in barest outline, to all seven plays. Indeed it is plain upon the face of it that the critical data are not at all points analogous. If the quarto *Taming of a Shrew* is a derivative text based substantially upon *The Taming of the Shrew*, as we know it in the folio, there has been far more elaborate writing up of the derived material than is found for example in *Henry V*. Certain features in *The Merry Wives* suggest that the quarto text may have been vamped up by the actor of a particular part, and the same theory has been applied to some other plays. On the other hand if an actor played the traitor in *The Merry Wives* it is clear that he relied on memory alone, whereas in *Hamlet* he may have made use of his written part. This possibility suggests that the first quarto of *Hamlet* at least may be a very composite text, and that, though undoubtedly a bad egg, it is of the curate's variety. The choruses of *Henry V*, which to some extent mark the act structure in the folio, find no place in the quarto: on the other hand *A Shrew* preserves the conclusion of the framework-action which it is natural to suppose must once have been present in *The Shrew*, though there is no trace of it in the folio.

But great as is the diversity of individual cases, there are, if the modern theory is correct, certain fundamental features in common. In all seven plays we have on the one hand an authoritative text derived by transcription or printing from the author's original, and on the other a vamped text at least one step in the transmission of which is memorial. The critical implications of these assumptions are obvious. Where the texts differ, one possesses vastly greater authority than the other: where they agree, we not only have direct transcriptional witness to what the author wrote, but we know, subject to certain possible exceptions, that this was what was actually spoken on the stage. In the latter case, before resorting to emendation, we shall be not only justified but bound to go to lengths of interpretation which would be altogether fantastic in Classes I and II, and would be doubtful even in Class III.

The seven plays of our fourth group fall into two

divisions. In *Romeo and Juliet* and *Hamlet* the bad quarto was superseded after about a couple of years by a good quarto containing a text substantially identical with that later printed in the folio. For these, therefore, we possess three several authorities, and to them I shall return. In the other five plays the bad quarto was only superseded by the good text printed in the folio. These present a rather simpler problem. Although, of course, each has features of its own, we can only on this occasion examine a single play as more or less representative of its class. *Henry V* will serve as well as any.[22]

There are of course a number of errors in the folio text, and it is only to be expected that in some instances the correct reading should survive in the quarto. Editors have indeed made pretty free use of the latter, sometimes with full justification, sometimes perhaps indiscreetly. When, according to the folio, Corporal Nym says:

It must be as it may, though patience be a tyred name, yet shee will plodde,

he is talking nonsense, and when for 'name' the quarto has 'mare', the graphic similarity suggests that it preserves the correct reading. On the other hand we may take such a passage as this:

Boy. Doe you not remember a saw a Flea sticke vpon *Bardolphs* Nose, and a said it was a blacke Soule burning in Hell.
Bard. Well, the fuell is gone that maintain'd that fire: that's all the Riches I got in his seruice.

In place of 'Hell' Capell introduced 'hell fire' from the quarto, and in view of Bardolph's reply all later editors seem to have felt constrained to accept the alteration. I do not think they were justified.

In one place the quarto supplies a speech of Nym's that seems necessary to the sense, and this perhaps excuses the insertion from the same source of a line in Henry's great speech on the feast of Crispian, though it is certainly not indispensable. I think the most interesting case is the passage which stands in the folio as follows:

Bedf[ord]. Farwell good *Salisbury*, & good luck go with thee:
And yet I doe thee wrong, to mind thee of it,
For thou art fram'd of the firme truth of valour.
   Exe[ter]. Farwell kind Lord: fight valiantly to day.
   Bedf. He is as full of Valour as of Kindnesse,
Princely in both.

The quarto gives the second and third lines in the mangled form:

> And yet in truth, I do thee wrong,
> For thou art made on the [t]rue sparkes of honour

and also alters the speakers; but what is significant is that it tacks these lines on to the words spoken in the folio by Exeter; and in so doing it is clearly right. How, then, did they get misplaced in the folio? One naturally supposes that they were a marginal addition in the manuscript, the position of which the compositor mistook. If so they afford further evidence that the quarto is dependent on the final version of the play, and not on an earlier draft.

As regards emendation, I cannot find that any reading rejected by editorial consensus is supported by a clear agreement of the original texts. But there are three cases of what I may call disguised agreement, and in each of these I think that editors have been wrong. I can only call attention to one now; the most interesting and perhaps the most doubtful. On the eve of Agincourt, Fluellen and Gower meet in the English camp, and the folio reads:

   Gower. Captaine *Fluellen*.
   Flu. 'So, in the Name of Iesu Christ, speake fewer: ...

Malone and modern editors alter this to 'speak lower'. But 'lower', which comes from the third quarto, is merely a compositor's emendation for 'lewer' in the first quarto, and this would seem to be a misprint for 'fewer' as in the folio. There is no difficulty in the reading 'fewer' itself, in the sense of less, 'fewer words'; the supposed necessity of reading 'lower' arises from Gower's subsequent promise 'I will speake lower', and from Holinshed's report of an order 'that no noise or clamor should be made in the host'.

It would be interesting to write a full commentary on the passage, but here it must suffice to observe that Fluellen does not censure Gower for shouting but for 'tiddle tadle' and 'pibble bable', and that the humour of it is that all the time it is Fluellen who babbles, while Gower can hardly get a word in edgeways.

In *Henry V* at least the textual phenomena are what we should expect from the assumed history. I may, however, repeat the warning that we must not expect the phenomena to be altogether constant throughout the group, and that in every particular play editorial practice should be governed by a detailed examination of the textual data.[23]

Our last two plays agree in possessing three several authorities for the text. But they differ markedly as to the nature of these authorities. In both cases we have a 'bad' quarto superseded by a 'good' one, but whereas in *Hamlet* the folio was printed from a manuscript and shows important differences, in *Romeo and Juliet* it was set up almost without alteration from the authorized quarto text. The latter, therefore, presents a comparatively simple problem, for the relation of the 'good' quarto to the folio is that of the simplest cases of Class II, and need not further concern us, while the relation of the quartos to one another is essentially the same as in *Henry V*.

There is, however, one peculiarity of *Romeo and Juliet* which gives it a unique interest for the critic, namely that the 'bad' quarto of 1597 served to some extent as copy for the 'good' quarto of 1599. This fact was first observed by a German writer half a century ago, but it has only recently shown signs of creeping into critical consciousness.[24] The evidence is supplied by a number of bibliographical peculiarities, the most obvious being that certain speeches are printed in italic in both quartos, and it is to my mind conclusive. But it applies to only a small part of the play, namely the first two sheets of the first quarto. It seems clear that some editor was commissioned to prepare the copy for an authorized quarto, and for this purpose was

provided with the 1597 edition and a playhouse manuscript. He began by taking the printed text and ela-
borately correcting and expanding it by comparison with
the manuscript, but when he got to the end of sheet B he
decided that it would be less trouble to make a transcript
of the latter. This he proceeded to do through the remainder of the play, though I will not say that he may not
have used other fragments of the printed text, and I am
certain that he consulted it on occasions when the manuscript was obscure.[25]

This bibliographical induction is borne out in a rather
remarkable way by the textual evidence of a number of
corruptions common to the two quartos. When Romeo
meets Capulet's servant he asks him whither the guests are
invited, and the conversation proceeds:

> *Serv.* Up.
> *Rom.* Whither?
> *Serv.* To supper; to our house.

This is Theobald's arrangement of the text, and it is
very likely correct: the quartos make the words 'to supper'
part of Romeo's speech. There are two other common
errors within a few lines of this, and the next scene is
marked by an agreement of the texts in several peculiar
spellings, the most notable being 'a leauen' (or 'a leuen')
for eleven. All these occur in sheet B. In the remainder
of the play, eight sheets, there is one common error (to
which I shall return), and one, or possibly two, partial
agreements in abnormal spellings. The conclusion is
obvious.[26]

This peculiar textual history should prepare us for something unusual in the readings. We find it in the frequent
use which editors have made of the 'bad' quarto in their
endeavour to emend the 'good' one. The cases are ten or
twelve times as numerous as in *Henry V* and mostly of
much greater importance. The Cambridge editors are
fairly conservative in the matter, but I have counted 118
instances (trivialities apart) in which they have replaced a
reading of the second quarto by what is substantially that

of the first, or about one in every twenty-five lines. Of course nothing like all these are really needed, but I think that about a third are inevitable; and if it is once admitted that the first quarto is right in two score cases, there is no particular reason to jib at six score.[27]

The most certain corrections supplied by the first quarto are not as a rule the most interesting, though they include such readings as 'chaples' (i.e. chapless) for 'chapels' and 'pay' for 'pray'. But there seems no reason to question the correctness of the line:

> Hence will I to my ghostly father's cell,

which editors have taken mainly from the first quarto, for the reading of the second, 'my ghostly Friers close cell', can only have originated, one supposes, in inability to decipher the playhouse manuscript. At the same time there are a few passages in which I think editors have done wrong to desert the primary authority, for instance in the Friar's reproof to Romeo:

> O she knew well,
> Thy loue did reade by rote, that could not spell:

where most editors since Pope have printed the less pregnant reading of the first quarto, 'and could not spell'.

The one common error in the later sheets of the play appears in a passage that raises a number of textual problems. Mercutio's conjuring of the invisible lover, so far as it can be quoted with decency, which happily will serve our turn, is printed by the Cambridge editors as follows:

> Romeo! humours! madman! passion! lover!
> Appear thou in the likeness of a sigh:
> Speak but one rhyme, and I am satisfied;
> Cry but 'ay me!' pronounce but 'love' and 'dove';
> Speak to my gossip Venus one fair word,
> One nick-name for her purblind son and heir,
> Young Adam Cupid, he that shot so trim
> When King Cophetua loved the beggar-maid!

I am not going to argue whether 'Adam Cupid' is right, though I think it may be: the point is that it is an emendation for '*Abraham: Cupid*', a reading in which the two quartos agree *literatim et punctuatim*. Now, two things are evident, namely that this as it stands cannot be correct, and that the second quarto must have copied it from the first. Is this, then, a passage for which the editor in 1599 used a fragment of the printed edition? The suggestion is ruled out by other readings which prove that the compositor of the second quarto had manuscript copy before him. Thus the fourth line is substantially taken from the first quarto; the second quarto reads:

> Crie but ay me, prouaunt, but loue and day,

where 'prouaunt' and 'day' are certainly graphic errors. It is clear that the editor was having unusual difficulties with the playhouse copy in this passage—it must have been mutilated or defaced—and that when he came to young Cupid he boldly turned to the printed text for guidance. But if this is so, we shall do well to examine very carefully the readings in which the second quarto differs from the first. Already, apart from the fourth line, editors have borrowed from the first quarto 'shot so trim' and 'son and heir', but they have followed the second quarto in the first line, where the first quarto has:

> *Romeo*, madman, humors, passion, liuer, . . .

Noting the slight change of order, which emphasizes the descent from man to his complaints, there seems a good deal to be said for the reading 'liuer', this being of course the seat of the disease of love. And again in the last line we may wonder whether 'begger wench', as in the first quarto, is not more in accord with Mercutio's humour than the rather conventional 'beggar-maid'. The latter, familiar from the ballad, would no doubt have come more readily from the editor's pen.[28]

Among the plays of Class IV *Romeo and Juliet* is remarkable in that the bad text seems a good deal better, and the good text a good deal worse, than we are accustomed to find. I fancy it offers opportunities of critical exploration which have not yet been exhausted.

Discussion of Shakespeare usually comes round in the end to *Hamlet*; and for us too the wheel is come full circle. *Hamlet* is not only, from the literary point of view, the most discussed play in the canon, it is also the one that presents the most complex problem to the textual student. It is the only play for which we possess three ostensibly independent authorities. And the earliest of these texts, the bad egg, appears to be of a more complex or variable badness than the other members of that addled sitting: or else its quality has been submitted to more minute examination. This is a topic upon which I cannot enter now. The theory which I wish to examine, without necessarily accepting, is that the 'good' second quarto was printed direct from Shakespeare's autograph, that the folio was printed from a playhouse manuscript copied from that autograph, which had undergone certain alteration in the course of two decades of constant use as a prompt-book, and that the 'bad' first quarto is in the main based upon a representation of the play, the actors' parts for which had been transcribed from the same prompt-copy in its original state. The actual textual history may be a good deal more complicated than this, but I wish at present merely to inquire how far this theory will 'work' in view of the variant readings found in the authorities and the emendations that have found favour with editors. In this investigation I have had the benefit of studying an important essay by Professor Dover Wilson on 'Spellings and Misprints in the Second Quarto of *Hamlet*'.

There are five classes of readings that throw light on our problem, namely: agreements of the first quarto and the folio against the second quarto, agreements of the two quartos against the folio, agreements of the second quarto and the folio which editors have rejected in favour of the first quarto, agreements of the second quarto and the folio which editors have rejected without seeking help from the first quarto, and agreements of all three texts which editors have rejected.

It is a curious fact that where the second quarto and the

folio differ the support of the first quarto is almost exactly balanced between them: in fifty-five instances it agrees with the other quarto, in fifty-seven with the folio. If our theory is correct its agreements with the folio are not of much significance, since both go back ultimately to the prompt-book; all that the first quarto can prove is that the folio reading is not due to the compositor and that it could pass muster on the stage. Analysis seems to show that the great majority of instances (44 out of 57) are due either to misprints in the second quarto or to small variants introduced in transcribing the prompt-copy. There are also three definite errors originating in that operation. The most interesting result is that the prompt-copy seems to have undergone some authoritative revision before the copying of the actors' parts, for there are ten passages or so in which readings of the autograph appear to have been deliberately altered. If Mr. Dover Wilson is right, one of the prompt-book errors was the substitution of snatches of old 'tunes' for 'lauds' through a misreading of Shakespeare's writing. The corrections or alterations are all instructive: I have only space to mention that Shakespeare seems originally to have written 'fearefull Porpentine', and that 'fretfull' was a happy second thought.

The variants in which the first quarto supports the second against the folio are of much greater importance, since on our theory agreement of the quartos establishes the reading of the prompt-book. Apart from chance coincidence, of which there may be a few examples, variation in the folio implies either a misprint in that text or an alteration subsequent to the preparation of the actors' parts. Misprints account for nearly half the cases; the rest are divided about equally between small editorial tinkerings, very likely made in preparing the playhouse manuscript for press, and alterations made in it in the course of its twenty years of use as a prompt-book. The distinction of these classes is of course conjectural. The most interesting misprint is the substitution of 'Landlesse' for 'lawelesse' resolutes, due it would seem to the easy

misreading of 'lawe' as 'land'. Among editorial changes
there are a couple that suggest that the speech with which
Hamlet leaves Ophelia, after consigning her to a nunnery,
had become partly obliterated in the manuscript. The
dozen or so major alterations are important. Shakespeare
himself, it would seem, altered 'quietly interr'd' to 'quietly
enurn'd', and perhaps made the necessary correction in the
'dayly Cast of Brazon Cannon', where 'cost' had got into
the acted version. But he surely had no hand in the 'too
too solid Flesh'. A vision of Burbage's waist-band should
suffice to prove that, editors notwithstanding, Shakespeare
can never have meant to write 'solid' here. It is a desperate
guess for the unintelligible 'sallied' of the quartos. The
problem is therefore one of emendation and I shall return
to it.

There are eight passages in which the Cambridge editors
have adopted a reading of the first quarto to the exclusion
of one supported by the second quarto and the folio. One
of these is clearly necessary, but the error is an easy one and
may well have arisen independently in the two more
authoritative texts. The other seven should be rejected.
Three or four are mere mischievous normalizations; one is
an exceedingly ingenious conjecture, for which the editors
have not been given the credit they deserve, but which is at
the same time rather hazardous. Of the rest the most
crucial is in the Play scene, where in reply to Ophelia's
'Still better, and worse', Hamlet snaps:

> So you must take your husbands.

Here 'must take' was introduced by Pope from the first
quarto in place of 'mistake' as in the other texts. But
surely Capell was right in printing 'mis-take': Hamlet
means: 'For better or worse! Why, that's the silly way you
choose husbands.'

There are ten instances, where the first quarto affords no
help, in which the Cambridge editors have rejected a
reading certified by both the second quarto and the folio.
Some are trivial; once or twice Shakespeare and the

prompter were both certainly nodding; but 'good kissing carrion' I am inclined to believe is correct, and 'cauiary' should not be altered to 'caviare', a form very rare in Shakespeare's day. Only one is of first-rate interest. Polonius hides behind the arras with the words: 'I'll silence me even here'. Hanmer emended 'silence' to 'sconce'. But, as Dowden remarked, only in death could Polonius be really silent, and it is just because he cannot 'silence' him that he dies. The emendation destroys the dramatic irony of the phrase.

There are even three cases in which the editors have rejected a reading which has the warrant of all three authorities. In one they did not venture on any emendation, and I propose to return to it in a moment. One is a trivial matter, a second-folio spelling adopted in the teeth of textual evidence. The last is very significant.

> White his shroud as the mountain snow,
>   Larded with sweet flowers;
> Which bewept to the grave did go
>   With true-love showers.

So Ophelia sings, at least according to Pope, and such no doubt were the words of the song she had in mind, supposing it to have been traditional. But in the third line all three texts read 'did not go', and we are bound to believe that not only is this what Shakespeare wrote, but what Ophelia actually sang on the stage. It is idle to talk of printers and their intrusive negatives; it would be equally idle to point out that Massinger once committed this very error in his own manuscript: the present case cannot be accidental, nor could it escape notice. Ophelia is suddenly struck by the inappropriateness of the words she is singing and twists them to a harsh discord.[29]

This completes what I have to say of the practice of editors considered in relation to the textual theory of *Hamlet* with which we began. If that theory is true it is clear that editors will have to modify their practice considerably. That it is true I will not assert, but we have found nothing in the textual evidence that necessarily contradicts it, and a good deal that is doubtful in editorial practice where this conflicts with it.

I wish in conclusion to consider two or three emendations or explanations of emendations suggested by Professor Dover Wilson in the paper already mentioned. As is well known he has based his work chiefly upon an analysis of Shakespeare's supposed handwriting and spelling, but he has pursued this line of inquiry in conjunction with textual theory.[30] For example he argues that where the second quarto gives us what may be a misreading of Shakespeare's autograph it is a facile abdication of critical function to accept instead a makeshift reading from the folio. Take for instance:

> The terms of our estate may not endure
> Hazard so near us as doth hourly grow
> Out of his lunacies.

The last word is supplied by the folio; the quarto has 'browes'. This of course is impossible, and we may suppose that it is just because it is impossible that the folio started guessing, but we are bound to do our best with it. Mr. Dover Wilson suggests a misreading of 'brawls'. I do not know whether his conjecture is right, but I am sure that his method is sound.[31]

So with the 'too too solid Flesh' already glanced at. The folio's 'solid' is a guess we must reject: the 'sallied' of the quartos is unintelligible. But 'sallies' occurs elsewhere in the second quarto as a misprint for 'sullies', showing that the words could be easily confused in Shakespeare's hand. Thus, when he intended 'sullied' flesh, it was twice misread as 'sallied' and finally mis-emended to 'solid'. Of this explanation I have little doubt.[32]

Lastly, what are we to make of the threefold witness to Polonius's words?—

> And they in France of the best rank and station
> Are of a most select and generous chief in that.

Mr. Dover Wilson tells us that 'of a' is a misreading of Shakespeare's attempt to write 'often'. I cannot discuss the details, but the emendation does not present any insuperable difficulty either graphic or metrical. What, however, are its textual implications? Granted that Shakespeare wrote 'often' in such a way that it would naturally be read 'of a': then we have to assume that the compositor of the second quarto so printed it, that the scribe of the playhouse manuscript so wrote it, that the scribe of the actors' parts accepted the reading, and likewise the actors who performed along with Shakespeare on the stage, the reporter of the representation, and the printer of his version; that meanwhile the reading remained unaltered in the prompt-copy, and passed muster with the editor and compositor of the folio. It would be idle to pretend that such a chain of error and persistence in error is not improbable; but where the facts are themselves unreasonable we need not be surprised if the explanation seems fantastic. It is the implications that are important, and it is Professor Dover Wilson's chief merit that he has courageously faced the consequences of his proposals. That renders his work significant even where it may prove mistaken, and I make no excuse for dwelling upon it here.[33]

Thus I come back at the end to the point with which I started, the interdependence of emendation and textual theory. We have considered the many aspects that the editorial problem assumes with the shifting relations of particular texts, but this interdependence is the one general principle that has emerged from, I fear, an o'er-lengthy discussion. To be fruitful the task of emendation must be pursued in the light of a clear perception of the possibilities of textual history; otherwise it is as a bow drawn at a venture. It is no revolutionary doctrine that I am preaching, and if, so far, it has been little reflected in the practice of editors, this has been perhaps less through deliberate neglect, than because the data for its application have been insufficient. For of one thing at least the preparation of this lecture has made me more than ever conscious, the need for a fresh and thorough investigation into the bibliographical history of the authorities for Shakespeare's text.

Postscript: June 1932

In the foregoing lecture I was more concerned to follow out the implications of certain current views than to inquire into the evidence in their support. I have, therefore, been content to reprint what I wrote with only minor alterations, and have made no attempt to bring it up to date as an account of Shakespearian textual theory. The last four or five years have, however, produced a considerable amount of fresh work in this field, and had I been writing to-day I should doubtless have put some things differently. I am particularly glad to see that my challenge on p. 140 has been taken up in an able study by Miss Madaleine Doran on *The Text of 'King Lear'* (Stanford University Press, 1931). While I am not convinced that her solution of the problems is in every case correct, I feel even less confident than before that the relation of the texts is that assumed in my lecture.

NOTES

QUOTATIONS from Shakespeare both in the lecture and the notes, except where they reproduce the originals, as a rule follow the Cambridge text of W. G. Clark and W. Aldis Wright (revised edition, 1891–3), and all references are to that edition. The collations there given are also my main source of information respecting the variant readings of the originals. In a few instances I have endeavoured to collect all variants of a particular type. If, as is probable, my lists are not complete, the responsibility lies, no doubt, mainly with my own carelessness, but, perhaps, also in part with imperfections of the record, for the collations of the Cambridge editors, though a monument of industry, are not invariably correct. It must also be remembered in using their apparatus that where the original editions present alternative readings, they do not, as a rule, specify which editors have adopted which alternative. The only attempt at a complete record is that in the Furness Variorum. A serious defect alike of the Cambridge and Furness editions is the absence of any proper index of sigla.

1 (p. 128). A. E. Housman, 'The Application of Thought to Textual Criticism', a paper read before the Classical Association, 4 Aug. 1921: *Proceedings*, xviii. 68.

2 (p. 129). *Henry V*, ii. iii. 13 ff. Theobald's emendation (*Shakespeare Restored*, 1726, p. 138) was suggested by the conjecture 'of a Gentleman sometime deceas'd', namely, 'and a' talked of green

Fields'. He proceeds: 'The Variation from *Table* to *talked* is not of a very great Latitude; tho' we may still come nearer to the Traces of the Letters, by restoring it thus', namely, 'and a' babled of green Fields'. 'To *bable*, or *babble*', he adds, 'is to mutter . . .' It is noticeable that this suggestion was first put forward tentatively as an alternative to supposing that the words were a stage-direction that had crept into the text. But in 1733 he adopted it in his text.

3 (p. 129). When in the same play Fluellen reproves Gower for babbling in the camp (IV. i. 71) the folio has the spelling 'bable'.

4 (p. 129). *Doctor Faustus*, i. 12.

5 (p. 130). The passage occurs in Greene's *Orlando Furioso*, ll. 1276–7 (Malone Society Reprint). See my *Two Elizabethan Stage Abridgements*, p. 240. The detection of the source is due to Mr. F. M. Cornford. The first edition actually reads '*lacusque laeosque*', and it is from the second that editors have taken '*locosque*'. The confusion of 'a' and 'u' is commoner than that of 'a' and 'o', so that the first edition slightly supports my emendation. I ought to say that I am by no means certain that these lines are Greene's, and should not be surprised to find that they were borrowed or at least adapted from some neo-Latin writer.

5a (p. 131). Dr. J. W. Mackail tells me that this instance, which I lifted from his Warton Lecture, is a bad one. It appears that the mistake is found in the only authorities that were accessible when Milton wrote.

6 (p. 132). See *The Library*, 1923, iv. 207 ff., 'Massinger's Autograph Corrections in *The Duke of Milan*, 1623'; and 1924, v. 59 ff., 'More Massinger Corrections'.

7 (p. 133). I make this admission deliberately, although it suggests that there may be some circularity in an argument that seeks to support textual theory by record of emendation, or to limit emendation by reference to textual theory. In some measure this is so. The number and to a certain extent the nature of the emendations made in any text naturally depend upon the condition of the text, and this is, of course, an important datum in the construction of textual theory. But it is far from being the sole basis. Textual theory, if it is to be in any way scientific, must take account of many kinds of evidence besides the readings which concern an editor; and it is clear that editors, in the preparation of their texts, have usually followed eclectic methods without regard to the relation of the authorities. In practice, therefore, textual theory and editorial practice are sufficiently independent to afford a check upon one

another, and there can be little doubt that, while textual conditions critically considered, may demand the revision of a theory, a textual theory constructed with adequate knowledge and care is a much sounder guide than traditional editorial practice. I think that both these features of our problem will come out clearly in the ensuing analysis.

8 (p. 134). The term 'independent manuscript' is rather vague, and critics have not always been careful to make their meaning clear. If they mean anything they must mean that the quarto and the folio were printed from *different* manuscripts, and they ought to mean that these were *independent*, in the sense that neither was a transcript of the other. More technically, the phrase should imply that, not only the printed texts, but the manuscripts used as copy, had a collateral and not an ancestral relation. It will be observed that, according to the textual theory of *Hamlet* with which we shall be concerned later, the folio was not printed from an independent manuscript, since this is assumed to have been a copy of the one used for the second quarto.

9 (p. 135). I must leave out of consideration for the present the interesting question of what, if any, authority attaches to the variant readings of the second folio.

10 (p. 135). In this country the investigation of manuscript forms and the closely related investigation of manuscript spellings have been mainly pursued by Professor Dover Wilson in his work in the eleven volumes of the New Shakespeare (Cambridge, 1921–8) that have so far appeared. See in particular his general 'Textual Introduction' to *The Tempest*; also his chapter on 'Bibliographical Links' in *Shakespeare's Hand in the Play of 'Sir Thomas More'* (ed. A. W. Pollard, 1923, pp. 113–41), his paper (in collaboration with Mr. Pollard) on 'What follows if some of the good Quarto Editions of Shakespeare's Plays were printed from his autograph manuscripts', summarized in the Bibliographical Society's *Transactions* for 1917–19 (xv. 136–9), and that on 'Spellings and Misprints in the second Quarto of *Hamlet*' contributed to the English Association's *Essays and Studies* in 1924 (x. 36–60). I may also refer to a paper on 'Elizabethan Spelling as a Literary and Bibliographical Clue' by Mr. A. W. Pollard, with supplements on Munday and Churchyard by Miss St. Clare Byrne, in *The Library* (1923–4, iv. 1, 9; v. 143), and to one by me on 'An Elizabethan Printer and his Copy' also in *The Library* (1923, iv. 102).

The most extensive investigation of the subject is, of course, that by Dr. Leon Kellner, *Restoring Shakespeare* (Leipzig, 1925). This is a most exhaustive and learned work, though it failed to produce any new emendations of importance that have been generally accepted by critics (cf. *The Review of English Studies*, 1925, i. 463).

11 (p. 136). An interesting, if conjectural, case occurs in one of the theatrical 'plots' discovered at Dulwich towards the end of the eighteenth century, which has since vanished, leaving only a print in the Variorum Shakespeare of 1803, namely, that for the play of *Tamar Cam*. In this one of the actors is given the absurd name of 'Denygten'. We know that the person intended was called Downton, and in one of the other plots he appears with the rather queer spelling 'Doughton'. It is clear that the impossible 'Denygten' is nothing but a misreading of 'Doughton', but it is a misreading which could only occur in English, and not in Italian, script. It seems likely, therefore, that the lost plot was drawn up by the same scribe as its fellow, but that, contrary to his custom, he used, at least for the name in question, the more old-fashioned secretary hand. The misreading is probably due to Steevens, from whose transcript the plot was printed, and it occurs three times over. How difficult it is to see a word right once it has been seen wrong may be illustrated by an entry in the Stationers' Register of 8 Nov. 1630, which includes the title 'Pericles'. The word is quite correctly written, but in such a way that at a casual glance it might be read 'Persiles'. Arber (iv. 242) actually so misread it, adding a note that it was an error for 'Pericles'.

12 (p. 136). In connexion with misreading and the theory of 'graphic emendation' there is one point to which I do not think that sufficient attention has been paid. It is, that where the forms of two letters or groups of letters resemble one another, the confusion does not necessarily work both ways. To take the simplest case: carelessness in the dotting of an 'i' will make 'in' or 'iu' indistinguishable from 'm', but no carelessness, only the imps of mischief, can convert 'm' into 'in' or 'iu'. Thus, to conjecture 'iuy' where the text reads 'my' is no violent emendation, but the opposite change is one which, on strict principles, would need further evidence to support it. Yet an examination of the work of those critics who have specialized in the graphic method shows that there is a constant temptation to treat what one may call asymmetrical resemblances as reversible; and undoubted instances of such reflex substitutions do occur. But they always call for explanation, and may, I think, be analysed under three heads. (1) In a particular writer

a particular miswriting may be so common that the compositor is led to assume it even where it has not occurred. For example, some writers, including Shakespeare it seems, were in the habit of occasionally using a particular form of the letter 'a', well known to palaeographers, which was liable to be mistaken for 'or', and, in fact, is so misprinted in two passages of *Hamlet* (Q 2: 1. ii. 96, 1. v. 56). We can imagine a writer using this form so persistently that a compositor might be led by force of habit to print 'a' even where 'or' was meant (cf. the similar error of 'daie' for 'doue', note 28, p. 181). Of course, the same principle makes the confusion of 'in' and 'm' reversible in practice. (2) One letter may be so much commoner than the other that it will tend to be used in all doubtful cases. In the secretary script, if a 'p' is carelessly formed it readily assumes a shape indistinguishable from 'x', but no malformation of 'x' will make it resemble a properly formed 'p'. Of course, compositors were well aware of this confusion, and 'x' being a comparatively uncommon letter, they appear always to have printed 'p' by preference if it made a possible word. Thus we may find 'axle-tree' transmographied into 'apple-tree', though I have never heard of an apple-tree masquerading as an axle-tree. (3) Lastly, there may be some particular association aroused by the context which suggests the reflex change to the compositor's eye. A good example occurs just at the end of *Every Man out of His Humour* (quarto version, Malone Society Reprint, l. 4363; Oxford Jonson, iii. 604). Jonson says, or is made by his compositor to say, that his detractors will

betray themselues

To Scorne and Laughter; and like guiltie Children,
Publish their *infancie* before their time,
By their owne fond exception.

There is no doubt, I think, that '*infancie*' should be altered to '*infamie*', an emendation lately proposed by Miss Evelyn Albright (*Dramatic Publication in England, 1580–1640*, p. 336) and made independently by Mr. Simpson in the Oxford edition. Now, alike in English and Italian script, a badly formed 'c' becomes a mere minim, or single down-stroke, and consequently there would always be a danger of 'nc' being misprinted as 'm' (cf. note 30, p. 200). The opposite confusion ought not to occur. But in this passage the idea of 'Children' was so dominant in the compositor's mind as to set up the association needed to make the confusion reversible.

13 (p. 136). In the case of common error, therefore, it is in the rigour of the evidence required to establish the error, rather than in the range of permissible conjecture, that the position differs from that in Class I. The reading must have passed muster at least to the extent of not causing active protest.

2 HENRY IV

14 (p. 137). Bardolph's speech, wrongly assigned to Poins, is at II. ii. 72. The correction was first made by Theobald. An amusing example of an error common to both texts occurs in the Induction (l. 35), where Rumour describes Percy's castle as

> this worm-eaten hole of ragged stone . . .

Of course, 'hole' should be 'hold'; it is the usual confusion of final 'e' and 'd', but it might not have been thus repeated without the unfortunate association of 'worm-hole'. Another seemingly clear case of twin error occurs at III. ii. 305, in Falstaff's description of Justice Shallow, which since Rowe has been printed:

> a' was so forlorn, that his dimensions to any thick sight were invisible:

whereas both Q and F have 'inuincible'. A significant case, as it appears to me, is that at IV. i. 34, where Westmoreland addresses the Archbishop in the words:

> If that rebellion
> Came like itself, in base and abject routs,
> Led on by bloody youth, guarded with rags,
> And countenanced by boys and beggary . . .

Here 'rags', now generally accepted in place of 'rage', is a fairly recent emendation, having been made independently by Collier and Walker about 1850. It is in a sense palmary, since it at once allows a more precise meaning for 'guarded' (i.e. trimmed) and supplies a parallel antithesis to the 'boys and beggary' of the next line. At the same time 'rage' can hardly be said to be necessarily wrong, and although it would not be an unlikely misprint it would hardly be a likely miswriting. If, therefore, F were printed from Q the emendation would be plausible enough, but if they are independent witnesses it must be held less convincing.

It should be remarked that Mr. R. P. Cowl, who prepared the edition of the play for the Arden Shakespeare in 1923, arrived 'with all diffidence' at the conclusion that F was printed, not from an independent source, but from a copy of Q which had been edited and collated with a manuscript.

Troilus and Cressida

15 (p. 137). Cressida's 'Comming in dumbnesse' occurs at III. ii. 129. The word 'coming' in this sense was actually misprinted 'cunning' in Massinger's *Bondman*, II. ii. (1624, sig. E 1ᵛ), where the printed text reads:

> your true Courtier knowes not
> His Neece, or Sister from another woman,
> If she be apt and cunning.

In this Massinger, with his own hand, corrected 'cunning' to 'cõminge' (*The Library*, v. 65, 87; see note 6).

A clear case of divergent error is found at II. iii. 75, where Agamemnon says that Achilles 'sate our messengers' according to Q, while F has 'sent'. It is clear that neither reading can be right, but it is not certain that they are misreadings of the same word. Theobald supposed that 'sent' was an error for 'shent'; Dyce that 'sate' was an error for 'rate', i.e. rated. If so, we have alternate readings, both of which have suffered corruption. Possibly another instance occurs in Cassandra's speech at II. ii. 104:

> Virgins and boys, mid age and wrinkled eld,
> Soft infancy, that nothing canst but cry,
> Add to my clamours!

Here 'eld' is an emendation of Theobald, where Q has 'elders' and F 'old'. Neither of these readings can be pronounced necessarily wrong, but the fact of variation itself perhaps favours the conjecture.

Common error is certain at II. i. 102, where Thersites says to Achilles:

There's Ulysses and old Nestor, whose wit was mouldy ere their grandsires had nails on their toes . . .

No doubt not 'their grandsires' but those of Achilles are meant, and Theobald was right to alter 'their' to 'your'. Presumably the error arose through the use of an abbreviation (see note 23, p. 174). Another is seen at I. ii. 8:

> Before the sun rose he was harness'd light,
> And to the field goes he;

where Q and F agree in the curious reading 'harnest lyte'. Other twin errors are, if we believe the Cambridge editors, 'scorne' for 'storm' (I. i. 37), 'yea' for 'you' (I. ii. 46), 'will' for 'wit' (I. ii. 82), 'indifferent, well', for 'indifferent well.' (I. ii. 215), 'staule' for

'stale' (II. iii. 186), 'goe' for 'giue' (III. iii. 178), and 'seale' for
'zeale' (IV. iv. 121). But I do not think that editors have always
been justified in their emendations. Take for example the following
(III. iii. 43):

'Tis like he'll question me
Why such unplausive eyes are bent? why turn'd on him?

Of course, it is quite possible that 'bent' and 'turn'd' were originally
alternatives, but the line is by no means impossible or even ineffective as it stands, and if it had no more than a single authority behind
it I should still question whether it was right to extrude the words
'why turn'd'. Similarly, I think that at III. iii. 168 Pope's deletion
of 'the' before 'welcome', and at v. i. 73 Rowe's substitution of
'sewer' for 'sure', are to be rejected, though the latter is ingenious
and even plausible.

OTHELLO

16 (p. 138). Textually *Othello* should be the most interesting of
the plays in Class III, for if the critics are right, not only were the
first quarto and the folio printed from independent manuscripts,
but in 1630 a second quarto, printed from the first, included passages
only found in the folio, but printed them, not from the folio, but
from another manuscript. Thus we appear to have two collateral
authorities for the shorter text of 1622, and likewise two collateral
authorities for the additional passages first printed in 1623.

There are, of course, a number of points at which editors have
altered details of arrangement in which Q and F agree, though they
have not always been happy in the result. But there seem to be
only four cases in which the Cambridge editors have seriously
interfered with a reading supported by double authority, and these
all deserve careful examination.

At II. iii. 307 Iago says that Othello

hath devoted and given up himself to the contemplation, mark and
denotement of her [Desdemona's] parts and graces ...

Here 'denotement' is an emendation proposed by Theobald in
place of 'deuotement', the reading of Qq and Ff. I think Theobald
and the Cambridge editors are right; though in this I find myself
unfortunately in disagreement with the *N.E.D.* (Murray), C. T.
Onions, and H. C. Hart, a formidable consensus. But the error is,
of course, a very easy one, and may well have arisen independently
in the two texts owing to the occurrence of 'deuoted' just before.

[Confusion has been introduced into the discussion by faulty collation. The *N.E.D.*, giving 'deuotement' (correctly) as the reading
of F 1, adds (incorrectly) that Qq and F 2 read 'denotement'. Hart
maintains that Q 2 alone reads 'denotement', adding that 'the
British Museum Q 2 has distinctly' this reading. I am sorry to
differ from so careful a scholar, but there are two copies of Q 2 in
the British Museum, and a comparison of them shows that the
reading is quite certainly 'deuotement'. I am afraid he relied on
Praetorius's facsimile of one of them, in which the reading is
certainly 'denotement', but it is clear that the plate must have
been tampered with. The collation as given by the Cambridge
editors is correct.]

The second instance is that cited in the lecture. It will be found
at II. iii. 373, where Q has 'awhile', F 'a while', and Theobald 'the
while'.

In III. iii. 67 Desdemona, pleading to her husband for Cassio,
says:

> in faith, he's penitent;
> And yet his trespass, in our common reason—
> Save that, they say, the wars must make examples
> Out of their best—is not almost a fault
> To incur a private check.

Here 'their best' is Rowe's correction for 'her best', the reading of
all previous editions. It is not, to my mind, altogether satisfactory,
for the plural 'the wars' is in any case rather unexpected and the
pronoun emphasizes this slight awkwardness. The original reading
is undoubtedly difficult, but, as Hart pointed out, there may be
some vague personification of 'wars', and in any case I feel that, if it
is a slip, it is probably Shakespeare's.

Lastly at III. iii. 444, when Iago is tempting Othello, we find this
passage:

> *Oth.* I gave her such a one; 'twas my first gift.
> *Iago.* I know not that: but such a handkerchief—
> I am sure it was your wife's—did I to-day
> See Cassio wipe his beard with.
> *Oth.* If it be that,—
> *Iago.* If it be that, or any that was hers,
> It speaks against her with the other proofs.

The last line but one is due to Malone: in the early texts it runs: 'If
it be that, or any, it was hers'. Malone's reading is the smoother
and more logical, but the original, even if the construction be a

little harsh, gives perfectly good sense—Whether it was that particular one or some other, yet I know it was hers—and the punctuation shows that this was in any case how it was understood, F even
emphasizing the interpretation by placing a full stop at the end of
the line. I have little doubt that this represents Shakespeare's
intention.

To these should be added I. i. 21, which is obelized as corrupt in
the Globe edition, though the editors do not venture on any
emendation. This famous line stands thus in Q:

> A fellow almost dambd in a fair wife,

and in F:

> (A Fellow almost damn'd in a faire Wife)

and, of course, many emendations have been suggested. None of
these are in the least convincing, and plenty of critics have sought
to explain the passage as it stands.

If any of these instances had occurred in 2 *Henry IV* or *Troilus
and Cressida*, we might not hesitate to adopt some emendation, but
when we are asked to accept them as practically the only evidence
that there are corruptions common to the two authorities, we may
be excused for feeling doubtful. It is to my mind remarkable that
so careful an editor as the late H. C. Hart, who prepared the play
for the Arden edition in 1902—an editor who thought that in
II. iii. 307 'The elder copies leave us no choice' but to read 'devote-
ment', though this is a reading in which agreement carries little
weight—should in the three other instances have altered the text,
though he was evidently not very happy about III. iii. 67. He retains and defends I. i. 21.

---

17 (p. 138). I have little doubt that *Love's Labour's Lost* really
belongs to Class IV, and that there was once an early 'bad' quarto of
which no copy is now known to exist. Mr. Dover Wilson, in the
edition in the New Shakespeare, accounts for certain confusions in
the extant text on the supposition that the manuscript had undergone revision, but Miss Hjort, writing in *The Modern Language
Review* (see note 24, p. 175), has pointed out that these may be due
to the quarto of 1598 having been printed, with extensive corrections, from its predecessor.

18 (p. 138). It is agreed that the folio text of *A Midsummer-
Night's Dream* was printed from a copy of the second quarto ('1600',
really 1619), and it has usually been assumed that this copy had
been used in the playhouse as a prompt-book. Mr. Dover Wilson,

however, has argued (New Shakespeare edition, p. 157) that it had not itself been so used, but was collated with a copy of the first edition (1600) that had. If this is true, it seems to me of some importance, for the collation may have been with a playhouse manuscript rather than with the earlier quarto. I do not think that the points supposed to prove that the prompter's notes were made in a copy of the quarto are conclusive, and I should like more evidence to show that printed texts were ever, in ordinary circumstances, used in the theatre.

King Lear

19 (p. 140). The evidence that F was printed from a copy of Q 1 containing sheets E, H, and K in their uncorrected state was first collected by P. A. Daniel (Introduction to the Praetorius facsimile of Q 1, 1885). The example of partial revision cited in the lecture occurs at II. iv. 100. Here the reading of F is intermediate between the original and the corrected forms appearing in Q 1, and the natural inference is that it was set up from an uncorrected copy which had been partly doctored by comparison with a text giving the correct reading. A second instance is found at IV. ii. 28, where the original reading, 'My foote vsurps my body', was altered to 'A foole vsurps my bed'; while F reads 'My Foole vsurpes my body'. This again may be a partial correction, although most editors have accepted it as the genuine text. A third is at V. iii. 47. Here the passage was first set up as:

> Sir I thought it fit,
> To saue the old and miserable King to some retention,

and altered to:

> Sir I thought it fit,
> To send the old and miserable King to some retention, and ap-
> (pointed guard,

obviously the proper arrangement being that of Q 2, which reads:

> Sir I thought it fit,
> To send the olde and miserable King
> To some retention, and appointed guard, . . .

In F it stands:

> Sir, I thought it fit,
> To send the old and miserable King to some retention,

which would appear to have been printed from an uncorrected copy of Q 1, while the alteration of 'saue' to 'send', though it might well have been made by the compositor, is more likely, in view of the foregoing examples, to have been again due to partial collation with the fuller text.

The instance of imperfect correction detected by Theobald, which was cited in the lecture, will be found at III. iv. 62. We might, no doubt, take 'ha's' as a contraction for 'has his' intended to replace 'his' ('What,' could stand as a foot by itself): however 'ha's' is a very common folio spelling of 'has' (cf. p. 185, note on I. i. 21). At v. iii. 289 Lear says in Q 'You'r welcome hither', while F prints 'Your are'. Apparently the corrector marked 'are' for insertion and forgot to delete the "r'. Again where, at I. i. 109, Q has 'The mistresse of Heccat', we may suppose that the corrector, wishing to alter the second word to 'misteries', wrote 'eries' in the margin, but accidentally drew his pen through the last six, instead of only the last five letters of 'mistresse'; hence F's reading 'miseries'. Similar agency may be seen in the confusion at II. ii. 70. Q reads:

Which are to intrench, to inloose smooth euery passion . . .

F corrects 'intrench' to 'intrince' and 'inloose' to 'vnloose:', but, evidently with an idea of mending the metre, reduces 'to' in both cases to 't'', oblivious of the fact that in the first it stands for 'too'. There may be yet another instance at III. vi. 68, a line which should read:

Hound or spaniel, brach or lym,

but for the last word of which Q prints 'him' and F. 'Hym'. It is possible that the corrector wrote 'Lym' in the margin, but made the capital indistinctly, so that the compositor, influenced by the printed word, misread it as an 'H'.

The *'Historica passio'* of II. iv. 56 seems to be the only quite certain verbal corruption common to the two texts, but there are, as we should expect, a number of common defects of punctuation. The most striking is one at II. iv. 289, where Q and F are in substantial agreement in reading:

'Tis his own blame hath put himself from rest,
And must needs taste his folly.

A heavy stop (editors put a colon) is needed after 'blame': the construction was evidently misunderstood.

The proposed emendation 'top the legitimate' occurs at I. ii. 21. Q reads 'shall tooth'legitimate', F 'Shall to'th'Legitimate'. The former rather bears out Edwards's conjecture, since, if the tail of the 'p' were for any reason obscured, 'top' would naturally be misread as 'too'. Another passage over which editors differ is in Poor Tom's song at III. iv. 118. The Cambridge Shakespeare has:

Saint Withold footed thrice the 'old;

on Theobald's assumption that F 'Swithold' (Q 'swithald') is a misreading of 'S. Withold'. But since 'Swithold' is said to be in any case a corruption of Saint Vitalis, it is hard to see the necessity of adopting an intermediate form, and in doing so editors have presumably been guided by what are surely mistaken notions of the requirements of metre. On the whole I think it would be best to read 'Swithald' after Q, on the grounds that the change in F is probably accidental, that the form is slightly nearer its supposed source, and that it avoids the repetition of the syllable 'old' in the line. It is worth noting that W. J. Craig, the very learned general editor of the Arden Shakespeare, who was himself responsible for *Lear*, rejected both the foregoing emendations.

---

20 (p. 140). The most elaborate investigations so far are those of Messrs. A. W. Pollard and J. Dover Wilson, which were made in the course of 1918 and 1919. There first appeared two articles by Mr. Dover Wilson on 'The Copy for *Hamlet*, 1603' and 'The *Hamlet* Transcript, 1593', published in *The Library* in July and October 1918 (ix. 153, 217), and reprinted the same year in pamphlet form. Meanwhile Mr. Pollard had been devoting his attention to textual problems in two articles on 'The York and Lancaster Plays in the Folio Shakespeare' that appeared in *The Times Literary Supplement* on 19 and 26 Sept. 1918. The following year they joined forces in a series of five articles on 'The "Stolne and Surreptitious" Shakespearian Texts', likewise printed in the *Literary Supplement*: namely, 'Why some of Shakespeare's Plays were Pirated', 9 Jan.; 'How some of Shakespeare's Plays were Pirated', 16 Jan.; 'Henry V (1600)', 13 Mar.; 'Merry Wives of Windsor (1602)', 7 Aug.; and 'Romeo and Juliet (1597)', 14 Aug. 1919. Their theories are far more complicated than those I have considered in my lecture, and involve in general a text of an early stage-version (possibly reported) expanded by recollection of performances of the play in its final form and at times by the use of actors' parts. But the Shakespearian problem does not stand alone; it should be attacked conjointly with that presented by a number of other abnormal texts of Elizabethan plays. I attempted a beginning of this larger investigation in an essay on *Two Elizabethan Stage Abridgements: 'The Battle of Alcazar' and 'Orlando*

Furioso, 1923. Several texts of this type have been reprinted by the Malone Society, and others remain to be issued; but a general survey of the subject is still a desideratum.

21 (p. 140). Mr. Alexander published his conclusions in *The Times Literary Supplement*, dealing with *2 Henry VI* on 9 Oct. 1924, with *3 Henry VI* on 13 Nov. 1924, and with *The Taming of the Shrew* on 16 Sept. 1926. As regards *Henry VI* Mr. Alexander's view has been accepted in the main by Sir Edmund Chambers, who developed the thesis in an address delivered before the Oxford Bibliographical Society. This was summarized in the Society's *Proceedings* (ii. 1), and he has defined his position and published one interesting point in a letter printed in the *Literary Supplement* on 8 Mar. 1928. The case as regards *The Taming of the Shrew* is much more problematic (but see the New Shakespeare edition, pp. 104 ff., and the *Literary Supplement* for 17 May and 7 June, 1928).

22 (p. 142). It is desirable to stress, more than was possible in the lecture, the necessity of recognizing that every play of this group presents to the editor an individual problem. The critical position is really determined, or at least profoundly modified, by the peculiarities of each several case. Moreover, the editor is embarrassed both by differences of critical opinion as to the nature of the individual peculiarities, and by uncertainty as to how far they are constant throughout a single text. It is to be hoped that fuller and more careful study will do something to remove the former difficulty by establishing some sort of consensus among bibliographers; but it is unlikely that full agreement on points of detail will ever be attained.

One particular minor problem of interest is presented by a number of alterations made in the text of *The First Part of the Contention* and *The True Tragedy of Richard Duke of York*, when these were reprinted together under the title of *The Whole Contention*; alterations which in several instances anticipated the yet unpublished texts of *2* and *3 Henry VI*. The same phenomenon is found less markedly in the '1608' edition of *Henry V*. This third quarto of *Henry V* and that of *The Whole Contention* belong, of course, to the rather mysterious Shakespearian collection of 1619, but the exact origin and significance of the alterations have never, so far as I know, been explained.

HENRY V

23 (p. 144). For this play I have had the advantage of consulting an excellent pamphlet on *The Text of Henry V*, published by

Mr. H. T. Price in 1921, which seems to me in the main correct, though I am not convinced that either shorthand notes or actors' parts were used in the preparation of the quarto.

The 'tyred mare' converted by the compositor into a 'tyred name' is at II. i. 23. A somewhat similar, though less certain instance occurs at II. iv. 107, in a passage rendered by F as follows:

> the Widdowes Teares, the Orphans Cryes,
> The dead-mens Blood, the priuy Maidens Groanes,
> For Husbands, Fathers, and betrothed Louers . . .

This is not necessarily wrong, if in the second line we understand the phrase to mean the hidden grief of maidens, but since Q supplies the word 'pining', of which 'priuy' might be a misreading, it is not surprising that editors have preferred to follow it.

Several of the corrections derived from Q are obvious, and would anyhow have been made by editors, as no doubt is the case with the tired mare. Thus, in the passage at I. ii. 212, where F has:

> So may a thousand actions once a foote,
> And in one purpose, and be all well borne
> Without defeat . . .

'And' is a fairly evident misprint for 'End' (as in Q) and was emended by Pope. So again at II. ii. 176, where Henry, addressing the traitors Cambridge, Scroop, and Grey, says according to F:

> But we our Kingdomes safety must so tender,
> Whose ruine you sought, that to her Lawes
> We do deliuer you.

The second line here is manifestly defective, a word being apparently lost before 'sought'. It is perhaps best, with Knight, to follow Q in reading 'you haue sought'; but it is to be observed that F 2 has 'you three sought', and this (adopted by earlier editors) may have more authority than Q, if we only knew it. Somewhat earlier F records the arrest of the conspirators in the following form (II. ii. 145 ff.):

> *Exe*[*ter*]. I arrest thee of High Treason, by the name of
> *Richard* Earle of *Cambridge*.
> I arrest thee of High Treason, by the name of *Thomas*
> Lord *Scroope* of *Marsham*.
> I arrest thee of High Treason, by the name of *Thomas*
> *Grey*, Knight of *Northumberland*.

Scroop's name was Henry, not Thomas, but if F was following its copy at all closely—and it looks as if it was—the wrong name was

obviously caught from two lines below. Q has it right: and moreover has the correct form '*Masham*' in place of '*Marsham*'.

At II. i. 70 F makes Pistol say:

Couple a gorge, that is the word. I defie thee againe. O hound of Creet,
think'st thou my spouse to get?

Q arranges the speech as verse, and so do modern editors, no doubt
rightly. They have also, since Capell, followed Q in reading 'thee
defy' rather than 'defy thee'. Both the verse and Pistol's style
require the inversion. Just below (II. i. 80) occurs an instance in
which an emendation, plausible though not absolutely necessary
in itself, receives indirect support from Q. Falstaff's boy enters with
the words, given thus by F:

Mine Hoast *Pistoll*, you must come to my Mayster, and your Hostesse:
He is very sicke, & would to bed.

It was Hanmer who first made the emendation 'and you, hostess': it
was Malone who pointed out the confirmation afforded by Q,
which has:

> Hostes you must come straight to my maister,
> And you Host *Pistoll*.

And once more, at IV. i. 35, F's reading '*Che vous la?*' was corrected
by Rowe to '*Qui va là?*' though whether he took account of
Q's 'Ke ve la?' may be doubted.

There are also certain passages of greater importance in which Q
has been called upon with more or less success. The crucial instance of the misplaced lines in the farewell to Salisbury will be
found at IV. iii. 11 ff. The problem is to some extent complicated by
the compression of the text in Q. Of the six lines quoted only
4, 2, 3 are represented, and they are assigned neither to Bedford
(who is not on) nor to Exeter, but to Clarence, of whom F knows
nothing. To take another example: there is in IV. v a passage spoken
by Bourbon under the smart of defeat, which runs in F (ll. 10 ff.):

> Shame, and eternall shame, nothing but shame,
> Let vs dye in once more backe againe,
> And he that will not follow *Burbon* now,
> Let him go home, and with his cap in hand
> Like a base Pander hold the Chamber doore,
> Whilst a base slaue, no gentler then my dogge,
> His fairest daughter is contaminated.

There are two errors here, one at the beginning, and one at the end.
The latter is evidently in the last line but one, for 'base' has been

repeated from the line above, and when this is ejected it also becomes clear that 'by' should be supplied after 'Whilst'. [It is possible that the line was originally set up with 'Whilst by a base slaue' (as it stands in F 2) and that 'by' was struck out on metrical grounds by a proof-reader who did not look beyond the single line.] Q, giving substantially the correct reading, merely corroborates what would in any case be plain. The other error is in the second line. This is manifestly defective, for to punctuate:

> Let vs dye: in once more: backe againe!

would not give a line consonant with Shakespeare's metrical usage, at any rate at this period; and moreover the last four words are linked together by the corresponding line of Q:

> A plague of order, once more to the field . . .

It follows that a word and a stop must be lost after 'in'. Now, at a somewhat later point in Q another speaker says:

> Lets dye with honour, our shame doth last too long

(this corresponds to F:

> Let life be short, else shame will be too long).

Editors have naturally been tempted to use this line of Q to emend the earlier line of F. At the same time they have hesitated to discard F's 'in' with a view to adopting the full reading of Q, 'with honour', and (since Knight) have tended to compromise on 'in honour'. But 'in honour' is a less natural phrase than 'with honour', and it assorts ill with the 'eternal shame' of the line before. I very much doubt, therefore, whether in this instance it is judicious to use Q for the correction of F.

The same uncertainty attaches to another passage, which has a double interest for us. It occurs in Henry's great speech before Agincourt, and runs thus in F (IV. iii. 40 ff.):

> This day is call'd the Feast of *Crispian*:
> He that out-liues this day, and comes safe home,
> Will stand a tip-toe when this day is named,
> And rowse him at the Name of *Crispian*.
> He that shall see this day, and liue old age,
> Will yeerely on the Vigil feast his neighbours,
> And say, to morrow is Saint *Crispian*.
> Then will he strip his sleeue, and shew his skarres:
> Old men forget; yet all shall be forgot . . .

and so forth. Now, the close repetition in the second and fifth lines will be noticed, and so will the fact that the latter is faulty. In Q the repetition is still closer, and the lines are reversed, thus:

> He that outliues this day, and sees old age, ...
> He that outliues this day, and comes safe home, ...

This has led most editors to follow Pope in emending F's line to:

> He that shall live this day, and see old age ...

But such a transposition is by no means a likely error to occur, and it might also be urged that the full parallelism of Q is more probable than so near an approach to it. For my own part I should prefer to adopt the simpler emendation proposed by Keightley and read:

> He that shall see this day, and live t'old age ...

I shall return to this speech. Meanwhile, here is another case in which Q should not be used to amend F. At I. ii. 173, one of the characters (which is not very clear) says, according to F, that if the eagle England leaves her nest unguarded, then

> the Weazell (Scot)
> Comes sneaking, and so sucks her Princely Egges,
> Playing the Mouse in absence of the Cat,
> To tame and hauock more then she can eate.

For 'tame' Q reads 'spoyle', which gives the requisite sense and was adopted by Rowe in his earlier edition. But 'tame' cannot be a mere misprint for 'spoil', and behind it (if corrupt) must lie a different, and presumably authoritative, reading. Rowe seems to have perceived this, for in his later edition he printed 'tear', an emendation that has been accepted by most modern editors. But this would only be plausible on the assumption of a spelling 'tare', which is very unlikely. I agree with Mr. Price that Theobald's conjecture 'taint' is preferable. It gives a pregnant sense, while the confusion of final 'e' and 't' is well recognized (I have lately met it in the work of three conscientious modern transcribers, including my own). [As a matter of fact *tame* (for *attame*, broach, break into) is perfectly correct.]

The hell-fire of Bardolph's nose in II. iii. 42 has been dealt with in the lecture. It only remains to note here that this is one of the readings in which Q 3 ('1608' = 1619) anticipates F. There are other minor instances of the injudicious use of Q. Several are due to Pope, but it is not clear whether they are restorations of readings of Q or metrical tinkerings of his own. At I. ii. 74 F has:

> Conuey'd himselfe as th'Heire to th' Lady *Lingare*,

where Q reads 'as heire', and Pope and the Cambridge editors
follow suit. Again at II. iv. 75, 115 F prints:

> From our Brother of England ? . . .
> Back to our Brother of England . . .

while Q, Pope, and the Cambridge editors in each case omit the
'of'. It is of course possible that it may have been inserted by the
compositor, though I see no reason to think so. It has also been
suggested that Theobald's famous restoration of quondam Quickly's
'a' babbled of green fields' receives some support from Q, which in
the corresponding speech of II. iii reads:

> For when I saw him fumble with the sheetes,
> And talk of floures, and smile vpō his fingers ends
> I knew there was no way but one.

But here 'And talk of floures' is not directly parallel at all, for it is
a perversion of the words 'and play with Flowers' in F. It is quite
possible, or even probable, that the babble suggested the talk, but
the former cannot receive confirmation from explaining what in
fact needs no explanation. This is immediately succeeded by a
passage which the Cambridge editors, following Capell, print thus
(II. iii. 21 ff.):

So a' bade me lay more clothes on his feet: I put my hand into the bed
and felt them, and they were as cold as any stone; then I felt to his knees,
[and they were as cold as any stone,] and so upward and upward, and all
was as cold as any stone.

I have enclosed within brackets a clause imported from Q. It is
clearly not needed, and by no means all editors have accepted the
addition. To my mind the phrase 'felt to his knees', following on
'felt them', points clearly to its being intrusive.

This last instance brings us to the question of possible omissions in
F. Near the end of II. i Pistol and Nym are quarrelling and the
dialogue, as printed by the Cambridge editors and most others
since Capell, runs (ll. 99 ff.):

Bard[*olph*]. Corporal Nym, an thou wilt be friends, be friends: an thou
wilt not, why, then, be enemies with me too. Prithee, put up.
Nym. I shall have my eight shillings I won of you at betting ?
Pist[*ol*]. A noble shalt thou have, and present pay . . .

Bardolph's speech is only in F, Nym's only in Q, but I agree that
both are necessary and consequently that there is here an omission
in the text of F. This granted, let us return to Henry's Crispian
speech already quoted (p. 170). The *textus receptus* since Malone

has introduced a whole line near the end from Q, which reads (at a rather later point):

> Then shall he strip his sleeues, and shew his skars
> And say, these wounds I had on Crispines day: . . .

The second of these lines is clearly not necessary to the sense, but it has a thoroughly genuine ring, and if the text of F is once admitted to be defective in this manner, it is natural to suppose that it is so here.

Of course, the appearance of a genuine line in Q alone could be explained on another theory, namely that Q was a reported version of a text that had not only been abridged for performance but had also undergone revision by the author. This theory was actually advanced, on other grounds, by P. A. Daniel in the introduction to the parallel-text edition (by B. Nicholson) issued by the New Shakespere Society in 1877. He based his argument on the fact that certain unhistorical features of F do not appear in Q. Further investigation has failed to add support to this view, which is rejected by Mr. Price. I have indeed noticed one textual point that might be cited in its favour. At iv. vi. 11 ff. is a passage which runs in F:

> Suffolke first dyed, and Yorke all hagled ouer
> Comes to him, where in gore he lay insteeped,
> And takes him by the Beard, kisses the gashes
> That bloodily did yawne vpon his face.
> He cryes aloud; Tarry my Cosin Suffolke,
> My soule shall thine keepe company to heauen . . .

There is nothing necessarily wrong here, for a slight pause after 'Beard' will readily disguise the absence of the conjunction. But when Q, placing a comma after 'face', gave the next line in the form:

> And cryde aloud, tarry deare cousin Suffolke . . .

it obviously offered a double temptation to editors, which none, I believe, since Pope and Steevens fell, have resisted. (The preterite 'cryde' is of course an error due to assimilation with the preceding line.) It is, indeed, difficult to suppose that the undoubted improvement is due to corruption: at the same time it is difficult to suppose that F can be merely misprinted. Revision would offer a solution.

This, however, affords very slender support for a rather revolutionary theory. I mention this here, not because I think it probable, but in order to draw attention to its textual implications. If the performance on which Q is based was of a version revised from that transmitted by F, editors would be placed in a truly unenviable position. They would namely be presented with the alternatives of either reproducing the unrevised version of F, only removing as best they might obvious errors of the scribe or compositor, or else of endeavouring, by an almost pure process of intuition, to recover such fragments of the author's second thoughts as may lie embedded in the corruption of Q, and weaving them into the texture of the earlier version. There is an all too common type of editor who would revel in such a problem as this, but one who took his task seriously might well be pardoned for giving it up in despair. Nor would it only be the choice of readings that would be affected: we should have in every instance to inquire whether an absurdity of Q could not be emended into something that might pass muster as a revision of F's reading. It is to be hoped that we are spared this nightmare.

From this digression I return to ask in conclusion whether, in any of the readings rejected by editorial consensus as corrupt, there is in fact agreement of the early authorities. I have not been able to find any clear case, but there appear to be three of what I have called disguised agreement. One in Fluellen's part at IV. i. 65 has been already considered. Another is at I. ii. 163, in a speech in which the Archbishop, addressing Henry, recalls how England once captured

> and impounded as a stray
> The King of Scots; whom she did send to France,
> To fill King Edward's fame with prisoner kings,
> And make her chronicle as rich with praise,
> As is the ooze and bottom of the sea
> With sunken wreck and sumless treasuries.

(Here 'wreck' is a thoroughly mischievous alteration by Theobald of F's 'Wrack'.) In this passage 'her chronicle' is an emendation of Johnson and Capell: F reads 'their' and Q 'your'. When we find a variant of this type we naturally suspect confusion over a contraction. Strictly, 'your' should be written as 'yor', and 'their' as 'y^{eir}', but various forms are found, and such a miswriting as 'y^r' could be interpreted either way. If this is the source of the trouble, it is possible that Q, resting on the spoken rather than the written word, may be the sounder witness: I assume, then, that 'your' is a reading really supported by both authorities. But the words 'your chronicle' give a quite satisfactory sense, for addressed to the King they mean 'the chronicle of your kingdom'. I think therefore that Steevens was right to adopt the reading of Q, and modern editors wrong to emend. What seems the clearest example is at

iv. v. 3, where the French nobles enter exclaiming on defeat, and one, according to F, says:

> *Mor Dieu ma vie*, all is confounded all . . .

In Q the phrase appears as 'Mor du ma vie', which I take to be substantial confirmation that what is intended is 'Mort Dieu! ma vie!' ['*Mort du*' occurs by itself, obviously for 'Mort Dieu', in Marlowe's *Massacre at Paris*, sc. xv (sig. C 1).] Nevertheless Rowe printed 'Mort de ma vie!' and I can only suppose that in following him modern editors have had some reason that escapes me.

I conclude that, as we should expect, a reading common to the folio and quarto texts is necessarily original. Where these differ, choice is open, and editors have varied considerably. If the usual modern theory of a derivative text preserved in the quarto is correct, there can be no question that in general editors have relied on its readings to a much greater extent than can be justified. The fact is that while critical opinion has for a century and a half been turning in this direction, editorial practice has remained unconsciously governed by the theory of an early draft, and particularly by Pope's belief that the folio represented indeed an enlarged, but at the same time a much corrupted and interpolated, version. The whole textual position needs carefully reviewing.

ROMEO AND JULIET

24 (p. 144). The bibliographical dependence of the second quarto on the first was originally suggested by Robert Gericke in an article printed in the *Shakespeare Jahrbuch* for 1879 (xiv. 207 ff., particularly 269–72). His theory was that the second quarto was printed from Shakespeare's autograph, with the sole exception apparently of i. ii. 45 to i. iii. 37, which for some reason was printed from the first quarto. The matter was recently brought to the fore again by Miss Gertrude Hjort in an important article on 'The Good and Bad Quartos of *Romeo and Juliet* and *Love's Labour's Lost*' in *The Modern Language Review* for 1926 (xxi. 140). In this the evidence is derived from the Nurse's part alone, though the writer appears to infer that the first quarto was used throughout as copy for the second.

25 (p. 145). The first hint of bibliographical connexion between Q 1 and Q 2 is afforded by the Prologue, which both print with some points of typographical similarity on a leaf by itself. Much more striking is the list of *invités* that Capulet's servant asks Romeo

to read; this list both print in italic, with a two-line initial and the heading 'He reads the Letter'—though letter it is not. But what seems to me the conclusive evidence is supplied by the Nurse's part. In Q 1 her speeches down to the end of the first act (I. v; sig. C 4) are consistently printed in italic. Whatever the explanation of this, I can recall nothing analogous in the whole of the Elizabethan drama: it is something quite peculiar and individual. Thus the fact that, up to a point, these speeches are similarly printed in Q 2 leaves no doubt in my mind that Q 1 actually served as copy for Q 2. And in any case the last shade of hesitation would be removed by the close similarity in spelling, punctuation, capitalization, and word division, and by the fact that the only two speeches of the Nurse in I. iii that Q 2 prints in roman (ll. 96, 106) are additional speeches that do not appear in Q 1 at all. But this bibliographical connexion does not extend very far. In I. v. Q 1 again prints the Nurse's part in italic, but here Q 2 does not follow suit. This might of course be due to a different compositor, or simply to realizing that there was no sense in doing so. But the minor resemblances of spelling and the like are equally absent. And I think we can determine, with considerable probability, the exact point at which the connexion ceases. It should be observed, to begin with, that if the textual links are most noticeable in the Nurse's part, this is because it is particularly well reported in Q 1 and could be used as copy almost without alteration. But they are traceable elsewhere too, particularly through most of the scene between Romeo, Benvolio, and Capulet's servant, which contains the list already mentioned (see I. ii. 54–101). All this is contained in sheet B of Q 1, and the same sheet contains almost the whole of I. iii, the scene made notable by the common use of italic. Almost, but not quite; for the scene just runs over on to C 1 with a speech by the Clown (or Servant), and this, like the Nurse's part, is printed in italic. It is remarkable that Q 2 prints this speech in roman, and the fact points to foot of B 4^v as the point at which Q 1 was discarded as copy.

26 (p. 145). The textual evidence for a bibliographical connexion between the quartos is confined to sheet B of Q 1. At I. ii. 57 we have the serving man's salutation 'Godgigoden' in both texts. If Q 1 is indeed 'reported' copy the chance of its having reproduced the word *literatim* as in the original manuscript seems infinitesimal. (Cf. III. v. 172, Q 1 'goddegodden': Q 2 'Godigeden'.) In the invitation list we have the name 'Vtruuio' (l. 66), which (assuming 'Utruvio' to be impossible) must be a twin error for 'Vitruuio'. The con-

fusion in the speeches that follow has been mentioned in the lecture. The lines stand in Q 2 thus (i. ii. 72–4):

> *Ser.* Vp.
> *Ro.* Whither to supper?
> *Ser.* To our house.

(Q 1 differs in the spelling 'Whether'.) A few lines later Romeo replies to his friend's promise to 'make thee think thy swan a crow' with the quatrain (ll. 88 ff.):

> When the devout religion of mine eye
> Maintains such falsehood, then turn tears to fires;
> And these, who, often drown'd, could never die,
> Transparent heretics, be burnt for liars!

So Pope, with due care for the proprieties of verse. But the quartos (and folios) spoil the rime by having the singular instead of 'fires'. The next scene supplies the very interesting spelling 'a leauen' (Q 1: 'a leuen' Q 2) for eleven (i. iii. 36). It is worth observing that this spelling (with an 'a' and in two words) occurs no less than five times in 'good' Shakespearian quartos (*Shakespeare's Hand*, p. 126). It is also important to note that a few lines before (l. 24) Q 1 and Q 2 leave 'eleauen' and 'eleuen' respectively.

In the later sheets of the play there is one reading of Q 2 that certainly comes from Q 1, though this was not used as copy (see note 28). Editors have also recorded a couple of spellings of possible though doubtful significance. At iv. i. 83 we have Juliet's line:

> With reeky shanks and yellow chapless skulls;

and in this Q 1 gives the form 'yeolow' and Q 2 'yealow', both unusual. Also Queen Mab's horses, the 'teame of little Atomies' as F has it at i. iv. 57, are called 'Atomi' in Q 1, and 'ottamie' in Q 2. But it is very doubtful whether these aberrant forms are related.

27 (p. 146). On the subject of Q 1 readings the Cambridge editors write that, while Q 2 'is unquestionably our best authority: nevertheless in determining the text, [Q 1] must in many places be taken into account'. They add: 'Pope felt this strongly, too strongly indeed, for he adopted the text of the first Quarto in many places where Capell and all subsequent editors have judiciously recurred to the second. Nevertheless there is no editor who has not felt it necessary occasionally to call in the aid of the first.' They themselves reject some of the Q 1 readings retained by Capell. In making the count of 118 readings even they have retained, I have as a rule excluded stage directions, and also a number of trivial cases, in

which the authority of Q 1 has been invoked for small normalizations, such as 'by the' for 'byth', which would equally have been
made without its sanction. The 118 are equivalent to one in every
25·5 lines of Q 2, or (a more significant figure) one in less than
19 lines of Q 1.

The distribution and necessity of these Q 1 readings are not
without interest. The distribution is of course far from even.
Only the odd 18 occur in the last two acts; a peculiarity due partly
to the relative shortness of these, partly to the fact that after IV. i.
the text of Q 1 goes badly to pieces. Also, while the third act is
considerably the longest, by far the greatest number occur in the
second. The question of necessity is important. If only, say, a
dozen (10 per cent.) of the readings could be regarded as tolerably
certain, the practice of editors would be open to serious challenge:
but with a rise in the number the credibility of the witness (i.e. Q 1)
appreciates rapidly, and if it reached, say, half, we should be justified in accepting almost any reading that seemed preferable. [Of
course, the percentages should properly be reckoned on the total
variants, not on those accepted by editors; but this is hardly
practicable and would not greatly increase the rigour of the argument.] It is impossible to discuss the readings individually, but I
may say that on a fairly generous count some forty Q 1 readings
seem to me pretty certainly correct, or approximately one third of
those admitted by the Cambridge editors. The precise value of this
I must leave others to estimate: the actual figures for the several
acts are, 8, 15, 9, 5, 6. The only marked variation from the average
is in the last act, in which all the accepted Q 1 readings but one
seem to be necessary. Since this is also the act in which Q 1 is
generally of least service, the fact seems to be to the credit of editors.
It may be worth while setting out the data in tabular form (the
bracketed figures refer to 'necessary' readings).

Act.	ll. in Q 2.	Q 1 readings.	ll. to each reading.	readings per 100 ll.	per cent. of necessary to total readings.
I	699	26 (8)	27 (87)	3·7 (1·1)	31
II	659	51 (15)	13 (44)	7·7 (2·3)	29
III	812	23 (9)	35 (90)	2·8 (1·1)	39
IV	400	11 (5)	36 (80)	2·75 (1·25)	45
V	437	7 (6)	62·5 (73)	1·6 (1·4)	86
Whole	3007	118 (43)	25·5 (70)	3·9 (1·4)	36

28 (p. 147). Among clear instances of corruption in Q 2, where
Q 1 supplies what is presumably the true text, may be instanced a
speech assigned to a character who is not on the stage (II. iv. 18:
'*Ro.*' being printed for '*Be.*' or '*Ben.*'), a speaker's name misplaced
(II. i. 7), appearing as part of a speech (III. v. 172), or omitted altogether (III. v. 173), a speech printed as a stage direction (v. iii. 71),
and such misprints as 'deuote' for 'denote' (III. iii. 110: cf. note 16,
p. 161), 'chapels' for 'chaples' (i.e. chapless, IV. i. 83), and 'pray' for
'pay' (v. i. 76). The more considerable blunder over 'my ghostly
father's cell' at II. ii. 189 has been quoted. Another occurs at
v. i. 15. 'News from Verona!' exclaims Romeo, and he begins to
ply his man with questions. Q 2 proceeds (v. i. 15):

> How doth my Lady, is my Father well:
> How doth my Lady *Iuliet*? that I aske againe . . .

Since the second line is clearly wrong, we may assume that the
compositor blundered through repeating part of the first. But
how much did he repeat? Q 1 seems to supply the answer by
reading:

> How doth my Ladie? Is my Father well?
> How fares my *Juliet*? that I aske againe:

and I think Steevens was justified in accepting this as correct.
    An instance in which the Cambridge editors followed Q 1, I think
injudiciously, has been quoted in the lecture from II. iii. 88. It is
worth observing that Dowden, who edited the play for the Arden
Shakespeare in 1900, retained the reading of Q 2. There is another
example at I. iv. 45, which seems worth discussing even at some
length. The passage is printed as follows by the Cambridge and
most modern editors:

> *Mer*[*cutio*]. . . . Come, we burn daylight, ho.
> *Rom*[*eo*]. Nay, that's not so.
> *Mer.*   I mean, sir, in delay
> We waste our lights in vain, like lamps by day.

For the last line Q 2 reads:

> We waste our lights in vaine, lights lights by day:

and Q 1:

> We burne our lights by night, like Lampes by day . . .

It was Capell who first combined the halves from the two sources
into the whole line of the received text. The view we take will
depend a good deal on the punctuation. Modern editors place no

point after 'delay'; Capell placed a semicolon. Q 2 has none, but its punctuation is unreliable; Q 1 has a comma, but its text is not wholly parallel. I think we may please ourselves. There is an appreciable difference in the sense. Modern editors would interpret: I mean that by delaying we waste our torches to no purpose. Capell evidently took 'in delay' along with what precedes, and understood the passage in the sense: I mean that we burn daylight through delaying; we are, in fact, wasting our torches. To 'burn daylight' was a common phrase for wasting time. With the modern punctuation Capell's emendation perhaps gives the best (though not the only) sense and construction that can be achieved. But personally I prefer Capell's punctuation, since I feel that 'in delay' and 'in vain' are a trifle clumsy if taken in close association. And with Capell's punctuation I think Capell's emendation can be bettered. Daniel followed Nicholson in reading:

> We waste our lights in vaine, light lights by day.

This is certainly the simplest emendation, but although it was on that ground accepted by no less a critic than Dowden, the resultant line is one I should be loath to foist on Shakespeare. I propose to read:

> We waste our lights in vaine, light lamps by day

that is, we are doing the equivalent of lighting lamps by day. This, I think, accounts better for the readings in the second half of the line. That of Q 1 (dependent on performance) would be an easy mishearing; while, as regards Q 2, I do not see how 'lamps' came to be corrupted to 'lights' except through repetition of a preceding 'light' or 'lights'.

The various problems raised by these rather perplexing texts appear in acute form in the passage, II. i. 7 ff., quoted in the lecture. The emendation 'Adam Cupid' was proposed by John Upton in his *Critical Observations on Shakespeare* in 1746, and adopted by Steevens in 1778. It means, of course, the archer Cupid, after Adam Bell, the famous bowman. The sense is palmary, and finds support in *Much Ado*, I. i. 222–4: 'If I do, hang me in a bottle like a cat, and shoot at me; and he that hits me, let him be clapped on the shoulder and called Adam.' But there is no need to enter on the great Adam-Abraham controversy. One may grant that 'Abram' or 'Abraham' was a current perversion of 'abron' or 'auburn', without feeling that we are much nearer explaining the reading. The significance of this, moreover, lies in its exact form and is unaffected by the interpretation we may adopt. The whole passage is printed as prose in Q 1, but the text there given is at various points superior. Q 2 makes Cupid shoot so 'true', where the original reading must be 'trim', as in the ballad—'The blinded boy, that shootes so trim'. It has 'sonne and her' for 'sonne and heire'. It has 'on rime' for 'one rime', and 'goship' for 'gossip'; but these may be copy-spellings. The fourth line editors have taken substantially from Q 1, which has:

> cry but ay me. Pronounce but Loue and Doue,

while Q 2 reads corruptly:

> Crie but ay me, prouaunt, but loue and day, . . .

In this 'prouaunt' must be a misreading of a Shakespearian spelling 'pronounc' (cf. *Shakespeare's Hand*, p. 124), and 'day' due to misreading 'doue' as 'daie' (cf. note 12, p. 158).

HAMLET

29 (p. 151). Only a very summary treatment of the textual evidence was possible in the lecture. It seems therefore worth while to set it out in detail in these notes. But I must repeat that I am not endeavouring to prove a theory but only to examine the textual consequences of its acceptance. Moreover, it is probable that any complete theory of the relation of the authorities would be considerably more complex than the one here under investigation. For example, I have taken no account of the possibility of Shakespearian lines appearing in Q 1 only. Nor have I considered explicitly those passages for which either Q 2 or F is our sole authority.

The readings which may be expected to throw light on the relation of the texts and upon the problem of emendation fall into five categories: (1) those in which Q 1 and F agree against Q 2, (2) those in which Q 1 and Q 2 agree against F, (3) those, if any, in which Q 1 preserves a correct reading where both Q 2 and F are corrupt, (4) errors common to Q 2 and F (Q 1 being absent), and (5) errors, if any, common to all three texts.

(1) **Q 1, F: Q 2.** The agreement of Q 1 with F against Q 2 is a very natural one on the textual assumptions we are making, since any reading in the prompt-book would naturally be copied into an actor's part, and would so find its way into performance. Indeed Q 1 only adds authority to F by showing that a particular reading stood in the manuscript and was not due to the compositor, and further that the reading was one that passed muster on the

stage. The distribution of readings of this type is fairly constant: of a total of 57 the numbers supplied by the several acts are 20, 15, 14, 4, 4; the falling off being naturally due to the greater divergence of Q 1 towards the end of the play.

Analysis of the readings suggests that variants of this form arise in four ways. Naturally critics will differ considerably in this analysis, and my own is at many points opposed to orthodox editorial opinion. Given for what it is worth, my classification of the readings is as follows: (a) misprints made by the compositor of Q 2, 25 cases; (b) readings of the autograph authoritatively corrected or altered in the prompt-copy, 10 cases; (c) variants due to the scribe of the prompt-copy, 19 cases; and (d) definite blunders of the prompt-copy surviving in the actors' parts, 3 cases. Of course in the first two categories (a, b, 35 cases) an editor would be bound to follow F, in the second two (c, d, 22 cases) Q 2. There are, however, many readings which it is difficult to assign with any confidence: in giving my list I add such notes as seem necessary.

(a) *Misprints of Q 2* (25). Mr. Dover Wilson finds the omission of words or word groups to be characteristic of the compositor of Q 2, and counts well over a hundred instances (see p. 38 of article cited). For this reason I have included several readings in this group which might otherwise have been regarded as variants of the playhouse scribe. I give first the reading of F (adding in brackets any differences in Q 1 that seem significant) and then that of Q 2.

I. i. 45. 'Question it': Q 2 'Speake to it'. The compositor may have been influenced by the preceding 'It would be spoke to'. But the reading of F, which seems an improvement, is possibly due to correction.

I. i. 73. 'why': Q 2 'with'.

I. ii. 224. 'Indeed, indeed Sirs': Q 2 'Indeede Sirs'.

I. ii. 236. 'Very like, very like': Q 2 'Very like'.

I. iii. 74. 'Are of a most': Q 2 'Or of a most'. Presumably due to the use of an 'a' with detached minim (cf. note 12, p. 158): 'ar' being misread as 'orr' and printed 'Or'.

I. iii. 115. 'I, Springes' (Q 1 'Springes'): Q 2 'I, springs'. Possibly a careless spelling by Shakespeare: 'spring' was a common variant of 'springe', but the verse needs a dissyllable.

I. v. 55. 'So Lust': Q 2 'So but'.

I. v. 122. 'I, by Heau'n, my Lord': Q 2 'I by heauen'.

II. i. 55. 'He closes with you thus' (Q 1 'he closeth with him thus'): Q 2 'He closes thus'. This is not very certain. The support of Q 1 is rather indirect, and Q 2 gives a regular line. But Polonius does run to alexandrines.

II. ii. 420. 'Byrlady' (Q 1 'burlady'): Q 2 'by lady'. Probably a letter has dropped out.

II. ii. 424. 'French': Q 2 'friendly'. Dover Wilson (p. 45) supposes that a badly written 'french' was misread as 'frenly' and emended to 'friendly'.

II. ii. 534-5. 'for a need': Q 2 'for neede'.

III. i. 83. 'Cowards of vs all': Q 2 'cowards'.

III. i. 129. 'arrant Knaues all': Q 2 'arrant knaues'.

III. i. 145. 'your Ignorance': Q 2 'ignorance'.

III. ii. 132. 'Miching *Malicho*' (Q 1 'myching Mallico): Q 2 'munching *Mallico*'. There seems no doubt what the word should be, but the compositor was not likely to be familiar with it.

III. ii. 247. 'Pox, leaue' (Q 1 'a poxe, leaue'): Q 2 'leaue'.

III. ii. 250. 'Confederate': Q 2 'Considerat'.

III. ii. 260. '*Ham*. What, frighted with false fire.' (Q 1 before l. 265): Q 2 omits.

III. ii. 362. 'though you can fret me': Q 2 'though you fret me not' (cf. (3), p. 195).

III. iv. 215. 'a foolish': Q 2 'a most foolish'. The compositor caught the word from the previous line.

IV. iii. 52. 'and so my mother': Q 2 'so my mother'.

IV. v. 37. '*graue*': Q 2 'ground'. Another misreading due to the use of an 'a' with detached minim (cf. p. 158): 'groiue' misinterpreted as 'ground'.

V. i. 188. 'my Ladies Chamber': Q 2 'my Ladies table'. The compositor seems to have caught the word 'table' from two lines above.

V. i. 202. 'as thus.' (Q 1 'as thus of *Alexander*,'): Q 2 omits.

(b) *Corrections in the prompt-copy* (10). There are some readings in Q 2 which cannot be regarded as errors of the compositor, but must be supposed to have stood in the autograph, and which are yet so manifestly inferior to those of F and Q 1 that we can only suppose the latter to have been author's, or at least authorized, corrections, introduced into the prompt-book previous to the preparation of the actors' parts. Naturally this is a group in which opinions will tend to differ sharply.

I. ii. 175. 'to drinke deepe': Q 2 'for to drinke'. Perhaps, however, the compositor of Q 2 accidentally omitted 'deepe', and 'for' was inserted in proof for the sake of metre.

I. v. 20. 'fretfull Porpentine': Q 2 'fearefull Porpentine'. The latter is quite a sound reading, since the porcupine raises its quills when alarmed; but it is easy to understand why Shakespeare should have preferred a pithier word.

I. v. 159–61. Neuer to speake of this that you haue heard:
    Sweare by my Sword.
        Gho. Sweare.

(Q 1   neuer to speake
    Of that which you haue seene, sweare by my sword.
    Ghost Sweare.)

Q 2 Sweare by my sword
    Neuer to speake of this that you haue heard.
    Ghost. Sweare by his sword.

This is a very difficult variant, but the two portions of it must be related. I think F is correct, and assume that the inversion in Q 2 implies an alteration or marginal addition which somehow betrayed the compositor into a partial repetition of the words. It is hard to know how to class it. The scribe of the prompt-copy may have straightened things out, but it is possible that we have both misprint on the one hand and correction on the other. Editors have reconstructed the passage in various ways.

II. ii. 73. 'three thousand Crownes': Q 2 'threescore thousand crownes'. The Q 2 reading must be rejected on the ground of metre, but it can hardly be due to the compositor. Probably Shakespeare altered his intention while writing the line and forgot to make the necessary correction.

II. ii. 440. '*Æneas* Tale to *Dido*': Q 2 '*Aeneas* talke to *Dido*'. 'Tale' certainly seems the preferable reading, but 'talke' may well have been the author's first shot. Or can Shakespeare have written 'talle' and the compositor misread it 'talke'?

II. ii. 535. 'some dosen or sixteene lines': Q 2 'some dosen lines or sixteene lines'. Possibly a first draft smoothed out later. It might, of course, be an error in Q 2, but the compositor seems more inclined to omit words than to insert them.

II. ii. 552. 'or he to *Hecuba*': Q 2 'or he to her'. The latter looks like a possible first attempt. Dover Wilson, however, has a different explanation, namely an abbreviation 'hec' misread as 'her' (p. 42).

III. ii. 218. 'If once a Widdow, ever I be Wife':
        Q 2 'If once I be a widdow, euer I be a wife'.
This must be a first draft.

IV. V. 36. '*Larded with sweet flowers*':

    Q 2 'Larded all with sweet flowers'.

Shakespeare must have started with the intention of writing 'Larded all with flowers', changed his mind, and forgotten to delete 'all'.

    V. II. 318. 'Is thy Vnion heere?': Q 2 'is the Onixe heere?' This is a very complicated variant, involving, I believe, both a correction and a compositor's error, or rather mis-emendation. The reference is to the pretended pearl which the King dropped into the poison cup. There seems no doubt that 'union' is the word aimed at, since this was in common use for a pearl of price, especially that which Cleopatra dissolved and drank. But it was certainly not the word that stood in the autograph. The pearl is mentioned at l. 264, and there Q 2 has the reading 'Vnice' (F 'vnion'). This Shakespeare probably connected with 'unique', which is the meaning of 'union'. I suppose that 'Vnice' was the word here too, but that the compositor, not understanding it and forgetting the earlier passage, emended it to 'Onixe'. Later Shakespeare discovered that 'union' was the word he meant, and altered it in the prompt-book. Perhaps 'the' was altered to 'thy' at the same time.

    (c) *Variations in the prompt-copy* (19). These are due to alterations, probably accidental, made by the scribe in copying from the autograph. Editors, particularly the Cambridge editors, have I think attached too much weight to the support which Q 1 affords to F in these readings.

    I. i. 21. '*Mar*[*cellus*]. What, ha's this thing appear'd againe to night.' Q 2 assigns the speech to '*Hora*[*tio*].' Recent editors follow F, but Capell adhered to Q 2, for what seems to me excellent reasons. It is part of Horatio's banter.

    I. i. 160. 'The Bird of Dawning': Q 2 'This bird of dawning'. A very doubtful case. I see no reason to suppose a misprint, but the reading of F may be a correction. A good many editors have followed Capell in retaining 'This'.

    I. i. 161. 'no Spirit can walke abroad' (Q 1 'no spirite dare walke abroade'): Q 2 'no spirit dare sturre abroade'. ['can' is a misprint of F, see (2, b), p. 188.] Editors are divided.

    I. i. 175. 'most conueniently': Q 2 'most conuenient'. Few editors have followed Capell and Q 2, but there is a slight difference of meaning, and the latter seems to me preferable.

    I. ii. 183. 'Ere': Q 2 'Or'. Editors are divided.

    I. iii. 63. 'Grapple them to thy Soule' (Q 1 '. . . to thee'):

Q 2 '. . . vnto thy soule'. Apparently Elze alone has followed Q 2, but there is no reason why it should not be what Shakespeare wrote.

I. v. 60. 'in the afternoone': Q 2 'of the afternoone'. Editors are divided.

I. v. 129. 'your busines and desires': Q 2 'your busines and desire'. The latter receives some support from the next line, which repeats the phrase as in Q 2 (only Q 1 reading 'desires' here). All recent editors follow Q 2.

II. i. 99. 'without their helpe': Q 2 'without theyr helps'. Editors are divided.

II. ii. 384. 'a Monday morning 'twas so indeed': Q 2 '. . . t'was then indeede'. Editors are divided, Capell being the first to follow Q 2; recent preference is for F.

II. ii. 435. 'there was no Sallets': Q 2 'there were no sallets'. Practically all editors, of course, have followed Q 2, except when they have emended.

II. ii. 496. 'But who, O who, had seen': Q 2 'But who, a woe, had seene'. Few editors have followed Capell in adhering to Q 2: yet it gives very good sense.

II. ii. 524. 'who should scape whipping': Q 2 'who shall scape whipping'. Editors are divided: curiously enough the Globe text has 'should', the Cambridge 'shall'.

II. ii. 584. 'About my Braine': Q 2 'About my braines'. Editors are divided: I see nothing against Q 2, even though it be the less familiar.

II. ii. 595. 'May be the Diuell': Q 2 'May be a deale'. ['deale' may be a mere misreading of 'deule'=devil.] A few editors have followed Capell and Q 2, but most, especially recent ones, have been biased in favour of F by the second half of the line (omitted in Q 1).

III. i. 128. 'crawling betweene Heauen and Earth': Q 2 'crauling betweene earth and heauen'. Editors are divided.

III. i. 147. 'no more Marriages': Q 2 'no mo marriage'. Apparently no editors have followed Q 2, though it gives a perfectly sound reading.

III. ii. 3. 'as many of your Players do': Q 2 'as many of our Players do'. Editors are divided. It is natural to compare I. v. 167 (see (2, c), p. 190), but there is no necessary relation.

v. ii. 235. 'shot mine Arrow': Q 2 'shot my arrowe'. Editors are divided.

(d) *Errors in the prompt-copy* (3). These do not differ greatly from class (c), but one can trace the reading of F more definitely to a misunderstanding of the autograph.

i. iv. 5. 'Indeed I heard it not': Q 2 'Indeede; I heard it not'. Only one editor has followed F, which is certainly wrong. The autograph probably gave little guidance.

iii. iii. 91. 'At gaming, swearing' (Q 1 'at game swaring'): Q 2 'At game a swearing'. Q 1 shows that the 'a' was accidentally omitted by the playhouse scribe: it was a later corrector, or else the compositor of F, who restored the verse by the emendation 'gaming' (cf. (2, c), p. 190).

iv. vii. 178. 'snatches of old tunes' (Q 1 'olde sundry tunes'): Q 2, 'snatches of old laudes'. Very few editors have followed Q 2; even Capell has 'tunes'. But Dover Wilson has pointed out (p. 50) that the variant is probably due to graphic confusion. I cannot believe that the compositor of Q 2 invented the reading 'laudes', and I therefore conclude that the playhouse scribe invented the much easier reading 'tunes'.

(2) **Q 1, 2: F.** The readings we have been considering so far really concern the general problem of the relation of the texts of Q 2 and F, for the agreement of Q 1 with F is of no great moment. It is very different with the readings of the present group, in which Q 1 and Q 2 agree against F; since, if our textual theory is correct, the agreement of the quartos must determine the reading of the prompt-copy. In this case the divergence of F can only be accounted for (coincidence apart) either by alterations made in the prompt-book subsequent to the preparation of the actors' parts, or else by errors of the compositor. Of course, if this is so, editors are bound to accept all the Q 2 readings of this group, except in so far as they may suppose the alterations in the prompt-book to have had the sanction of the author. I shall, therefore, discuss all cases in which the Cambridge editors have followed F.

Curiously enough the number of readings in this group is almost the same as in group (1), namely 55; but the distribution is strikingly different, the numbers in the several acts being 37, 6, 7, 1, 4. The fact that more than two-thirds of the readings come from the first act must, I feel sure, have some important significance for the textual problem, but what this significance can be I am at present unable to imagine.

I divide the variants of this group according to their origin as follows: (a) possible accidental agreements between Q 1 and Q 2, 3 cases; (b) misprints in F, 24 cases; (c) small alterations which may have been made in the prompt-copy or may have arisen in printing from it, 15 cases; and (d) alterations certainly made in the prompt-copy between the preparation of the actors' parts and the printing of F, 13 cases. I give first the reading of Q 2 (adding in brackets any significant differences in Q 1) and then that of F.

(a) *Accidental agreements* (3). It would not be safe in these instances to argue that the reading of Q 1 lent any additional support to Q 2.

I. i. 33. 'What we haue two nights seene': F 'What we two Nights haue seene'. I do not think that in such a case as this the evidence of Q 1 is worth considering, but the variant may, of course, be due to the compositor of F.

I. v. 113. 'Heauens secure him': F 'Heauen secure him'. If Q 1 depends on oral authority the reading is of no significance as the difference would not be heard.

IV. v. 184. 'Thought and afflictions' (Q 1 'Thoughts & afflictions'): F 'Thought, and Affliction'. The passage in Q 1 is really too divergent to carry any weight. Editors have followed the folio as giving the smoother reading.

(b) *Misprints in F* (24).

I. i. 98. 'lawelesse resolutes': F 'Landlesse Resolutes'. This is a graphic error, 'lawe' being misread as 'land'.

I. i. 150. 'trumpet to the morne' (Q 1 'trumpet to the morning'): F 'Trumpet to the day'.

I. i. 161. 'dare sturre' (Q 1 'dare walke'): F 'can walke' (cf. (1, c), p. 185).

I. i. 164. 'so gratious is that time': F '. . . is the time'. Editors have, on the whole, preferred F, but there seems no reason to do so.

I. ii. 35. 'For bearers of this greeting': F 'For bearing of . . .'. An anticipatory assimilation.

I. ii. 183. 'Or euer I had' (Q 1 'Ere euer I had'): F 'Ere I had euer' (cf. (1, c), p. 185).

I. ii. 204. 'distil'd Almost to gelly': F 1 'bestil'd Almost to Ielly'.

I. ii. 247. 'tenable in your silence': F 'treble in your silence'.

I. iii. 57. 'my blessing with thee': F 'my blessing with you'. The folio assimilates the pronoun to what precedes instead of what follows.

I. iv. 9. 'Keepes wassell' (Q 1 'Keepe wassel'): F 'Keepes wassels'.

I. v. 71. 'tetter barckt about' (Q 1 'barked, and tettered ouer'): F 'Tetter bak'd about'. Possibly the prompt-copy had 'barkt', which the compositor misread as 'backt'.

i. v. 133. 'whurling words' (Q 1 'wherling words'): F 'hurling words'.

i. v. 136. 'but there is *Horatio*': F 'but there is my Lord'. The words were caught from the line above.

i. v. 162. 'can'st worke it'h earth': F 'can'st worke i'th' ground'.

i. v. 177. 'there be and if they might': F 'there be and if there might'. The compositor apparently did not understand the passage. I do not know what sense the few editors who have adopted the reading of F attached to it.

ii. ii. 106. 'haue while she is mine': F 'haue, whil'st she is mine'. Of course, in such a case the evidence of Q 1 is very slight, and the reading might be classed under (a).

ii. ii. 418. 'thy face is valanct' (Q 1 'thy face is vallanced'): F 'thy face is valiant'. It is astounding that three modern editors should have adopted the obvious misprint of the folio.

ii. ii. 427. 'What speech my good Lord ?': F 'What speech, my Lord ?'

iii. ii. 12. 'I would haue such a fellow whipt': F 'I could haue . . .'.

iii. ii. 239. 'You are as good as a Chorus': F 'You are a good Chorus'.

iii. ii. 268. 'Thus runnes the world away': F 'So runnes . . .'.

v. i. 137. 'the heele of the Courtier': F 'the heeles of our Courtier'. A double misprint.

v. ii. 236. 'And hurt my brother': F 'And hurt my Mother'. For the extravagance of which conjecture is capable see Hunter's note quoted by Furness.

(c) *Uncertain variations* (15). These are probably more than mere misprints, being modernizations or conscious tinkerings of the text where it appeared for some reason unsatisfactory. It is impossible to say whether they were made in the prompt-copy while in use, by an editor preparing the same for press, or by the compositor of F.

i. i. 65. 'and iump at this dead houre': F 'and iust at . . .'.

i. ii. 200. 'Armed at poynt, exactly *Capapea*' (Q 1 'Armed to poynt, exactly *Capapea*'): F 'Arm'd at all points exactly, *Cap a Pe*'. There are two variants here. The first is either due to unfamiliarity with the phrase, or else to a desire to avoid making the '-ed' syllabic. The second is presumably a modernization, and as such has apparently been adopted by all editors. Webster has '*Cap a pea*' in the 1615 *Characters* (ed. Lucas, iv. 23), and no doubt this was the spelling Shakespeare intended. Moreover the *N.E.D.* cites an instance of the form 'Capa peia' as late as 1650, which suggests that the variant may be more than orthographic.

I. ii. 242. 'I warn't it will' (Q 1 'I warrant it will'): F 'I warrant you it will'. The spelling of Q 2 shows that the word was meant to be one syllable. But F had no love for such forms, and therefore added 'you' to make a regular alexandrine.

I. iii. 57. 'And you are stayed for, there my blessing with thee': F '. . . for there: my . . .'. The punctuation may not have been very clear in the manuscript, but F definitely took the passage in another sense.

I. iii. 62. 'Those friends thou hast': F 'The friends thou hast'. This seems more likely to be a deliberate change than a mere misprint.

I. v. 167. 'in your philosophie': F 'in our Philosophy'. Presumably F failed to get the force of 'your'.

I. v. 173. 'at such times seeing me': F 'at such time seeing me'. Perhaps a misprint; but the folio may have supposed it was giving a smoother reading. However, the support of Q 1 counts for very little here.

I. v. 174. 'thus, or this head shake': F 'thus, or thus, head shake'. F evidently understood the passage differently.

II. ii. 415. 'my abridgment comes': F 'my Abridgements come'. Hamlet's interruption is the entrance of the players, and F therefore thought it necessary to use the plural.

II. ii. 574. 'I should a fatted': F 'I should haue fatted'. A modernization which has tempted editors.

III. i. 142. 'I haue heard of your paintings': F '. . . your pratlings'. Also—

III. i. 143. 'God hath giuen you one face': F '. . . one pace'. Something had gone wrong here with the prompt-copy, for the readings of F are guesswork; 'pace' being suggested by 'jig' and 'amble', and 'pratlings' by 'lisp' and 'nick-name'.

III. ii. 254. 'On wholsome life vsurps immediatly': F '. . . life, vsurpe . . .'. The support of Q 1 is not very weighty, but such as it is it points to the reading of F being one of its usual small normalizations of which editors are so fond. In that case it at least disposes of the suggestion that 'usurp' is imperative.

III. iii. 91. 'At game a swearing' (Q 1 'at game swaring'): F 'At gaming, swearing'. As we have already seen (1, d; p. 187) F's 'gaming' is due to an attempt to restore the verse injured by the loss of 'a'.

(d) *Alterations in the prompt-copy* (13). These appear to be deliberate alterations made in the prompt-book while in use, but subsequent to the preparation of the actors' parts. They require to be carefully considered in view of possible authorization by Shakespeare.

I. i. 73. 'dayly cost of brazon Cannon': F 'dayly Cast . . .'. Presumably the reading of F, accepted by practically all editors, is correct, though it appears to be the only instance of this use. It is possible (perhaps, indeed, most likely) that the agreement of Q 1 and Q 2 is due to coincidence, since the unusual word 'cast' would easily be misunderstood.

I. ii. 129. 'too too sallied flesh' (Q 1 'too much grieu'd and sallied flesh'): F 'too too solid Flesh'. Burbage was getting a little portly, for Hamlet we learn was 'fat' (v. ii. 279), but though Shakespeare might safely poke fun at him in the fencing match, to begin a serious speech by emphasizing the defect would have been disastrous. It follows that, in spite of editorial consensus, he cannot possibly have intended to write 'solid' here. (Of course, with a slimmer actor 'solid' would be unobjectionable.) On the other hand, I do not think that 'sallied' can be right, though it has found defenders, and it is clear that the prompt-book ultimately rejected it as unintelligible. The problem, therefore, is to emend 'sallied' (see note 32, p. 200).

I. iii. 65. 'each new hatcht vnfledged courage' (Q 1 'euery new vnfleg'd courage'): F 'each vnhatch't, vnfledg'd Comrade'. [Here 'vnhatch't' is, of course, a misprint.] No editor has printed 'courage', though it has occasionally found defenders. But 'Comrade' gives very poor sense, and is presumably a makeshift for an impossible word in the prompt-book. Dover Wilson has suggested that 'courage' is a misreading of 'cocnaye' (cockney), and 'Comrade' an erroneous emendation (*Times Literary Supplement*, 14 Nov. 1918).

I. iv. 49. 'quietly interr'd': F 'quietly enurn'd'. Few editors have followed Capell in preferring the reading of Qq, though that of F has sometimes been challenged as unsuited to the context. However, 'urn' is used for grave in *Henry V* (I. ii. 228) and *Coriolanus* (v. vi. 145), and since F gives a much pithier reading, I see no reason to doubt that the alteration is Shakespeare's.

I. iv. 61. 'It waues you': F 'It wafts you'. I can only suppose an alteration in the prompt-book, but the reason for it is obscure. F has 'wafts' again at l. 78, but 'waues' at l. 68 (Q 2 'waues' in both cases, and Q 1 absent).

I. v. 18. 'Thy knotted and combined locks': F 'Thy knotty . . .'. Several editors, including Capell, have preferred the reading of F, though it has fallen into disfavour recently. It is just possible that Shakespeare felt the repeated participles to be clumsy.

I. v. 33. 'rootes it selfe in ease': F 'rots it selfe in ease'. This may be a misprint, but both readings are so excellent that one hesitates to assume such an origin. Again Capell followed F, and so have many others, and the passage has been freely annotated. If 'rots' is not a misprint (or misunderstanding) it must be Shakespeare's revision.

I. v. 62. 'Hebona': F 'Hebenon'. Only one editor has followed Qq. It seems clear that ebony (*hebenus*, ἔβενος) and not henbane is meant, but neither of the given forms is recognized. Since we can hardly suppose a misprint, it is probably an intentional alteration. Shakespeare may have come across a Greek accusative.

I. v. 69. 'eager droppings': F 'Aygre droppings'. These are really only alternative spellings, but F's emphasizes the literal (and French) sense. It is not likely to be due to the compositor.

I. v. 107. 'My tables,' (Q I '(My Tables)'): F I 'My Tables, my Tables;'. This is an interesting variant if one allows speculation its head. These duplications are rather characteristic of Hamlet, and they are more in evidence in F than in Q 2. If omission of words is a characteristic of Q 2, this is not surprising, but in the present instance Q I and the redundant metre combine to point to addition in F rather than omission in Q 2. It was suggested by De Groot that such repetitions were a trick, not of Hamlet, but of Burbage (*Hamlet and its Textual History*, 1923, pp. 35–6). This view Dover Wilson waves aside (p. 39), and Granville-Barker points out a subtler use of the same device in *Lear*, where it is not confined to one character (*Prefaces to Shakespeare*, first series, 1927, pp. 160–1). But because Shakespeare adopted and developed the trick, it may have been Burbage's nevertheless, and the present reading of F perhaps betrays him.

II. i. 114. 'By heauen it is': F 'It seemes it is'. F suggests a casual compliance with the laws against profanity: but the original phrase may have been felt to be rather too emphatic for Polonius.

v. i. 257. 'Which let thy wisedome feare': F '. . . wisenesse feare'. I can only suppose a deliberate alteration, but I fail to catch the intent. Sundry editors have followed the folio, but none seem to have explained why.

I have reserved to the end one exceedingly small point, which, however, seems to me very significant of the relation of the texts. My excuse for classing it here is that there is undoubtedly a correction in F, however minute.

1. i. 44. 'it horrowes me with feare' (Q 1 'it horrors . . .'): F 'It harrowes . . .'. Of course 'harrows' is meant. I conjecture that Shakespeare wrote 'harows', with the peculiar 'a' that was liable to be mistaken for 'or' (p. 158), and hence it appeared as 'horrowes' in Q 2 and as 'horrows' in the prompt-book; that this 'horrows' was mistaken for 'horrors' in the actor's part (hence Q 1), but correctly restored as 'harrowes' in F.

[The foregoing analysis of readings in groups (1) and (2) affords some guidance in dealing with these variants between Q 2 and F on which Q 1 throws no light. Such variants may be expected, if the theory we are examining is correct, to fall into four classes, and it is essential that an editor should make up his mind to which of these a particular one belongs before he considers what his choice should be. To begin with we shall have (a) variants in which the reading of Q 2 is clearly a misprint of that preserved in F, and (b) those in which the reading of F is a misprint of that preserved in Q 2. (There may, of course, be cases in which the readings are evidently varying misprints of a common original.) Then there will be (c) accidental or trivial variations arising in the preparation of prompt-copy. In all these cases an editor's course is clear: in (a) he will adopt the reading of F, and in (b) and (c) that of Q 2. There remain (d) what may be called genuine or intentional variants, and these will all require individual attention. But there is one very important consideration to be borne in mind. No genuine variant is to be dismissed because it is obviously corrupt. An evident error, which cannot be a mere misprint of the other reading, must first be itself emended before it is presented for criticism. It is not enough to compare the readings of Q 2 and F and adopt whichever makes sense, though this has been all too commonly the practice of editors. For the corruption of Q 2 we must first substitute the presumed reading of the autograph, for the corruption of F the presumed reading of the prompt-book, and then compare these corrected readings and consider our choice between them (cf. p. 152).]

(3) Q 1 : Q 2, F.   We must now examine those readings of Q 1 which editors have adopted against an agreement of Q 2 and F. This is obviously a drastic measure, and it is rather surprising to find as many as eight instances in the Cambridge text. Apart from accidental convergence in the more authoritative texts, such a

choice could only be justified on the supposition of an error in the autograph, remaining uncorrected in the prompt-book, but detected and corrected in performance. This would be by no means impossible, but frequent recourse to the assumption would raise grave suspicions as to the theory that necessitated it. Actually in only one out of the eight cases do the editors appear to be justified, while in several they have fallen into quite manifest error.

I. ii. 209 supplies the only inevitable example. As now printed the passage runs:

> And I with them the third night kept the watch:
> Where, as they had deliver'd, . . .
> The apparition comes:

but only Q 1 reads 'Where as'; Q 2 and F have 'Whereas'. Even Q 1 has no punctuation, and in the absence of clear direction the compositors of Q 2 and F may have fallen into the trap quite independently.

I. ii. 198. 'In the dead vast and middle of the night': Q 1 'vast': Q 2, F 'wast', i.e. 'waste' (as in F 2–4). It should be noted that, while Q 4 (1611) also reads 'wast', Q 5, 6 (n.d. and 1637) read 'vast', though whence they derived it is unknown. (Q 3 of the Cambridge notation, i.e. 1605, is identical with Q 2, 1604.) Even with this dubious support I can conceive no valid reason for preferring the reading of Q 1.

I. iii. 67. 'Bear't, that the opposed may beware of thee': Q 1 'the opposed': Q 2, F 'th'opposed'. Theobald and most modern editors appear to have printed 'the opposed' as a normalization of their own, but it is, in fact, the reading of Q 1.

III. ii. 237. 'let the galled jade wince, our withers are unwrung': Q 1 'wince': Q 2, F 'winch'. The spelling of Q 1 was adopted by Steevens, but it should be observed that on the only other occasion that Shakespeare uses the word (*King John*, IV. i. 81) the folio again spells it 'winch'. This is one of the many passages on which the *N.E.D.* has thrown light. It seems that 'wince' and 'winch' are distinct words, going back to different forms in Old French, and that, at the time Shakespeare wrote, 'winch' meant what we mean by wince, while 'wince' meant to kick.

III. ii. 246. 'So you must take your husbands': Q 1 'must take': Q 2, F 'mistake'. This has been discussed in the lecture. Much that has been written on the subject seems beside the point: whichever reading we adopt the allusion is to the marriage service. Pope's version means: That is how the Church bids you take husbands! Capell's: That's the silly way you choose husbands! The latter seems to have more point, but any one who failed to catch it might easily mishear 'mis-take' as 'must take'.

[Curiously enough there occurs a few lines later (l. 252) a passage in which I think it is quite possible that Q 1 may preserve the author's intention:

> Thou mixture rank, of midnight weeds collected,
> With Hecate's ban thrice blasted, thrice infected . . .

This is possible; and 'Ban' or 'ban', curse, is the reading of F and Q 2: Q 1 has 'bane', poison (so also Q 6 and F 4). But Shakespeare had a trick of leaving out a final 'e', and was quite capable of writing 'ban' when he meant 'bane'. If he did so here, the comparative familiarity of 'ban' would aid its retention by the scribe and compositors, but it is possible that Q 1 represents the stage tradition, preserving in performance the sense the author intended.]

III. ii. 362. Hamlet, toying with the recorders and his tormentors, says:

Call me what instrument you will, though you can fret me, yet you cannot play upon me.

The word 'yet' is borrowed from Q 1, it is not in Q 2 or F. Its introduction is a peculiarity of the Globe and Cambridge texts, which appear to have found no followers. It seems at first sight wanton, and only on close examination does the reason for it become apparent. The three authorities read as follows:

> F   though you can fret me, you cannot play vpon me.
> Q 2 though you fret me not, you cannot play vpon me.
> Q 1 though you can frett mee, yet you can not Play vpon mee, . . .

The natural assumption is that the omission of 'can' in Q 2 is a compositor's error (cf. (1, a), p. 183). When this is restored, Q 1 and Q 2 only differ from F by the addition, at the same point (if we disregard the comma), the one of 'not', the other of 'yet'. The former makes no sense; but if the tail of the 'y' were obscure, 'yet' might look very like 'not', and 'yet' may thus claim the hypothetical support of both quartos. The argument is extremely ingenious; but it is perhaps simpler to suppose that the compositor of Q 2 altered a phrase he failed to understand, and that 'yet' got into Q 1 through an unconscious addition by the actor.

iv. v. 139. The King asks Laertes:

> is 't writ in your revenge
> That, swoopstake, you will draw both friend and foe,
> Winner and loser?

Q 1 'Swoop-stake-like' (in very divergent text): Q 2 'soopstake': F 'Soop-stake'. The form 'swoopstake' is a variant of 'sweepstake' through the influence of the verb 'swoop', and in the seventeenth century 'soop' was a very common form of 'swoop'. There is no doubt that 'soopstake' is what Shakespeare wrote, and to be consistent modernizing editors should print 'sweepstake'.

v. i. 59. As the gravedigger knows,

> the houses that he makes last till doomsday

but Q 2 and F agree that he said that they 'lasts'. The normalization, which editors would in any case have made, has been introduced ostensibly on the authority of Q 4 and F 4, but it happens to be already found in Q 1. It has, of course, no significance whatever.

(4) **Q 2, F: X.** We now pass from the question of choice to that of emendation. There seem to be eleven passages in which the Cambridge editors have admitted an emendation in place of a reading supported both by Q 2 and F (Q 1 being either absent or impossibly divergent). In a few cases they are clearly wrong in deserting the transmitted text; several instances are trivial; and the remainder are certainly not more numerous than on our theory we should expect.

ii. i. 3. 'You shall do marvellous wisely': Q 2 'meruiles': F 'maruels' [Q 4 'maruelous': Q 5, 6 'marvellous']. The agreement of Q 2 and F is probably only apparent. No doubt 'marvellous' is the word intended, and I should not be surprised to learn that 'meruiles', or something like it, was Shakespeare's spelling, and 'maruels' a mistaken normalization.

ii. ii. 181. 'being a god kissing carrion': Q 2 &c., Ff 'good' [Warburton 'God']. Johnson thought it 'a noble emendation, which almost sets the critic on a level with the author'. It is facile and plausible, but I think unnecessary. Hamlet's fancies are not always as nice as editors would have them.

ii. ii. 430. ''twas caviare to the general': Q 2 'cauiary': F '*Cauiarie*'. The alteration is wholly unwarranted: 'caviáry' or 'caviály' was the original form in English; the earliest evidence in the *N.E.D.* for a trisyllabic form (through weakening of the last syllable) is not earlier than 1620–30, though as early as 1612 Webster has the ambiguous line (*The White Devil*, I. i. 21): 'Only for Cauiare.—Those noblemen'.

II. ii. 482. 'Aroused vengeance sets him new a-work': Q 2 'A rowsed': F 'A ro wsed'. The readings might easily have arisen independently (or accidentally); but the emendation, which was first proposed by Collier, is clearly not inevitable, since all earlier editors accepted the text. There seems, indeed, little to choose.

II. ii. 489. 'Break all the spokes and fellies from her wheel': Q 2 'follies': F 'Fallies'. Q 2 evidently gives a compositor's misreading of the form preserved in F, which is a recognized, if rare, seventeenth-century spelling, and it is probably due to Shakespeare. Editors, in reading 'fellies', have followed F 4.

III. iii. 18. 'the summit of the highest mount': Q 2 'somnet': F 'Somnet'. Cf. I. iv. 70, where Q 2 again has 'somnet', and F misprints it 'Sonnet'. There can be no doubt, therefore, that 'somnet' was Shakespeare's spelling. The *N.E.D.* gives it as a recognized though erroneous form.

III. iv. 4. '*Pol*[*onius*]. . . . I'll sconce me even here': Q 2, F 'silence me'. This has been discussed in the lecture.

III. iv. 121. 'Your bedded hairs . . . Start up and stand an end': Q 2, F 'haire'. An awkward use of the collective in place of the plural, but no doubt due to the author.

IV. v. 116. 'between the chaste unsmirched brows Of my true mother': Q 2 'browe': F 'brow'. A similar slip presumably due to the same.

V. i. 215. 'Fordo its own life': Q 2, F 'it'. The well-recognized use of 'it' as possessive was habitual with Shakespeare. It occurs fifteen times in the first folio and is the only form found in the quartos; the later folios substitute 'its' or 'it's'. On the other hand 'it's' occurs nine times, and 'its' once, in the first folio, but significantly confined to plays first printed in 1623. (See *N.E.D.*, s.v. 'its'.)

V. ii. 303. 'Ho! let the door be lock'd': Q 2 'how let': F 'How? Let'. The reading of F is clearly due to a misunderstanding by the compositor. In Q 2 'how' is apparently Shakespeare's spelling of the exclamation, since at l. 295 it prints: 'Looke to the Queene there howe', where F has 'hoa'.

(5) **Q 1, 2, F: X.** Lastly we have those passages in which the Cambridge editors have emended a reading which has the support of all three authorities.

IV. v. 37. 'Which bewept to the grave did go': Q 1 'did not goe':
Q 2 'did not go': F '*did not go*'. This has been discussed in the
lecture. It should be mentioned that Malone and Dowden are
among the editors who retain the negative. None of those who
reject it have attempted to explain the facts. The idea of its
intrusion has, however, been supported by reference to *Much Ado*,
III. ii. 25, where both the quarto and folio have 'cannot' by mistake
for 'can'. But there the textual data are not analogous. Reference might also be made to the autograph manuscript of *Believe as
you List* (l. 2011), in which Massinger makes his prisoned and
famished king exclaim:

> and warnde by my example, when your tables
> cracke not with the waight, of deere, and far fetchd dainties
> dispute not with heavns bounties.

Here it is evident that the author, making a fair transcript of his
revised play, accidentally caught the 'not' from the line below, and
the sentence is one in which the error is easily overlooked, as is
shown by the fact that the piece has been repeatedly edited without
its rousing suspicion (see the Malone Society Reprint, in which
Dr. Sisson duly notes it). Neither of these instances is in the least
relevant to the discussion.

Editors have without exception, I believe, adopted for one of the
minor characters in the play the spelling 'Voltimand', which first
appears in F 2. He only comes on twice, in I. ii and II. ii, and the
textual evidence is as follows: Q 1 'Voltemar' (twice), Q 2 'Valtemand' (twice), F 'Voltemand' (twice) and 'Voltumand' (twice). It
is obvious that (whatever the vowel of the first syllable) the
evidence is conclusive in favour of 'Voltemand' as against 'Voltimand' for the Shakespearian form. (There is, however, no such
name as Voltimand or Valtemand in Danish: it is presumably a
corruption of Valdemar, and Q 1 may indicate that the actors
attempted to correct Shakespeare on the stage. Mr. J. H. Helweg
writes to suggest that several queer names in *Hamlet* are per-
versions of Danish.)

Besides these there is the line I. iii. 74, which the Cambridge
editors retain for lack of any acceptable emendation. That they
regard it as corrupt is clear from their obelizing it in the Globe
edition. It is considered below, note 33. It is significant that the
four other readings in *Hamlet* obelized in the Globe edition have
only a single authority behind them.

30 (p. 152). Professor J. Dover Wilson's paper on 'Spellings and

Misprints in the Second Quarto of *Hamlet*' is printed in *Essays and Studies* by members of the English Association, 1924. In it he has particularly investigated those errors which arise through mis-interpretations of Shakespeare's spelling and handwriting.

Where errors are common to Q 2 and F the origin must be sought in a reading of the autograph. That errors should occur in the author's own manuscript is natural enough. I suppose we have all had the experience of finding that we had written a word quite other than what we intended: in preparing this lecture I caught myself writing 'source' where I meant to write 'seat'. And I do not imagine that Shakespeare was immune to such human weakness. But it is also possible for a scribe actually to write the word he intends, but for his hand to form the letters in such a manner that even a careful reader may mistake them for other letters. He may even form them so that for practical purposes they are other letters —in such a way, that is, that several different readers will inevitably read them as other letters. For instance a typist and a compositor, working on the same manuscript of this lecture, made five identical mistakes. This is one side of the problem, the genesis of error. The other is the persistence of error. The appearance of such a mis-reading in F means that it originated with the scribe of the prompt-copy, remained uncorrected during the use of that copy in the play-house, and was thus perpetuated by the compositor. The appear-ance of such in Q 1 implies a yet longer and more surprising chain of error. It is useful to keep these two aspects of the problem distinct.

It is the possibilities of such malformation of letters to which Mr. Dover Wilson has directed attention. The general nature of the question has already been glanced at above in notes 10 to 12. Here we are particularly concerned with the possibility or proba-bility of repeated misreading by several persons. The probability is usually not great, but the possibility undoubtedly exists. We possess three pages of writing in what some people believe to be Shakespeare's hand, and in these there are several words which are capable of being misread. When Shakespeare tried to write 'mountainish' (so Mr. Dover Wilson assumes) he formed one minim too few in each half of the word, which as it stands can only be read as 'momtanish'. And when he tried to write 'order' he tacked on an unneeded 'e' and formed it so large that there would be nothing surprising in several independent compositors printing 'orderd'. Miss W. Frijlinck has lately called my attention to a similar instance in the manuscript play of *Richard II* (or *Thomas of*

Woodstock) in MS. Egerton 1994 (fol. 169ᵇ; l. 1040 in her edition for the Malone Society). Here we find a word which three successive scholars, who have edited or collated the text, agree in reading 'paleing', and this has been interpreted as a participial adjective from the verb 'pale', to enclose or surround. In this sense it has found its way as a solitary example into the *N.E.D.* But a careful examination shows that what the scribe wrote was 'pooleing'; 'poole' being a variant of 'poll', to shave or fleece. Any one who has had experience in editing manuscripts could multiply examples. The phenomenon is not confined to Elizabethan script: medievalists will recall the 'caitif' of *Aucassin et Nicolete*, that looks exactly like 'antif', and the Green Knight's name 'Bernlak', that is now believed to be 'Bercilak'. I will only add one rather striking instance from Massinger. In a passage in *The Emperor of the East* (IV. iv) he used the word 'cancer', but when the play was printed in 1632 the compositor set it up as 'camer'. In a copy of the play still extant, Massinger with his own hand rewrote the word 'cancer' in the margin—but in doing so he amply justified the compositor, for sense apart no one would read it as anything but 'camer' (*The Library*, v. 67, 80, see note 6; and cf. note 12, p. 158).

31 (p. 152). For the method cf. note 29, p. 193. The passage occurs at III. iii. 7. The contention is that Shakespeare either accidentally wrote 'browes' when he meant to write some other word, or wrote another word in such a manner that the compositor of Q 2 and the scribe of the prompt-copy both misread it as 'browes'. In the former case emendation must be an affair of pure guesswork, in the latter we may hope for some hint from a study of the graphic forms. In either case the original reading was lost, and 'browes' being impossible, some substitute had to be found. It should be observed that a substitute-reading may nevertheless be Shakespeare's. Confronted by a corruption of the original word, he might quite possibly forget what that had been and supply another. It is, however, not very likely that the present is a case in point, for 'lunacies' is decidedly weak as well as metrically redundant.

32 (p. 152). Hamlet's sullied or solid flesh is at I. ii. 129 (cf. p. 150, and note 29, p. 191). The illuminative misprint of 'sallies' for 'sullies' in Q 2 (F 'sulleyes') will be found at II. i. 39.

33 (p. 153). The line in question, I. iii. 74, runs in the three texts thus:

> Q 1 Are of a most select and generall chiefe in that:
> Q 2 Or of a most select and generous, chiefe in that:
> F Are of a most select and generous cheff in that.

(For Q 2 'Or' cf. note 29, p. 182.) Mr. Dover Wilson remarks that
'Most editors cut the knot by simply omitting the words "of a";
thus at once making sense and seemingly restoring the metre'. But
he points out that Polonius is rather fond of alexandrines. He
therefore proposes to retain the words, but pitches on them as the
seat of corruption. His emendation is 'often', which he supposes
Shakespeare to have written 'ofen'. We elsewhere find 'heauen'
misread and printed 'heaue, a' (Q 2, III. iv. 59), which proves that
Shakespeare's 'n' could look very like an 'a'. Also (in the hand he
accepts as Shakespeare's) a final 'f' often ends with a flourish remarkably like one form of 'e' (though this does not occur in the
particular hand). He argues, therefore, that it need not surprise us
to find 'ofen' misread as 'of a'.

Now, supposing the double error to have arisen in Q 2 and the
prompt-copy, I do not think that its persistence through the actors'
part and in Q 1 and F need trouble us. The reading has a certain
specious air about it that might disguise the fact of its being nonsense. It is over the genesis, especially the double genesis, of the
error that doubt arises. The assumed spelling 'ofen' is, I think,
likely enough, but the step from 'ofen' to 'of a' presents difficulties.
For although a change from final 'f' to 'fe' would (on the assumption) be reasonable enough, the opposite change appears doubtful.
It is an instance of what I have called reflex substitution, and it
hardly falls into any of the categories in which I have argued that
this is likely to occur (see note 12). We should have to suppose that
both the compositor and the scribe were so familiar with a peculiar
form of 'f' that they assumed it even where it was not used. This
seems to me somewhat improbable. There is, however, another
possibility. I should not be more than mildly surprised to learn that
Shakespeare sometimes spelled 'often', not only 'ofen', but even
'ofn', and the conversion of 'ofn' into 'of a' would be not merely
easy but probable. If any evidence could be produced for Shakespeare having so written the word I should be quite content to
accept the emendation: but so far as I know there is none.

Of course, such evidence might be claimed if another textual
crux could be solved by assuming the same misreading. This is
supplied by Mr. Dover Wilson where, in place of 'the noble substance of a doubt' (I. iv. 37), he proposes 'the noble substance often
dout', but I am afraid that I do not find this emendation in itself
sufficiently convincing to cite it in support for another.

THE ELIZABETHAN SHAKESPEARE

By J. DOVER WILSON [1]

BEN JONSON accused Shakespeare of lack of art and Samuel Johnson complained that 'he seems to write without any moral purpose'. In different language and with differences of emphasis both criticisms are being loudly repeated at the present day, and since Dr. Bridges published in 1907 his essay on 'The Influence of the Audience on Shakespeare's Drama',[2] an essay recently re-issued as the first number of his *Collected Essays*, much has been heard of the barbarous and brutal Elizabethans who thronged Shakespeare's theatre, and of the moral and artistic improprieties occasioned by the need of pleasing them. I propose this afternoon to say something under both these heads, and I shall begin by considering the first charge, that of lack of art.

No one at this time of day is going to defend Shakespeare as the perfect artist. He wrote many pedestrian and even some foolish lines, and taking the folio as a whole Ben Jonson's wish that he had 'blotted a thousand' is probably just and reasonable. But the faults now complained of are not those of style or diction, still less that mixture of dramatic types which Jonson tilts at in his induction to *Bartholomew Fair*; they are faults of dramatic inconsistency, inadequate motivation, careless contradiction, faults of which Jonson seems to have been completely unconscious. Modern critics all over the world, scholars like Professor Schücking in Germany, Professor Stoll in

---

[1] First delivered 1929. Save for a few slight changes this lecture is here reprinted as originally published in 1929.

[2] The Stratford Town edition of Shakespeare, vol. x. The essay is in a sense the development of a lecture by Professor Andrew Bradley delivered two years earlier on *Shakespeare's Theatre and Audience*, and this lecture, in turn, when printed in 1909 in *Oxford Lectures on Poetry*, contained a footnote commenting upon Dr. Bridges's essay (pp. 366–7).

America, and Mr. J. M. Robertson in this country, are busy going over the plays with their microscopes and bringing to light countless flaws of structure and character, flaws which they interpret as evidence either that Shakespeare was a crude or careless dramatist, or that he worked with indifferent collaborators. The latter explanation may pass muster in respect of plays like *Measure for Measure* or *All's Well that ends Well*, which are almost certainly the result of collaboration between Shakespeare and some second-rate dramatist to whom was entrusted the final shaping of the material. But collaboration of this kind is, I believe, rare in Shakespeare, and in any case it must be carefully distinguished from the far more frequent phenomenon of revision. The distinction has important aesthetic implications, since it is (or should be) a cardinal principle in the criticism of plays belonging to this period that the dramatist who last handles a text must accept full artistic responsibility for it. I make a point of this because those who detect, or think they detect, revision in the plays have on that account been accused before this Academy and elsewhere of disintegrating Shakespeare.[1] I confess that I find this attitude a little difficult to understand. To show, for instance, that *Hamlet* had been rehandled once or even twice by Shakespeare is not surely to injure it in any way as a work of art. Nor, provided that one dramatist had the final revision in his complete control, is it reasonable to refuse the title of artistic unity to a play because it happens to be composed of strata written at different times or even by different hands. For, what Shakespeare rewrote he presumably imagined he was improving, and what he left alone he presumably thought good enough for his purposes.

Yes, but what exactly were his purposes? That is the crux, a crux which is the root of much confusion in present-day Shakespearian criticism. It can never be too often emphasized that Shakespeare wrote his plays not for the printing-house but for the theatre, and that the texts

[1] Cf. pp. 23-48, above.

he left behind him were not books but prompt-books or, if you will, theatrical scores for the performance of moving pageants of speech, action, and colour, upon a particular stage by a particular troupe of actors for a particular audience. It is doubtful whether any play of Shakespeare's was ever revived in his lifetime in exactly its original form. The widely different versions of plays like *Hamlet* and *King Lear* should have long ago warned the world of this fact. But what is palpable in *Hamlet* and *King Lear* is scarcely less obvious in every other text that has come down to us in two good playhouse forms, and may even be detected sometimes in plays of which no more than one text has survived. For example, had *A Midsummer-Night's Dream* been preserved in the 1600 quarto alone, we could still feel tolerably certain that this play, originally written for one occasion, had been rehandled by Shakespeare for another and later one.[1] As it is, we have the folio text as well to proclaim still further adaption. For whereas in the quarto the interlude is set for a theatre with an inner-stage and a traverse which can be drawn to hide the bodies of Pyramus and Thisbe, in the folio no traverse is available, so that the killing has to be enacted on the open stage, and is therefore perforce followed by Bottom's resurrection. Thus we must imagine Shakespearian playbooks in a constant state of flux, and if they come to rest when they pass out of the theatre into the printer's hands, their final state does not represent any considered preparation by the author for publication, but merely records the conditions of the last performance before the printing was taken in hand. In the modern world theatres exist to perform the plays of literary gentlemen called dramatists; in the Globe an actor made his living by providing plays, new, retouched, or reconstructed, for the performances of a repertory company.

[1] The chief evidence for this rehandling is the disarrangement of eight passages in the first eighty-four lines of verse in Act V, passages which may be omitted without injuring the sense of the context though certainly not without detracting from its beauty, v. edition of the play in the 'New Shakespeare', pp. 80–6.

It follows that to criticize a play by Shakespeare in the same fashion and from the same point of view as we criticize a play by Mr. Bernard Shaw is as absurd as it would be to blame the polyphonic musicians of the sixteenth century for not observing the rules of harmony. It is not merely that the structure of the theatre has profoundly changed in the past three hundred years, the very meaning of the word 'play' has altered. With Shakespeare a play was first and foremost a performance; with us—at any rate since Mr. Shaw set the fashion of publishing drama—it has become first and foremost a printed book. But some of the critics I am considering go even farther; they actually take Shakespeare to task for ignoring the literary proprieties which we expect in a modern novel, biography, or history, quite oblivious of the fact that to bring forward loose ends and contradictions which can only be discovered by the close study of the printed texts and make them the basis of an aesthetic judgement on the plays as stage-productions is an entirely illegitimate proceeding, and withal a dangerous one likely to recoil upon the critic's own head. When, to take a famous instance, we read *Hamlet* the book, we may be puzzled to observe that the hero is apparently about eighteen years old at the beginning of the play and thirty years old at the end: but as we sit and watch *Hamlet* the play we are disturbed by no such discrepancy, for the simple reason that we have the hero before us in the shape of an actor made to look a certain age, which we accept of course entirely without question. Thus, though the discrepancy is there and, as evidence of textual revision, is interesting to scholars, it can in no way be regarded as a technical flaw in a drama which was written solely for performance and thought of by its creator from first to last in terms of the company which he served. Indeed, it is conceivable that the discrepancy arose merely from the fact that Burbadge, the impersonator of Hamlet, had grown older and stouter between the original and the final draft of the play. In other words, the pointed reference in the Grave-yard scene to the Prince of Denmark's thirty years may have been intended as a piece of 'fat' for the actor in two senses of the word.

Again, when Dr. Bridges writes 'The tragedy of *Othello* is intolerably painful; and that not merely because we see Othello being grossly deceived, but because we are ourselves constrained to submit to palpable deception. The whole thing is impossible',[1] we must remember that he is speaking of a book, every nook and cranny of which has been explored and thrown into high relief by the relentless light of modern analytical criticism. In particular, he is looking at the book through the eyes of Professor Andrew Bradley, one of the greatest of Shakespeare's critics, yet at the same time apt to be misleading to readers who follow his penetrating curiosity into the very viscera of a tragedy and overlook his constant warning that these matters are often irrelevant as far as the theatre is concerned.[2] Indeed, this play which Dr. Bridges in his study finds 'impossible' is generally regarded on the stage as the most effective and technically the most perfect of all Shakespeare's tragedies. The two points of view are in startling opposition; and yet they are really complementary. For the swiftness and brilliance of *Othello* as a theatre-piece are, at least in part, brought about by those very contradictions and deceptions which would be rightly stamped as defects in a novel. The tempo of the play, for example, has been much praised. Its rapidity at once symbolizes, and heightens our sense of, the torrential passion that rages through the hero's mind;

---

[1] Op. cit. *Collected Essays*, i. p. 23.

[2] Dr. Bridges might have found *Othello* less intolerable had he pondered a sentence towards the end of the very note of Professor Bradley's upon which he founds his condemnation, a sentence which admits that no one 'either in the theatre or in a casual reading of the play' is likely to notice any of the impossibilities and contradictions that the writer had been discussing for the past six pages. (*Shakespearean Tragedy*, pp. 423–9). The proviso destroys the whole validity of Dr. Bridges's case. For, if they pass thus unnoticed in the theatre, such contradictions are of no dramatic significance whatsoever, however interesting they may prove in connexion with the history of the text.

but this sense of speed has been purchased by just that foreshortening of time which, did Shakespeare allow us to consider it in the theatre as we are able to do in our studies, would be recognized as absurd. Or—to take a point of detail—critics who find Emilia guilty of 'gross stupidity'[1] or 'sinful levity'[2] for not confessing the theft of the kerchief to Desdemona, when Othello taxes her with its loss in her presence, are surely themselves displaying some stupidity of dramatic perception.[3] Shakespeare sees to it that Emilia shall be there when Othello cross-examines Desdemona about the kerchief, in order to heighten the feeling of tension, to keep his audience upon the rack of what Professor Bradley has called 'sickening hope', which it is one of his chief purposes in this play to evoke. But if we watch the scene upon the stage, there is (or should be) nothing in the least flat or obtuse in the conduct of Emilia. She does not confess the theft, partly of course because it was a theft, but partly also because she is a woman, a woman married to an over-jealous husband, and therefore amused to see her young mistress getting a taste of what she considers the ordinary run of married life. It never occurs to her to connect Othello's jealousy with Iago's desire for the kerchief. Why should it? Her mind is busy not with handkerchiefs but with husbands:

Desdemona.	Alas the day! I never gave him cause.
Emilia.	But jealous souls will not be answered so:
	They are not ever jealous for the cause,
	But jealous for they are jealous: 'tis a monster
	Begot upon itself, born on itself.[4]

[1] Bradley, *Shakespearean Tragedy*, p. 240.
[2] Schlegel quoted in Furness's Variorum *Othello*, p. 432.
[3] Dr. Bridges writes: 'Exasperation is the word that I should choose to express the state of feeling which the reading of the *Othello* induces in me: and seeing how cleverly everything is calculated to this effect, I conclude that it was Shakespeare's intention, and that what so hurts me was only a pleasureable excitement to his audience, whose gratification was relied on to lull their criticism. What else can be the meaning of Emilia purloining the kerchief, and then being present at the enquiry concerning it?'
[4] Act iii, sc. iv, 158–61.

Any actress would make it clear if she were worth her salt, since the signposts in the text are plain enough.[1]

Verisimilitude, not exactitude or consistency, is required of dramatists and novelists; for they are artists, not historians. They may fool their public to the top of its bent, on one condition—that the deception is completely successful. But the two arts are different, and means which are available in one are denied to the other. The freedom of the novelist is in many ways far greater than that of the dramatist. As regards consistency, however, he is more restricted: his readers can pause, ponder, and even turn back to check him. In the theatre, on the other hand, especially in Shakespeare's theatre without drop-curtain or act-pauses, the play moves forward from beginning to end and gives the audience no opportunity of examining the coherence of events too curiously. From the very outset of his career Shakespeare took advantage of this freedom, but as time went on and as his sense of mastery of his instrument, the Elizabethan stage, grew upon him, he availed himself of it, I think, more and more boldly—not because he was becoming careless, but quite legitimately in the service of his art, in order to heighten his effects and to increase the volume and complexity of his theatrical orchestration. Vasari writes of Titian:

'His first works were finished with great diligence, and might be looked at near or far, but the last were worked with great patches of colour, so that they cannot be seen near, but at a distance they look perfect. This is the reason that many think they are done without any trouble, but this is not true. And this way of working is most judicious, for it makes the pictures seem living.'[2]

Shakespeare's works must also be looked at and heard 'at a distance', the distance which the theatre provides, if they

[1] For the most thoroughgoing treatment of the so-called defects and inconsistencies of this play the reader may be referred to *Othello: an Historical and Comparative Study*, by Elmer Edgar Stoll: Studies in Language and Literature, University of Minnesota, 1915.

[2] Vasari, *The Lives of the Painters*.

are to be justly appreciated; 'seen near' in the book they may lose their whole perspective.

Nevertheless, despite the blind eye which they turn towards the theatrical conditions of Shakespeare's art, the modern school of Shakespearian critical analysis is doing work which carries us some way towards an understanding, not of Macbeth, Iago, Cleopatra, and Hamlet, but of the craftsmanship which went to the creation of these characters, and deliberately concealed or blurred their motives so as to render them more convincingly human upon the stage. Such analysis is nothing to Shakespeare's purpose; it does not add a whit to our enjoyment or appreciation of the plays themselves. On the contrary, by its exposure of tricks and deceptions, loose threads and gaping flats, inconsistencies and vaguenesses, in a word of the whole seamy side of the dramatist's production, a side he never intended us to see at all, it appears to 'sully all his gloss of former honour' and leave his dramas 'things of shreds and patches'. It appears so, but only to the dull-witted and the faint-hearted. For what it means is that even Shakespeare, at long last, is being brought to the judgement-bar of criticism, must submit like every other poet and artist to the dissecting-table and the scalpel, and will in the end be forced to yield up to our scrutiny the very heart of his mystery. 'Others abide our question; thou art free!' It is no longer true.

But the end is not yet; and before the end is in sight the present generation of critics must themselves submit to judgement—the judgement of the theatre. It is not enough to be a scholar, a poet, or even a modern dramatist to pass verdict upon the craft of Shakespeare. True, there is still much to do in the field of scholarship. Despite the work of men like Mr. W. J. Lawrence, Sir Edmund Chambers, and many others, we are not yet sure about the details of the Elizabethan stage, and until we have mastered the stops of Shakespeare's recorder we cannot hope to command it 'to any utterance of harmony'. As to the original texts, it was only the other day that Professor

Pollard discovered their real significance for us, and it will take another decade of labour by as many students as may be pressed into the field before we can expect even to spell them out to our satisfaction. Then too, there is the whole vast continent, mostly unexplored so far, of the Elizabethan mind, the mind of Shakespeare's audience and of Shakespeare himself, with its alchemical and astrological prepossessions, its demonology and its ghost-lore, its barbarous medicine and its bizarre psychology, to say nothing of its political and topical interests. How much light may be shed upon the plays by a week-to-week account of London gossip while they were being written is being amply demonstrated by Mr. G. B. Harrison.[1] Unless I am very much mistaken, he will succeed in disposing for ever of the myth of the impersonality of Shakespeare's art. He seems already to have discovered an unmistakable contemporary original for the Bastard in *King John*, and as he continues to unroll his film before our eyes we may expect to catch likenesses to other familiar Shakespearian figures. How far astray, on the other hand, scholars may wander in their aesthetic judgement through ignorance of the elements of Elizabethan spiritualism may be shown by recent pronouncements on the ghost-scenes in *Hamlet*.[2] For example, three of the historical critics already mentioned, Professor Schücking, Professor Stoll, and Mr. J. M. Robertson, unite in fastening upon that old crux, Hamlet's reference to

> The undiscovered country from whose bourn
> No traveller returns,

as an illustration of Shakespeare's carelessness, since, they assert, such words are absurd on the lips of one who has himself interviewed the returned spirit of his own father. A little knowledge of Elizabethan ghost-lore would have

[1] v. *An Elizabethan Journal, being a record of those things most talked of during the years* 1591–4, by G. B. Harrison (Constable, 1928)—followed, since the above was written, by a *Second Journal* for the years 1595 to 1598.

[2] v. Introduction to Lewis Lavater's *Of Ghostes and Spirites*, Shakespeare Association, 1929.

shown them that the passage in question is simply an expression of the contemporary Protestant refusal to believe
that apparitions could be the spirits of the departed, and
that it falls in with the despondent mood of the 'To be or
not to be' soliloquy as the most positive utterance of the
doubt which haunts the student of Wittenberg until
the end of the Play-scene and which he voices plainly
enough in the preceding soliloquy when he surmises that
'the spirit that I have seen may be a devil'.[1]

Further, since the universe of man is the creation of
human thought and human imagination, Shakespeare
quite literally lived in a different universe from ourselves.
We inhabit a house founded by Copernicus and roofed in
by Newton; and we are about to quit it for another
designed by Einstein. We are told that the new building
can only be described in mathematical formulae, or that
it is unimaginable. It may be so for us, but it will certainly
not be so for our grandchildren. Language will adjust
itself to the new conceptions, and babies will grow up
understanding the Einsteinian cosmos because they will
assume it from the start. But what is happening in our
own day teaches us to appreciate the gulf that divides us
from Shakespeare. He would find our universe as unimaginable and inexpressible as we find Einstein's. His
very language is Ptolemaic.[2]

Yet when learning has solved these and a hundred
kindred problems, when the last ounce of meaning has been
extracted from the last word of the text, and when the
poetic critic has joined the commentator and laid bare the
secrets of Shakespeare's diction, the nervous system of his

---

[1] The foregoing sentences and what follows on pp. 214–216 below gave
rise to a controversy between Mr. Robertson and myself in *The Criterion*
for Jan. and July 1930.

[2] Physiological notions have likewise completely altered. 'A plague of
sighing and grief! it blows a man up like a bladder' exclaims Falstaff
(1 *Henry IV*, II. iv. 365), and we laugh, without noticing that half the jest
has died with the death of the doctrine, frequently referred to by Shakespeare, that 'sighing and grief' impoverished the blood and so led to
emaciation.

verse and the complete history of his stylistic development, the serious study of his dramatic intentions and effects may still remain untouched. For such study is to be undertaken, not by solitary men poring upon books in their libraries, but by scholar-players in the traffic of a Shakespearian theatre. This living criticism of a living art might be inaugurated to-morrow if we had the courage and the faith to furnish the means. The adventure does not lack its leader. An actor-dramatist of our day, himself a profound Elizabethan scholar, has set himself, like Jacob with the angel, to wrestle lovingly with his fellow actor-dramatist of three hundred years ago, in the hope of forcing him to reveal his secret. I need not tell you that I am speaking of Mr. Granville-Barker. Nor do I need to remind you of those brilliant *Prefaces to Shakespeare*, essays towards the new critical method, in which he has sketched out his ideas on the staging of certain plays. To me, as doubtless to many others here, the preface to *King Lear* in particular came like a fresh revelation. Here is a tragedy, labelled by the literary critics from Charles Lamb onwards as too vague and too terrible for the stage, and now shown by a man of the theatre to be full of situations and dramatic values which pass unnoticed by the reader, because they are only given being in the visible movement and interplay of flesh and blood. Even that ancient stone of stumbling, the blinding of Gloucester, finds its due and fitting place as an inevitable buttress in the mighty structure. A strange paradox, is it not, that we who with Dr. Bridges class this as one of the 'scenes which offend our feelings, so that we cannot endure to see them in representation' never give ourselves the opportunity of putting those feelings to the test ? And thus Shakespeare is condemned, unheard, unseen.

Mr. Granville-Barker should be allowed to prove his case, to demonstrate by stage-production the superiority of the Elizabethan *King Lear*, Shakespeare's *King Lear*, to the dramatic poem which at once astonished and pained Victorian readers. But lacking both theatre and an established company to experiment with, he is obliged to fall back on the pen and the lecturer's desk, and we remain in ignorance of Shakespeare's art, and are for the most part content to remain so. Still, something can be done even by lectures and prefaces. You will not easily forget, I think, the discourse delivered before you in 1925. Let me pick out a passage particularly relevant to my present theme.

'I do not pretend', he said, 'that I have fathomed Shakespeare's secret; my contention is that it has not been fathomed yet, and that it cannot be given to the world by such means as we have now at hand. The scholar, at best, will be in the case of a man reading the score of a symphony, humming the themes. He may study and re-study a play, and ever find something new. . . .' Yet, 'who will not confess with me that at any performance some quite unsuspected effect (unsuspected often by the interpreters themselves) may suddenly glow into life before him ?'[1]

'A man reading the score of a symphony, humming the themes!' If Mr. Granville-Barker with all his theatrical experience and his incomparable theatrical sense thinks of himself in such terms as he ponders over Shakespeare at his desk, how parlous must be the condition of us literary interpreters, with no practical knowledge of the stage and too often unconscious that the stage has any bearing at all upon the problems we discuss. When the New Globe is built—it is bound to come—and the King's Men—King Shakespeare's this time, not King James's—get to work, their purpose will be of course to perform the plays as they ought to be performed. But first they will study much and experiment often, because no one yet knows how Shakespeare 'ought to be performed'. Their primary task, in short, will be the discovery of Shakespeare's technique. Now in the course of this discovery they will also be led to consider those contradictions, inconsistencies, and loose ends, which modern criticism is so busy with. It is my belief that they will not only find most of them disappearing in the true stage-perspective, but even that a

[1] Cf. above, pp. 81–2.

large proportion, as I have suggested already, so far from being defects, were deliberately employed by the master-craftsman as means of dramatic grace. In this connexion it may occur perhaps to some antiquarian among them—the librarian of the theatre, shall we say?—that writers on Shakespeare during the first quarter of the twentieth century were much occupied with matters of this kind. If he turns us up, how much will he find of our theorizing and discussion that is relevant to the purpose of his company? How many halfpence worth of daily bread for the player to this intolerable deal of literary sack, of German, American, and English vintage, which has so blown up the Shakespeare of our day that he appears to be bursting at the seams? Truly a judgement awaits the present generation of those who sit in judgement on the Man of the Theatre—the judgement of the theatre itself. It is a chastening reflection, which sometimes troubles me in the watches of the night!

Even now, on our picture stage and in our commercialized playhouse, we may occasionally be lucky enough to check or correct the deductions of the academic theorist, if we observe performances of Shakespeare closely. And sometimes a blunder on the part of the producer will actually expose a bookman's fallacy. I have come across at least one amusing instance of this, which may be quoted as a 'cautionary tale'. Mr. Granville-Barker is scathing on the subject of Shakespeare in modern dress, but for my own poor part I found Sir Barry Jackson's *Hamlet* at the Kingsway a few years ago so instructive on the play I happen to know best that I went four times and learnt more on each successive occasion. The Birmingham Repertory Company possess one shining virtue which most other modern companies lack. They play as a team, and the quality of the acting is not proportioned to the size of the part. Moreover, Mr. Poel has taught them that the traditional act-pauses are devoid of Shakespearian authority and may be treated with a high hand. But the modern dinner-hour cannot, alas, be so treated by any manager with the smallest regard for his box-office, so that the *Hamlet* was cut, in places pretty drastically. One of the scenes thus sacrificed was that at the beginning of Act II in which Polonius dispatches his man Reynaldo to Paris with instructions to spy upon Laertes. It is not a complete scene, since, as you will recollect, Ophelia's account of Hamlet's invasion of her closet follows immediately; but it is readily excised and its riddance saves seventy-two lines. Moreover, in making this cut the Birmingham players were well in line with the latest findings of Shakespearian scholarship, inasmuch as Mr. J. M. Robertson has classed the episode among 'superfluous' and 'irrelevant scenes' and declared that it 'clearly derives somehow from a pre-Shakespearian source'. Indeed he continues, 'as our play now stands, the only conceivable motive for the Reynaldo scene is the theatrical need for comic relief after the tremendous Ghost scene'.[1] Yet by following Mr. Robertson (consciously or unconsciously), Sir Barry Jackson's producer succeeded in confuting him and entirely vindicating Shakespeare. For omit the Reynaldo episode in the theatre, and it is seen to be absolutely vital to the whole structure of the play. The effect at the Kingsway was that Hamlet rushed straight from the interview with his father's spirit to the interview with Ophelia; and her description of him,

> Pale as his shirt, his knees knocking each other,
> And with a look so piteous in purport
> As if he had been loosèd out of hell
> To speak of horrors,

only confirmed the impression. Thus Hamlet's behaviour to Ophelia at this juncture was provided with an excuse for which there is no warrant in Shakespeare, the two months' interval vanished into air, and the sense of delay was weakened to such an extent that it was difficult to understand what Hamlet's self-reproaches concerning his procrastination were about. My friend Mr. Robertson will, I hope, forgive me for employing a slip on his part to

[1] J. M. Robertson, *The Problem of Hamlet*, 1919, pp. 57–8.

illustrate the general thesis that we literary critics run great risks in passing judgements on Shakespeare which involve questions of theatrical values. I fear I have myself made many slips as bad or worse; and though I shall continue to live dangerously, I cling, like a shipwrecked sailor on a raft, to memories of experience as a producer of amateur Shakespearian performances, and strive to keep those memories green by as frequent visits to theatres playing Shakespeare as a busy man can find time for. And however wooden the company or slipshod the production, I never come away without fresh light, new hints.

Yet the theatre, even the ideal theatre of our dreams, cannot claim a monopoly of Shakespeare. He had passed beyond the charmed circle of the art he served, and those disgracefully printed little quartos of his plays which he himself took no interest in and probably utterly despised have proved the first-fruits of a line of printed texts which, as far as eye can see, will stretch out till the crack o' doom. And so the reader has his rights in Shakespeare as well as the actor and the spectator, rights too which must be respected. It has been the burden of this lecture that these rights, at any rate since the time of Coleridge, have been overmuch respected, to the contempt of Shakespeare's craft and the misapprehension of his purposes. But 'the whirligig of time brings in his revenges', and there are signs in some quarters of an arrogance which, if it got its own way, would imprison the man of the theatre within the walls of the theatre and deny the laity access to the sacred text except as interpreted by the ministration of the stage. At all such talk of hierophantic exclusiveness an editor can afford to smile, for his function is to make Shakespeare available to readers, and he knows that readers will always outnumber spectators by more than ten to one. But he cannot afford to quarrel with the theatre, for he knows too that once cut the connexion there and the springs of his truest inspiration are dried up. Most of all does he need the freshening influence of the living art of the play-house in the most thankless, the most dangerous, the almost impossible part of his task, the framing of stage-directions. Editorial stage-directions will always evoke the laughter of the actor and will never completely satisfy the judgement of the scholar. Yet no editor can avoid the responsibility; he must either compose them himself or endorse those of his predecessors by reproducing them. Stage-directions of some kind are essential if a dramatic text is to be intelligible, while to make it easy to read, as Mr. Shaw has demonstrated, some degree of elaboration is required. And of all the reader's rights in Shakespeare, the greatest, after that of being presented with a true text, is the right of easy access.

After nine years of mining operations in the text of Shakespeare it is a relief to an editorial 'pioner' to emerge from the cellarage for an afternoon and exercise his lungs— 'lungs faintly powdered with coal-dust' as one critic has been good enough to describe them—by blowing his horn a little on the battlements. But Dr. Jekyll the editor has now had his outing, and it is time for Mr. Hyde the professor of pedagogy to take up the tale. I might have suppressed him altogether, were it not that with an ex-president of the Board of Education in the Chair[1] he refused to keep silence and were it not too that he claimed to be specially briefed in respect of the second of the two charges against Shakespeare I am asking you to consider. Certainly there can be no doubt that in the essay already referred to, Dr. Bridges was primarily addressing those whose business lies with the care and instruction of the young, and that, profoundly as he reverences Shakespeare, he is gravely concerned at the prospect of his plays becoming the basis of our national English culture, as they inevitably must become with the growing neglect of the Bible at home and the Classics at school. For though his pamphlet is mostly taken up with dramatic points similar to those above discussed, they are only brought forward as illustrations of his main thesis, that the influence of the barbarous Elizabethan audience led Shakespeare to deface

[1] Dr. H. A. L. Fisher, President of the British Academy.

his plays not merely by flaws of character and construction but also by moral improprieties which are offensive to modern taste and contaminating to youthful minds. And the purpose with which he set out is made clear in the 'practical corollary' with which he concludes, namely

'that Shakespeare should not be put into the hands of the young without the warning that the foolish things in his plays were written to please the foolish, the filthy for the filthy, and the brutal for the brutal; and that, if out of veneration for his genius we are led to admire or even tolerate such things, we may be thereby not conforming ourselves to him, but only degrading ourselves to the level of his audience, and learning contamination from those wretched beings who can never be forgiven their share in preventing the greatest poet and dramatist of the world from being the best artist'.

Here is a challenge indeed! Here is matter, and to spare, for a dozen lectures! More than half-way through one I have only time to take up a single issue, an issue closely allied with that theme which has hitherto occupied us this afternoon, and also, as we shall discover, not unrelated to education.

Let me broach it with a question. What kind of a Shakespeare is this that Dr. Bridges asks us to commend to the young? Phrases like 'veneration for his genius', 'conforming ourselves to him', 'the greatest poet and dramatist of the world' are hints enough that he subscribes without question to what may be called the Victorian conception of Shakespeare. And in this matter we are most of us still Victorian. When we think of Shakespeare, we tend to think of him in the last two acts of his career—acts in which, as Mr. Lytton Strachey has reminded us, we have carefully suppressed certain scenes which mar the symmetry of the picture. We think of him in the period of *Lear*, *Othello*, and *The Tempest* as a great tragic poet, facing the vastidity of the universe, wrestling with the problems of evil and disaster—a man of brooding temper, of lofty thought, of grave demeanour, and, after passing through the fire, of joyful serenity of temper. In a word, we think of him as a kind of Prospero, swaying a whole world of imagination by the aid of his attendant genius, and banishing all the Caliban elements of human nature to a rockbound dungeon beneath his cell. It is a pretty notion; but it minimizes the greatness of his achievement, ignores the miracle of his development, and in paying him semi-divine honours does him grievous wrong as a man. Dr. Johnson said of Isaac Watts: 'For children he condescended to lay aside the scholar, the philosopher, and the wit, to write little poems of devotion and systems of instruction adapted to their wants and capacities.' The Victorian Shakespeare also condescends to lay aside the philosopher, but not for the purposes of devotion and instruction. No: he stoops from the heights of his serene omniscience to tickle the palate of a degraded audience, to pander to the taste of Caliban himself with dish after dish made savoury with the spice of 'the foolish, the filthy, and the brutal'. And if we ask why, the answer must be, to get his living, to make money, to purchase New Place, a coat of arms and other trappings of gentility, since if we are to believe Sidney Lee—'his literary attainments and successes were chiefly valued as serving the prosaic end of making a permanent provision for himself and his daughters'.[1]

Now if this be a true account of the author of the plays, then I for one am frankly a Baconian. For the eyes that peep through the mask of this fawning philosopher and Olympian cynic can surely be no other than those of the sagest and most cold-hearted of Lord Chancellors. But it is not true. I deny it, not because I do not wish it to be true, or because I shudder to think of the young 'conforming themselves' to such an ideal, but simply because it does not fit the facts. Or rather it represents a hybrid monster begotten of an honest though ill-considered attempt to reconcile the Victorian conception of Shakespeare with certain facts which the Victorians overlooked or found it convenient to ignore. Modern criticism, from Coleridge to

[1] Sidney Lee, *Life of Shakespeare*, p. 503.

Dr. Andrew Bradley, has been mainly occupied with the tragedies; the comedies have been comparatively neglected and in consequence, as I have said, we have tended to look at Shakespeare through the tragic end of the biographical telescope. But the comedies came first; the Shakespeare of *King Lear* and *The Tempest* grew out of the Shakespeare who gave us Berowne and the Bastard, Juliet's Nurse and Mistress Quickly, the clowns Lance and Lancelot, Sir Toby Belch and Sir John Falstaff, to name only a few of the greatest rout of unseemly disreputables that ever teemed from a dramatist's brain. Were these characters created merely 'to please the foolish, the filthy, and the brutal ?' The question answers itself. They are immortal, because of their amazing vitality; and their vitality is an indisputable testimony to the enormous satisfaction that went to their making. To attack the 'wretched' Elizabethans for degrading Shakespeare is to attack the Elizabethan Shakespeare for not living up to Victorian standards. And when I say 'the Elizabethan Shakespeare' I am now speaking by the history-book; the Jacobean Shakespeare became not more respectable but more serious.

During the quarter of an hour or so that remains, will you allow me to stress one or two well-known facts about this Elizabethan Shakespeare which have, I think, been too little regarded ? He steps into the limelight of history with a flattering, not to say deferential, testimonial from a fellow-writer and fellow-dramatist. The dying Greene had attacked him in the famous passage on 'the upstart crow', and Henry Chettle, who edited the pamphlet containing this passage, felt himself bound, in a book published a few months later, to offer a public apology. 'I am as sorry', he writes, 'as if the original fault had been my fault, because myself have seen his demeanour no less civil than he excellent in the quality he professes, besides divers of worship have reported his uprightness of dealing, which argues his honesty, and his facetious grace in writing that approves his art.' The words were printed in December 1592, and they prove not only that Shakespeare was already recognized as 'honest and of an open and free nature', to quote another testimonial found among Ben Jonson's papers after his death forty-five years later,[1] but that he had also made a name in influential circles as a writer of comedy. Indeed 'facetious grace' most happily describes those qualities in Shakespeare's early plays which would especially appeal to the cultured men of high rank, who, as Chettle hints, were interesting themselves in the rising dramatist's fortunes. We have not, I think, allowed sufficiently for the presence of such men in Shakespeare's audience. Certainly he wrote with his eye particularly upon them, for as he tells us in *Hamlet*, in his opinion their 'censure' must 'o'erweigh a whole theatre of others'. Nor is it difficult to guess from the fare which he provided that these noble patrons were young. Play after play at this period contains its party of dashing young bucks. They are come abroad to see the great world in *The Two Gentlemen of Verona*, *The Comedy of Errors*, and *The Taming of the Shrew*. They seek to combine this with university studies in the last named, or they found a little 'academe' of their own in *Love's Labour's Lost*. Or yet again, as in *The Merchant of Venice, Romeo and Juliet*, and *Much Ado about Nothing*, they are just men of the town or gentlemen about the court, revelling and roistering and chaffing each other. Almost always too, like young men of whatever rank or whatever period, they hunt in threes. Mercutio, Romeo, and Benvolio; Berowne, Longaville, and Dumain; Antonio, Bassanio, and Gratiano; Petruchio, Lucentio, and Tranio— so persistent is the triangle that it is hard to resist a suspicion that the same triangle existed among the 'divers of worship' for whose eyes the dramas were primarily written.

On the other hand, such groupings are highly convenient dramatically, since they provide dialogue, and I need not remind you how large a proportion of the dialogue in Shakespearian comedy is taken up with young-mannish

---

[1] The striking similarity between Chettle's tribute and Jonson's is noted by Dr. A. C. Bradley, v. *Oxford Lectures on Poetry*, p. 317.

conversation. These students, courtiers, or inns-of-court men—always thoroughly English and of London, whatever be the name of the Italian city to which they ostensibly belong—chat together, or with their servants, worrying the language and getting entangled in it, like puppies with a ball of string. They quibble and jest, endlessly and untiringly, while their jesting, after the manner of undergraduates, is frank and unseemly. They skirt philosophy, write poems and read them aloud, and above all discuss love, discuss it lightly, sometimes cynically, often indecorously. For the atmosphere is essentially a bachelor one, and the general attitude towards the great enemy of that state is best expressed in the words of the serving-man in *The Two Gentlemen of Verona*: 'Though the chameleon Love can feed on air, I am one that is nourished by my victuals and would fain have meat' (ii. i. 178).

As a precipitate for this atmosphere, and as whetstones for these blades, Shakespeare introduces his 'mocking wenches'—a type which he invented and reproduced with variations in one play after another. And there can be no doubt that his 'facetious grace' appeared most brilliant to his contemporaries in the 'sets of wit well played' between the young bachelors and these sprightly women-folk. *Love's Labour's Lost* is richest in this dialogue, is indeed little more than a succession of such 'sets of wit'; but it is to be found, of course, in many other plays. Petruchio and Katherine, for instance, carry on an elaborate duel of the kind at their first encounter, while with Benedick and Beatrice the steel is at the brightest and the thrust and parry at the swiftest. Skirmishes of this sort are more exciting than mere 'volleys of words' shot off by the men among themselves, since the element of sex gives a sense of danger to the fencing; the buttons are off the foils, a slip and one or other may be wounded—to the heart. It pleased Shakespeare to underline this peril, so to speak, by steeping his dialogue in *double entendre*. The conversation is not coarse, as it often is between the men, but it is frequently highly indelicate, though the equivocal sense is generally so obscure as to escape the casual modern reader entirely, and must sometimes also have escaped all but the keenest witted amongst the judicious in the original audience.

And as with the early comedies, so in a slightly different way with the poems, which also belong to this period. *Venus and Adonis*, which was authorized for publication, remarkably enough, 'under the hands of the Archbishop of Canterbury', was clearly aimed at the young, and the six editions of it that appeared between 1592 and 1602 show that it hit its mark. 'Affluent in beautiful imagery and metrical sweetness,' writes the standard biographer of Shakespeare, 'it is imbued with a juvenile tone of licence, which harmonizes with its pretension of youthful origin'.[1] The theme of *Lucrece* is graver and the treatment more mature, while one or two of the Sonnets express some of Shakespeare's deepest thoughts on life; but the general tone of all these poems is the same as that of *Venus and Adonis*; they were written in the same mood and addressed to the same public.

The Elizabethan Shakespeare was, then, not an Olympian pandering to a barbarous audience; he was a light-hearted dramatic poet in his early thirties who succeeded in securing what all poets of that age strove to secure, namely the admiring patronage of a powerful circle of cultivated noblemen at Court. For them he wrote his poems, and chiefly for them too, as I believe, he wrote his comedies and histories. And though he wrote to please, he did so to please himself quite as much as his patrons, for he admired them as much as they admired him. Their tastes were his own, and the mutual admiration sprang from 'the marriage of true minds'.

What then—to return to Dr. Bridges's corollary—are we to say about Shakespeare when we place his works in the hands of the young? I am not thinking, and I do not suppose Dr. Bridges was thinking, of children, who read their selected plays in school editions and ask no questions

[1] Sidney Lee, *Life of Shakespeare*, p. 143.

about the author. I have in mind boys and girls in upper sixth forms at school, or of college age, of the age of Southampton when Shakespeare wrote *Venus and Adonis* for his delight. Well, if we elders are to say anything at all, let us at least tell the truth and the whole truth. We must make it clear, for a beginning, that poetic and dramatic genius has no necessary connexion with moral propriety at all, and that Shakespeare right up to the end of his life was never a very decorous person. But we must explain, on the other hand, that moral sanity and moral propriety are two utterly different things and that few men have ever lived possessing more moral sanity than Shakespeare. Thus he whose laugh is 'broad as ten thousand beeves at pasture' spreads no contamination, and though, to quote Dr. Johnson once again, 'so much more ready to please than to instruct that he seems to write without any moral purpose', has yet become one of the greatest moral forces of the world.

And if the young people protest that this paradox is too hard for them, let Shakespeare be allowed to speak for himself. Let him speak through the play which above all others belongs to the young, his *Romeo and Juliet*. Written at the height of his Elizabethan gaiety, this tragic tale of star-crossed lovers is shot with comic colour and rich in comic characters, among whom Mercutio and the Nurse stand out pre-eminent. By what right have these reprobates thrust themselves into so tender, so sublime a drama of young love ? The answer is that they are the two pillars which support the whole dramatic structure. For the lovers, in the great scenes where they are together, scenes more like opera than drama, chant their passion to each other in immortal verse but tell us little about themselves. Yet somehow Shakespeare must convince us of their reality, must assure us that they are creatures of flesh and blood. He does so by placing characters of the utmost vivacity at their side—the Nurse beside Juliet and Mercutio beside Romeo. Furthermore, both Mercutio and the Nurse are coarse and harp upon the physical basis of love. He is full of the bawdy talk that hot-blooded young men affect; and she prattles after the manner of old peasant women. Is not Shakespeare stooping to tickle the palate of 'those wretched beings' his audience? Are not such passages just 'sallets to make the matter savoury',[1] outrageous excrescences upon the greatest of modern love-poems? On the contrary, they are as essential to the tone of the play as the characters which speak them are to the play's structure. Once again the magician is assuring us of reality. He is proving that the marvellous blossom of love which forms the main theme of the story is not a mere poet's dream, a pleasing fancy, but a piece of real life rooted deep in the crude common soil of human nature, the nature we all know so well, too well. He is persuading young readers or spectators, boys and girls of all types, that the passion of Mercutio's bosom friend for a mistress suckled at the Nurse's breast is a passion possible for themselves; and by making such splendour seem possible he is adding meaning and sanctification to their own little loves. It is just because Shakespeare conceals nothing and condemns nothing—because he is so utterly unlike a school-master or a preacher or a professor—that the young feel safe with him. And having gained their confidence he may lead them where he will, to endure the purging fires of *Macbeth* and *Othello*, to share the crucifixion and redemption of Lear, to win through to the haven of atonement and forgiveness in the enchanted island.

For as the virility of Mercutio helps us to accept the raptures of Romeo, so the Elizabethan Shakespeare gives guarantee for the Jacobean. The passage from Falstaff to Hamlet, from *Venus and Adonis* to *King Lear*, is a passage from one world to another; yet we are with the same Shakespeare in both. He has grown—grown out of all

---

[1] Dr. Bridges takes these words of Hamlet as 'a confession' by Shakespeare 'that he had himself deliberately played false to his own artistic ideals for the sake of gratifying his audience'. Until we know a good deal more about the Aeneas speech than we are ever likely to know it is surely risky, to say the least of it, to found arguments upon it.

knowledge, as the saying is—but he has not recanted or denied one whit of his former self. And so we trust him as we trust no other writer. For he has proved himself one of us, has shown that however foolish or brutal or filthy we may be, he understands us and claims us as his brothers. Thus too, when he confronts us with the deepest and gravest problems of life and death, we know that he will deal fairly, neither beguiling our eyes with false hopes nor blinding them with the mists of despair.

But on May Day, the festival of youth and fecundity, I would not leave you thinking of the grappler with problems, or even of the healer and reconciler. Rather I would remind you once more of that teeming comic imagination, that inexhaustible spring of geniality and fun, that prodigality of enchanting word-music, that tender and humorous observance of human frailty, that irresistible gusto and delight in every manifestation of life, which go to make up what I have called the Elizabethan Shakespeare. I have dwelt at some length on one aspect of his work because it seemed to me that the time had come to be honest about it. But that is only a small element of the whole, an occasional eddy as it were on the racing leaping torrent of virility which beats like a tide of pulsing blood through the great comedies. To give a picture of the complete Shakespeare at this period of his development would be impossible. I have essayed a hint or two, nothing more. Let me borrow another from himself and end with that piece of unconscious self-portraiture which he gives in the description of his Antony:

His voice was propertied
As all the tunéd spheres, and that to friends.
... For his bounty,
There was no winter in't; an autumn 'twas
That grew the more by reaping: his delights
Were dolphin-like; they showed his back above
The element they lived in: in his livery
Walked crowns and crownets; realms and islands were
As plates dropped from his pocket!

A PLEA FOR THE LIBERTY OF INTERPRETING[1]

By LASCELLES ABERCROMBIE

I NEED not remind this audience of the several revolutions that have occurred in the history of Shakespearian criticism; and I suppose it will be admitted that they have not yet brought us to anything like stability. The Romantics were fond of asserting the infinite in Shakespeare: certainly there seems no end to the criticism of him. But perhaps the endlessness of Shakespearian criticism is like the endlessness of Einstein's space—you keep on going round and round. Lately, as every one knows, the tendency has been to discredit that boundless liberty of interpretation which the Romantics claimed. We mistrust nowadays what one of the most eminent of our scientific critics has called 'mere connoisseurship'; we prefer to rely, for our interpretation of Shakespeare, on patient and exact understanding of his conditions—the conditions under which he worked, and the conditions under which his work has been preserved to us. Instead of soaring into the Empyrean, we attend to the theatre and the printing-house. Nevertheless, I have sometimes thought I could detect signs that the process of Shakespearian criticism is once more on the turn: we may perhaps have come to the beginning of another revolution, which will land us once more where the Romantics stood. Not in their posture; I suggest no return to romantic adoration of the miraculous poet and the infinite genius: such conceptions belong to the nature of romanticism, not to the criticism of Shakespeare. No: it is not to romanticism, but to the ground on which the romantic attitude to

[1] First delivered 1930, this lecture is reprinted as originally published in 1930.

Shakespeare stood, that I look for the next revolution to take us. And that, I submit, is safe ground: safer, I believe, than the ground we stand on now. For, however romanticism may have rolled its eyes and rhapsodized, it did at any rate stand on this: that Shakespeare is to be regarded, first and foremost, as an artist, and his compositions as works of art. But, instead of prophesying, I had better plead; since, after all, the movements of criticism are, to some extent at least, in the power of the critics, and this is eminently an occasion on which one may appeal to the critics. Humbly then, but with a due sense of the privilege this occasion gives me, I put my plea for a return to that liberty of interpreting which must follow when Shakespeare is considered primarily as an artist. I will proceed, first by meeting some particular objections to that way of considering him, then by attempting a general view of what is involved in such a consideration.

Do not suppose I am unaware of the dangers of 'mere connoisseurship', which means, no doubt, purely aesthetic criticism. They are the dangers of ungoverned subjectivism. A critic, let us say, dislikes the sort of person Shakespeare drew in his character of Henry V. The critic is a pacifist, a Little-Englander, a detester of that militant patriotism which finds it easier to attack than to create. Accordingly, the critic proceeds to show with what subtlety and refinement of irony Shakespeare holds up Henry V to reprobation. This, of course, will not do; but it is a very old mistake to put down liberty because it is sometimes confused with licence.

Do not suppose, either, that I am suggesting we should abandon what we have gained during the ascendancy of scientific criticism. We have gained invaluable things, and there is no reason in the world why we should not take them with us and make all possible use of them. As a matter of fact, scientific criticism itself took over several things from romanticism—not always to its advantage. Nor must it be thought that I am accusing science of indifference to art. It was no doubt an inevitable revolution, it was certainly a salutary one, that brought us to prefer a few small facts, solid and verifiable, to noble gestures of enthusiasm, which might tell us a great deal about the performer, but very little about Shakespeare. A sense of beauty need not always express itself in a rapture, and there is nothing incompatible between digging for facts and enjoying poetry. But there is one capital kind of mistake to which scientific, or realistic, criticism seems peculiarly liable. It is to suppose that when you have accounted for the conditions under which an artist worked, you have thereby accounted for the artist. An aesthetic critic greatly admires some remarkable stroke of art: 'admire it as much as you like', says the realist, 'but what you call a stroke of art was simply dictated by perfectly explicable conditions'. The conditions may indeed be explicable, but conditions do not explain an artist. To understand the means which an artist used is not in itself to understand the effect he got out of them; to think that it is so, is not only to ignore the artist—it may also be, what is much worse, to discredit and belittle the effect. There is a good instance of this in G. H. Lewes's *Life of Goethe*. Lewes is comparing Goethe's Prometheus with Aeschylus', and very unwisely does so by decrying the latter. Aeschylus, you will remember, begins his characterization of Prometheus in an extraordinarily impressive way. Lewes himself shall describe it: 'Aeschylus has in the first scene made him imperturbably silent, disdaining to answer the taunts of Power and the pity of Vulcan, as they bind him to the rock. These draw from him no groan, no word, no gesture; he has no defiance for the one, nor friendly gratitude for the other. It is not until he is left alone that he appeals to Earth, Air, and Ocean. This silence, followed by this passion, produces a sublime effect. 'But', says Lewes, with the air of a man going on to make his deadly point, 'but the sublimity was *not* the poet's intention. It was an accidental effect'; and he points out that at this period 'more than two speakers were never together on the stage'; consequently, at the opening of the play, Prometheus '*must* be silent, for there is no one to speak for him'. Thus this 'sublime effect' is not to be included in the character which Aeschylus *intended*.

What is the answer to this ingenious realism? A very simple one: it is the business of an artist to accept the conditions under which he works and *use* them for his own purposes. Just that is what Aeschylus did here: by means of the conditions imposed on him, he produced a tremendous effect, entirely to his purpose; that is to say, it is entirely in accordance with the rest of the play, and contributes something essential to the understanding of the whole. But Lewes, finding he can explain the conditions, thinks he has thereby explained the art and disposed of its effect; and he naturally proceeds to a hopeless misinterpretation of the whole play, having decided to dismiss the crucial thing as something accidental and unintentional.

It must be admitted, I think, that we have had something like this in the interpretation of Shakespeare during the reign of scientific or realistic criticism. And it must surely be admited, too, that the person who is dealing with certainties in this business is not the realist but the aesthetic critic. For the one thing certain in a work of art is the effect it has on us. Even Lewes acknowledged that the effect he dismissed *is* sublime; he dismissed it, because he supposed it was not intended. But *judge by results* is the grand principle of aesthetic criticism. The vice of realism —of the interpretation based on the scientific study of conditions—is its noticeable tendency to substitute for that principle some attempt to *judge by intentions*, as if knowledge of the conditions could confer any right to say what was intended. The conditions may be ascertainable fact; but to proceed from them to intentions is to take a blind jump into pure theory. You can never be sure what the intentions of an artist were, whereas you always know what he actually did. And if aesthetic criticism is to take over the invaluable things our scientific criticism has gained for us, it will not be to let *judgement by results*, which are

unmistakable, give way to *judgement by intentions*, which
can only be speculations, often very vain and impertinent;
it will simply be to sharpen and intensify our *judgements by
results* by our understanding of the means used to obtain
them.

After these preliminaries, the first thing I have to do is
to meet some typical objections which realistic criticism,
moved by the sort of animus I illustrated just now in G. H.
Lewes, has to offer to the purely aesthetic interpretation
of Shakespeare, and to the liberty such an interpretation
involves. I need not stay long over the most general and,
if it could be made out, the most radical of them all: the
objection, namely, that Shakespeare could not have been
an artist, because he was just a professional man who had
learnt the trade of supplying the actors with plays that
would go well on the stage and make money. This is
radical enough, but it is not an objection at all; it is radical
only in being a radical misconception. It is worth while
mentioning it, however, because in various disguises it
does occasionally crop up in connexion with particular
points. Of course, Shakespeare was a professional man;
only, he was a professional artist. Dislike the fact as you
will, make of it all the psychological mystery you can, it
is nevertheless the fact that an artist can quite well make
a business of his art. Economic pressure and the pressure
of artistic inspiration need not be alternatives; a man may
work under both kinds of pressure at once. Michelangelo
did; Titian did; why not Shakespeare? An artist must eat
his dinner; it is not the only thing in which he resembles
Caliban. If it happens that he must earn his dinner,
and can do so by his art, be sure he will. Michelangelo
and Titian found patrons who would pay for their art:
so did Shakespeare. It is true that his payment came
to him less directly; namely, as a 'sharer' in a company
whose prosperity depended in part on the success of the
plays he wrote for it; but it is precisely under such conditions that the pressure of inspiration could most easily work
in with economic pressure.

Sane realism, however, does not go in for these swashing blows; it does not put its objections in anything like so radical and general a fashion. Yet it does sometimes look with suspicion on Shakespeare's obvious care that his plays should succeed. But what does *success* here mean ? It means *pleasing the audience*; and did any dramatist ever wish *not* to please his audience ? Did Ibsen, the greatest, the most scrupulous dramatic artist of recent times ? He may not have always managed it; but since he knew his business, in the end he did: he had made a strange mistake in his vocation, if he could not have done so. Is it to Shakespeare's discredit that, as far as we can tell, he began by pleasing his audience and, on the whole, went on as he had begun ? The truth is, that this stage success, this pleasing of the audience, is one of the conditions of his art which a dramatist must accept, and use—use to his own ends. It is not even a condition peculiar to dramatic art; in some kind or degree, it is a condition of any art whatsoever. Certainly, a dramatist indifferent to his audience is a contradiction in terms.

But still, says the realist, this is surely not the end of the matter. The whole thing is, *how* does he please his audience ? and *what* audience does he please ? Shakespeare was an artist, no question; but not wholly an artist; is he not also very often the mere tradesman of the theatre ? When he is amusing wits and groundlings with his classical allusions, his conceited logic-chopping, his plays on words, his obscenities, is he an artist then ?

The point we are considering is not whether these things are good or bad, but whether they can accord with the conscience of an artist; and that, I am afraid, depends simply on whether the artist himself liked them or not. Plainly, no one has any right at all to suppose that Shakespeare ever invited his audience to enjoy anything he did not enjoy himself; and since that is so, all this kind of objection is nothing. Tastes change; but it does not need much knowledge or sympathy to see how it might be quite as much to please himself as to flatter his audience, that

Shakespeare made Suffolk face his death with this roll of
rodomontade in his mouth:

> Great men oft die by vile bezonians:
> A Roman sworder and banditto slave
> Murder'd sweet Tully; Brutus' bastard hand
> Stabb'd Julius Caesar; savage islanders
> Pompey the Great; and Suffolk dies by pirates.

Does that seem nowadays the language for a man to die in?
Perhaps not, but it is exactly how an Elizabethan noble
would like to die in such a case: the speech is the very
quintessence of the culture and ethic of the time's
aristocracy. And all Shakespeare's classical allusions, even
the most incongruous of them, can be put on a similar
footing to this. The kind of pleasure they could give to
Shakespeare and his audience has gone past us; but that
gives us no right to say it was not so artistically intended
as the pleasure that has proved perennial. So with the
other things: the ingenious obscenity, for instance; though
to be frank, it is not Shakespeare who shocks me here so
much as the critics who are not amused. As for the things
that really are shocking, the frigid conceits and chop-logic
in the midst of emotional crises, we can of course refer
them to the taste of the time; but that must not exclude
Shakespeare's own taste, as if he was giving his audience
something he knew was beneath him: any more than when
Bellini perpetrates the intolerable conceit of making a
slaughtered martyr write with his finger, in his own
streaming blood, the word 'credo' on the floor, we can
assume he was pleasing his patrons rather than himself.

But perhaps Shakespeare made too much money? Well,
once allow an artist to make any at all, and I see not where
the limit is to be put. What has it got to do with the
status of anything as a work of art, whether it made money
or not, or how much it made? I have heard that Herr
Richard Strauss has been blamed, in some inconsequent
fashion, for making too much money out of his music; but
I never heard that his music was said not to be art *because*
it made him a fortune. It is surely time we dropped all

this knowing talk about 'Shakespeare the business-man'; it has nothing whatever to do with anything that can conceivably concern criticism.

'But still', says the realist, 'there is the question of his retirement: does that not make it look as if money was the incentive? For when he had made enough money, he simply dropped what you call his art, and withdrew to live at his ease in Stratford'. Judging from his signature, however, it might just as well be that he retired because he had become a nervous wreck. But in fact we know nothing whatever about it. He certainly retired; so did Rossini, just as enigmatically: does that throw any doubt on Rossini's career as an artist? All we know about Shakespeare is, in substance, this: he left Stratford, wrote plays, made money, and went back to Stratford. Seeing what those plays are, is it not the obvious thing to suppose, that what this represents is just the career of an artist—that, whatever might be the reason for his retirement, he left Stratford because he wanted to write plays, and managed to make his life the fulfilment of his artistic ambition? No one, I believe, would ever have thought of anything else, had it not been for the Romantics. For we touch here one of the things which realism has unconsciously taken over from romanticism, and oddly perverted: the tendency to make Shakespeare altogether exceptional, not to be understood as other men may be understood. If it had been anybody else, what we know of Shakespeare would have fallen naturally and inevitably into the obvious explanation: a young man in the provinces has poetic ambitions, and goes up to the capital to see what he can make of them. This, in fact, as we find in Aubrey, who had excellent information to draw on, was the explanation that actually was given, before the miracle-mongering began. But to the Romantics, Shakespeare was a preternatural genius, or, if you like, one to whom nature had given everything and culture nothing; by some divine accident he dropped into the theatre, and carelessly took the scope for his genius he found there, without in the least realizing the miracle that was happening. Absurd, of course; but just as absurd, to suppose that the man from Stratford went into the theatre to make money, and wrote the plays he did write. That way Bacon lies—nay, Oxford!

No: he went into the theatre because he wanted to write plays—*his own* plays; he knew the conditions of his art and how to use them; he knew how to please his audience by writing what he wanted to write; and thus he paid his way. *Entia non sunt multiplicanda.* But that is not only the simplest explanation, it is the only explanation that fits the facts, so far as we can tell them. *Henry VI*, a colossal success, is followed by *Richard III*: a huge success again; but look at the difference, the immense artistic difference, between them. He is not content, as the business man in the theatre would have been, to repeat his success; he goes on to something prodigiously better, an extraordinary advance in art, but—he carries his audience with him. And so all through his career. I do not believe it possible to arrange the plays in a rigid and precise chronological series; for the probability is—and until it is disproved it makes any such series to a great extent illusory —the strong probability is, on the analogy of other artists whose output was anything like comparable, such as Beethoven or Goethe or Michelangelo, that Shakespeare often had several things on hand at the same time. But no doubt a general chronology can be established in which we can feel reasonably secure: and the most striking thing about it is the continual advance it shows in the scope and subtlety and elaboration of dramatic art. It might be difficult to make out that the later plays are absolutely *better* than some of those which plainly belong to early or middle stages of his career; it is hard to see how anything could be absolutely better than *A Midsummer-Night's Dream*. It might be difficult to argue that Beethoven's last quartettes are *better* than the lovely Rasumofski set; but they are certainly an immense advance in their art. Just so Shakespeare is not content with perfection of achievement at any stage of his career; he must always go

on to a stage beyond. After *A Midsummer-Night's Dream*
comes *Twelfth Night*; and after *Twelfth Night*, *The Tempest*—each perfection in its kind, but each kind an astounding advance in art. I shall have some more to say shortly
about this progress; for the moment, look only at the way
he exploited popular sentiment, in order to make it contribute to his stage-success. Think of his appeal to patriotism in the Joan of Arc scenes in *Henry VI*; the critics have,
I think, been a little too squeamish about them, but they
are certainly pretty crude. Compare them with the noble
use he made later on of a much more ignoble feeling—the
anti-Jewish feeling in *The Merchant of Venice*. Nothing
could be sillier than the notion that Shakespeare meant by
Shylock a mere long-nosed ogre, an odious figure of fun.
If that was what he meant, why did he write Shylock's
speeches? We may read into the character more than an
Elizabethan audience would have found in it; but Shylock
can never have been anything else than the odious Jew
made an understandable human being: that is to say, a
profoundly tragic figure. An original figure, too; up till
then, there had been nothing like it. And when we come
to Shakespeare's use of the feeling against puritanism in
Measure for Measure, we find that the antagonist who
brings into odium the popular idea of puritanism in
Angelo, is actually puritanism itself—the splendid and
terrible puritanism of Isabella. Now if stage-success was
all he wanted, he knew exactly how to exploit popular
sentiment to that end when he wrote *Henry VI*; he had
only to go on in that style. He does not; he goes on to
exploit popular sentiment in such a way as to serve his own
continually developing requirements. These three instances are typical of his whole career: it is only intelligible
as the career of an artist.

'But I think we go too fast!' the realist puts in here.
'Regard *him* as an artist if you like; that may be right
enough, as a general proposition. But when you descend
from *him* to his *work*, in order to regard *that* aesthetically,
surely first and foremost must come scholarship. Aesthetic

criticism of Shakespeare's work will be a very floundering
affair, if it does not know what that work is—if, for
example, it lumps together the whole of *Henry VI* as
Shakespeare's. The canon of Shakespeare must first be
settled; and only scholarship, strict and scientific, can
settle it.'

The importance of this objection can hardly be over-
rated. If it be true that Shakespeare was only responsible
for part of the work which goes under his name, then
aesthetic criticism becomes, properly speaking, impossible.
It might be thought that we need only wait until scholarship shall have decided which is Shakespeare's work and
which is not. But if we must wait for that we must wait
till doomsday. There will never be agreement; we shall
never be sure of our ground. For there is no real evidence
on which the question *can* be decided. There are pre-
judices, preferences, analyses, comparisons, statistics, verse-
tests, word-counts, sense of style, poetical feelings, intui-
tions—but we must not call all this evidence, unless we
add the compromising epithet 'internal'. And internal
evidence, by its very nature, has only subjective weight;
it puts no obligation on any one but the person who brings
it forward. This is a somewhat desperate state of affairs
for aesthetic criticism. We are told that the works of
Shakespeare, as they have come down to us, are not pure
metal. The alloy may be old work taken over by Shakespeare, or it may be the work of collaborators or of inter-
polators. And when we look for scholarship to dissolve out
the alloy and leave us the pure metal to deal with, we are
met with assurances that the work is going forward and we
hear of many most interesting experiments. But we find
that these experiments can only be of such a kind as cannot
possibly give any certainty of result. So that it seems we
shall never know whether what we are criticizing is Shakespeare or not; and our fine explanations of deep motive
and subtle characterization may be no more than failure
to detect bad joints between Shakespeare's work and the
other man's.

The contention, then, that aesthetic criticism must base itself on scholarship's settlement of the canon, practically amounts to a very grave objection to the validity of aesthetic criticism at all. How is this to be met ? Here, of course, only in very general terms, which cannot do justice to the intricacy of the problem. Note first that there is no question, in Shakespeare's case, as there is in the case of Marlowe, of *claiming* work for him, unless it be in respect of *Pericles*; the question confines itself to detecting what is not Shakespeare's and proving it not to be his, and that by internal evidence. It is scientific criticism itself, in its latest and finest development—the keen and rigorous criticism of Professor Pollard and Dr. Greg and, more recently still, of Mr. Alexander—that has made it clear how entirely we must rely on internal evidence if we wish to purge the first folio. Mr. Alexander, for example, has conclusively shown that the notion that *Henry VI* is a sort of *suovetaurilia* of Marlowe, Green, and Peel (or whatever the mixture may be) can find no support from the existence of *The Contention* and *The True Tragedy*; and consequently if we wish to exclude Shakespeare from all or any of the trilogy, that must be done on internal evidence within the folio version. This brilliant piece of work disposes of what has long been the worst scandal in Shakespearian affairs; for Mr. Alexander's argument makes it irresistible, that the simplest and completest account of the whole situation in respect of *Henry VI* is to accept Shakespeare as the author of the folio trilogy. This goes a long way to discredit the general supposition that Heminge and Condell admitted as Shakespeare's, work which they must have known was not his; and this latest development of scientific criticism is one of the things that make me believe Shakespearian affairs may be once more on the verge of another revolution.

For what is the strength of internal evidence ? Ultimately, it is the strength of the critic's own conviction; and we usually find that his conviction depends on how he likes this passage or that. If he must have in George Peele

for the Joan of Arc scenes, it is because he cannot bear
those scenes. There is nothing new in this; the scientific
critic is doing just what the romantic critics did. The
function of romantic criticism was to admire the divine
poet: what it could not admire could not be Shakespeare.
We do not now talk about divinity; we admit that Shakespeare, being a man, might err as an artist; but apparently
there is a limit: if he err too much, once more from dislike
we proceed to rejection. Thus we still have critics who
boggle at *Titus Andronicus*. Even the critic who rejected
the superb quarrel between Brutus and Cassius was careful
to tell us that he found it poor stuff. Now any argument
against authenticity that is unmistakably, and indeed from
its very origin, coloured by prejudice, must be regarded
with the most cautious suspicion. We must very strictly
ask ourselves, what is its logical status? And the argument from internal evidence—that is to say, from *style*, in
the widest sense of the term—must necessarily be of the
self-contained or self-supporting kind. If we accept the
theory of the composite authorship of the plays we know
as Shakespeare's, we can only accept as *his* the work which
conforms to our notion of his style. And on what do we
form our notion of his style? On his work. And what is his
work? That which conforms to our notion of his style.
Where does this take us? Logically, nowhere: all the
argument from internal evidence can do, is to bite its own
tail. The only force in it is the prejudice from which it
starts, the only direction it can take is to return whence it
came. Its full scope is to come full circle.

When I look at some of the editions in which Shakespeare's genuine work is discriminated from that which
merely goes under his name, I am reminded of that sternly
scientific scholar—a German, I think he was—who was
determined to produce a model edition of Theocritus, to
the pages of which no spurious line should be admitted.
But in the end, the edition had to be abandoned, since
every page of it turned out a blank. Nothing whatever of
Theocritus had survived, he discovered, which strict

criticism could allow to be truly Theocritean in style. Not
otherwise in logic do our Shakespearian editors form their
criteria for deciding, on internal evidence, the authenticity
of their text. They have not yet carried their convictions
as far as that eminent German carried his; but there seems
no reason why they should not. An argument that has no
logical standing has no logical limits. This is not mere
fantasy. A scientific editor has seriously assured us that
the first scene of the first act of *Macbeth* cannot be Shakespeare's. Whence does his argument proceed? Whither
does it take us? The answer to both questions is the same:
this scene happens to offend this particular editor. Similarly, another editor dislikes the masque in *The Tempest*;
and Shakespeare accordingly must be relieved of that mis-
fortune. These verdicts are not, of course, put so crudely:
prejudice, whether it be mere dislike or some preconceived
notion of Shakespearian style, is discreetly veiled by precise and dispassionate considerations. But it makes no
difference; the kind of argument which rejects

> When shall we three meet again?

might just as well reject.

> How all occasions do inform against me,

or

> Ill met by moonlight, proud Titania.

Nothing is safe from it. For in fact this realistic attitude
to Shakespeare, in spite of its imposing apparatus of
scientific exactitude, turns out to be in essence pure
subjectivism. It simply depends on taste—alas! too often
it depends on bad taste. A learned gentleman has lately
been investigating the nature of poetry by recording the
reactions of quite unpoetical persons to it. I recommend
him to add some Shakespearian editors to his bag.

Let me remind you that I am speaking now solely on the
question of authenticity. As regards the text, no one,
I believe, is more sensible than I am of the debt we all owe
to realistic methods of elucidation. But the question of
the canon of Shakespeare's work is, as I have said, crucial in

aesthetic criticism. What then is to be its attitude to this question?

There are really two questions here. When we speak of the composite authorship of Shakespeare's plays we may, in the first place, mean collaboration and interpolation. Obviously, for whatever these introduce, Shakespeare himself cannot be held responsible. It is plainly impossible to say that Shakespeare did not collaborate and was not subject to interpolation. But what one can say is that there is no real evidence for either. And what is to be gained by assuming a composite authorship that can never be proved —that can never even have the advantage of probability? Drop the assumption, then; once more, *Entia non sunt multiplicanda*. What comes down to us, under good authority, as Shakespeare's work, we have a right to take as his, and so criticize it; and the authority of the Folio is good enough. When we read in it

> The gaudy blabbing and remorseful day
> Is crept into the bosom of the sea,
> And now loud-howling wolves arouse the jades,
> That drag the tragic melancholy night;

we may well be tempted to exclaim, Marlowe! But to proceed from that to the conclusion, Therefore not Shakespeare, involves the assumption that Shakespeare could not write like Marlowe: an unsupported and unsupportable assumption, which, so far as evidence goes, is perfectly countered by the reply, But here we have Shakespeare doing it!—There is, then, no need for aesthetic criticism to allow itself to be put out of its stride by the questions of composite authorship, when this means collaboration or interpolation. It is fair to say that the effort of scientific criticism here is nothing else than to give apparent logical form to feelings that can have no logical validity: it is always the rationalization of prejudice of one kind or another.

But when by composite authorship is meant the taking over by Shakespeare of other dramatists' work, and the remodelling of this, then quite different considerations apply.

And still aesthetic criticism need not be put out of its stride. For if Shakespeare did take over other people's work and convert it to his own use, he thereby made himself responsible for it: he made it his, and as his we may justly criticize it. Is not Berni responsible not only for what he actually did to Boiardo, but for the whole *rifacimento* as it stands? If we criticize Berni's poem, can we leave the story out of consideration on the ground that this is Boiardo's? If we did, we should certainly be failing to criticize the total effect Berni's poem has on us; for any one can see, by comparing it with its original, that the effect of the story in Berni is quite different from the effect in Boiardo. Just so with Shakespeare; only in his case we have no original with which to compare his remodelling. Supposing, to save himself trouble, or whatever the reason was, he took over a Hamlet from Kyd. This, then, was his material, and as such it is no concern of ours. It does not matter to us what Kyd made of Hamlet; whatever was Kyd's has become Shakespeare's. Our business is with the effect Shakespeare produced, and in that effect, everything he used participates. Conceivably, it might have suited his purpose to leave Kyd unaltered here and there, but, even if these passages could be detected, that would make no difference. They belong now to Shakespeare's *Hamlet*; the purpose they serve now is Shakespeare's; he has taken them over and he must be responsible for them. Aesthetic criticism ought not to allow itself to be in the least perturbed about them. And it would be merely evading its duty, besides allowing improper weight to internal evidence, if it sought to dispose of difficulties of interpretation or apparent inconsistencies in *Hamlet* by indicating lumps of undigested Kyd. I take this purely speculative instance in order to put the question in an extreme form. Even in *Pericles*, if we give it to Shakespeare (and, were I playing the scientific game, I could detect Shakespeare's hand in it throughout)—even in *Pericles* Shakespeare cannot be relieved of responsibility for the 'mouldy tale'. The man who wrote the last act is the rightful owner of the play as it now exists; for it is the last Act that gives the play whatever artistic purpose it has. But if this man was Shakespeare, as I suppose every one believes he was, then all the wretched stuff he took over becomes his, by virtue of the effect he got out of it. The business of aesthetic criticism is to consider that effect, which does not mean merely to appraise the poetry and pathos of the shipwreck, and the brilliant prose and savage realism of the brothel-scenes, and the thrilling recognition of Marina, with that sublime stroke 'The music of the spheres!', but to take the whole play, and to acknowledge the preposterous conditions Shakespeare was willing to accept and make his own in order to exercise his finest powers, and say the thing he had to say.

The case would be a good deal more difficult if it were the other way round, as it may be in *Henry VIII*. If, instead of Shakespeare taking over other men's work, we have Fletcher taking over Shakespeare's work, what would then be the attitude of aesthetic criticism? As regards the whole effect of the play, it must be admitted that, whatever the reason may be, it goes to pieces. But as to whether Shakespeare is responsible for that, and as to what may be Shakespeare's in the play and what not, the question is precisely the same as when collaboration is asserted. All rests on internal evidence, and that has whatever weight you like to give it. But since in any case the play is radically incoherent, criticism must perforce be content here with that kind of piecemeal appreciation which everywhere else in Shakespeare—even in *Pericles*—is not only inadequate but likely to be falsifying.

Now my plea is for that liberty of interpreting which, as I suggested at the beginning, necessarily follows when Shakespeare is regarded primarily as an artist. This claim for liberty has, I know, a somewhat dubious sound; and in order to arrive at it I fear I must seem to have trespassed unduly on your patience; for, after all, who, if it were put as a general proposition, would seriously deny that Shakespeare must be regarded as an artist? Nevertheless, as

Shakespearian scholarship in this age has developed, criticism has, in fact, tended to discover, or to make, a good
many difficulties about that way of looking at him, whether
in reaction against the previous age, or on account of
certain otherwise salutary lines of study. It was first of
all necessary to deal with these difficulties; but having, as
I believe, shown that they may be surmounted, I proceed
now to what I have to say on this question of liberty in
criticism.

Let me begin with what I do not mean by it. An acute
and much-to-be-admired critic once discussed the fourth
book of the *Aeneid*, to the effect that the humane and en-
lightened Virgil had, by drawing the character of Dido,
marked a stage in the emancipation of women. This was
certainly taking a liberty with Virgil, and to prove it an
unwarrantable liberty there is no need to appeal to the
unknowable, Virgil's *intentions*. We merely have to appeal
to what Virgil did—the *result* to which his art worked.
And what he did is this: he compels his readers to feel with
the utmost poignancy the terrible dilemma in which
Aeneas found himself, by making the woman who had
entangled him, and sought to divert him from his noble
purpose, not a mere wanton adventuress, but a splendid
and adorable creature. But our critic was an enthusiast
for female enfranchisement; and he could not encounter
a splendid and adorable woman anywhere without thinking, 'She ought to have the vote!' For all I know Virgil
may have thought so too; what is certain is, that to associate Dido with the emancipation of women is to go clean
outside anything Virgil's art has to give us.

Again, another critic interprets *Paradise Lost* as a revelation of the spirit of Calvinism. We need not be so scrupulous here about appealing to the poet's intentions. We
may be pretty sure that, had anything remotely like
Calvinism occurred to Milton while he was composing
Paradise Lost, he would not have dictated it to his
daughters; he would have spat it out, while 'hatefullest
disrelish writhed his jaws'. But Milton (with very doubt-

ful propriety) is called a Puritan; for some reason Puritanism carried, for this critic, a strong suggestion of Calvinism; and so he interprets *Paradise Lost* not by taking what
the poem has to give him, but by allowing this private
association of his own to intrude and attach itself in
accordance with a habit of mind which has nothing whatever to do with the art of Milton. In short, by liberty of
interpretation, I do not mean liberty to read into a play
of Shakespeare's whatever feeling or idea a modern reader
may loosely and accidentally associate with its subject:
associate it, that is, not because he found it in the play, but
because some idiosyncrasy of his own suggested it and
irresponsibly brought it in from his private world. But
I do mean that anything which may be found in that art,
even if it is only the modern reader who can find it there,
may legitimately be taken as its meaning. *Judge by results*,
I say; not by the results of reverie, which the poem merely
sets going, and in which attention may ramble anywhere
it pleases, for that is not criticism at all; but certainly by
any result that may come of living in the art of the play
and attending to everything it consists of: and I say that,
so long as it keeps within that boundary, there is no proper
ground for objection, if this attention seems to be modern
in its nature. To put it more precisely, instead of 'modern'
I might say, a species of attention at once more analytic
in its scrutiny of detail and more comprehensive in its
synthesis of the play into a unity, than the author ever
intended his work to undergo. But note! I have used the
word *intended* here; and that should warn us we are on
dangerous ground. I said advisedly, that to plead for
liberty might be to plead for an attention that *seems* to be
modern in this sense; for we cannot *know* that Shakespeare
was careless of his detail—for instance, in his time-schemes
—or introduced matter without troubling about its
function in the play as a whole, because he counted on
having only to appeal to some not very exacting kind of
attention.

But to come to a concrete instance. When, at the end

of *Henry IV*, the Prince, on his way to his coronation, so brutally and yet, all things considered, so justly, rejects Falstaff, we have an incident that most readers find startling, and many shocking: an incident, at any rate, which, if the play is to be criticized at all, cries out for comment and, if possible, interpretation. Now its interpretation seems not only possible but inevitable, if we look for it in the right place: not in the mechanics of play-construction, namely, but in the character of Henry. The incident, in fact, throws back, over the whole of his character as it has so far been (somewhat enigmatically) presented, a sudden and brilliantly transforming illumination. Some such revelation as this Shakespeare had indeed more than once unobtrusively warned his audience to expect; but scarcely to expect anything like so remarkable and complete a transfiguration. For we now understand what the scapegrace Prince has been all through the two parts of *Henry IV*. He is the kind of person who can touch pitch without being defiled; or rather he is the kind of personality that can no more be smircht by circumstance than white-hot iron by dust. Avid of experience, he is so sure of his own integrity, that he can mix with cheerful scoundrels, and like them enjoy the most reprehensible behaviour, knowing that he will finally emerge untarnished. An admirable but not very lovable psychology: and drawn to perfection when this incident of the rejection of Falstaff concludes and retrospectively illuminates the whole series of previous incidents.

Now this, I submit, is what the play actually does give us: this interpretation is nothing extraneous, it is simply a possible way of understanding what is to be found in Shakespeare's art. However, it will, I am sure, be objected to it, that it is too *modern*. It will probably be said, that there is here no psychology at all worth speaking of; all the rejection of Falstaff means is, that Shakespeare had somehow or other to get rid of Falstaff as far as Henry's dramatic future was concerned, and he saw the chance of a striking moment of stage-effect in doing so. His Elizabethan audience would never see more in it than that, and he never expected more than that to be seen in it.

This way of reasoning is typical of the mood which realistic criticism opposes to what I call liberty of interpretation; and it may be noticed that, though it professes to explain, it gives up the very notion of interpretation. It is to be met with on any aspect of Shakespeare; but it has perhaps made itself especially noticeable in questions of characterization. Probably not many critics would agree that Cleopatra is to be regarded merely as an unco-ordinated series of moments of striking stage-effect: Cleopatra was an unfortunate instance to choose for pushing this method to extremes, since nowhere does apparent inconsistency of behaviour make a more convincing impression of single personality. No conceivable audience of human beings could watch this series of moments without connecting them; and if Shakespeare had intelligence enough to stage the incidents themselves, one after another, he might easily have had intelligence enough to design a connexion which no one can help seeing. But Professor Schücking's way of dealing with Cleopatra merely shows to what lengths the methods of realistic criticism can be taken. It is, however, precisely the same in kind as the criticism which warns us not to meddle too nicely with the psychological subtleties and problems which a modern mind may discover in Shylock, say, or in Hamlet. And why not? Because—so the warning goes—Shakespeare is to be judged as what he actually was, not for what we can make of him. That is to say—and these are the two great reasons alleged against liberty of interpreting—he is to be judged as a man writing for the stage (and for a particular kind of stage) and as an Elizabethan poet writing for Elizabethan audiences. To interpret him in terms which would not come off on the stage, or could not be understood by an Elizabethan audience, is, strictly speaking, not to interpret Shakespeare's work at all, but our own superfluity of sophistication.

Well, and is he not an Elizabethan? So much so, that,

unless he is regarded rather as an Elizabethan dramatist than as a world poet, the development of his art, and therewith the animating spirit of it, cannot possibly be understood. In studying Elizabethan drama, there is one factor of capital importance which must always be borne in mind. What Elizabethan audiences chiefly delighted to see, and what an Elizabethan dramatist had to give them (and, being himself an Elizabethan, delighted to give them) was a spectacle of the *variety* of life. The more variety that could be crowded into a couple of hours—the greater the range of the possibilities of life—the better the play, in Elizabethan taste. That was the main end Elizabethan drama had to serve; that was why a dramatist would not scruple to jam together into one play (as in *The Changeling*) two utterly unconnected stories; that was why Elizabethan drama became the greatest exhibition of human character the world has ever seen, from the heights to the depths of it, from its most tragic splendour to its most imbecile absurdity; that was why, as swiftly as it grew up, Elizabethan drama decayed, 'strangled in its waste fertility'. This demand was the governing condition under which Shakespeare worked. It was not good for some poets—Marlowe, for instance; but it exactly suited Shakespeare—nay, it was as much the inspiration as the condition of his work. The whole development of his drama is a continually exploring effort to bring larger and richer and finer variety into the unity of dramatic form. The effort is the secret of his failures as well as of his successes; *Measure for Measure* is a characteristic instance of both. Very generally, his dramatic development may be described as proceeding from the method perfected in *A Midsummer-Night's Dream*—the method of bringing together into one action a set of sharply contrasted groups of fixed characters—to the method of which *A Winter's Tale* may be taken as typical—where character itself changes under the changes of fortune which it brings upon itself. This is the prevailing direction in his perpetual endeavour to dramatize the endless variety of life; but of course the two methods overlap, for as early as *The Two Gentlemen of Verona* we find him experimenting with the mutual influence of character and fortune, and even in *The Tempest* the persons are displayed in contrasted groups. But whatever form it takes, the development of his art is a direct response to the taste of his time.

Thus, it is hardly possible to exaggerate the importance of Shakespeare's Elizabethanism, since, as I say, it not only conditions but inspires his work. But it seems to me the queerest misconception of that importance, to make it impose limitations on the interpreting of his poetry. Granted that it fired his genius to work under such conditions: still, it was *his* genius: it was Shakespeare who was inspired. Even if we suppose that his Elizabethanism did, in some way or other, circumscribe his meaning to his contemporaries, why should that limitation be maintained now that the Elizabethan mind is dead and gone? Why not let him mean all he can mean? Why impose on Shakespeare limitations which no one would think of imposing, say, on Homer? And after all, what are the grounds for supposing that what Shakespeare meant to the Elizabethans need be limited at all? Who knows that he did not mean to them what he means to us? Indeed, there are two very serious deficiencies in the argument that Shakespeare ought not to be understood except as an Elizabethan audience would have understood him. In the first place, what is meant by an Elizabethan audience? For presumably there would be in it as many kinds and degrees of intelligence as there are in an audience to-day. In the next place, what was an Elizabethan audience really like? And that, I venture to think, is not in the power of any one to answer, except in terms so broad as to be here quite useless. Until, however, these two questions are completely answered, this argument against the liberty I plead for can hardly be sustained. Its abstract validity seems extremely questionable; and it fails to make itself intelligible in any concrete form.

But Shakespeare wrote for the theatre; and we read him

in a book—at least, it is a hundred to one that the Shakespeare we criticize is the Shakespeare we read. Here we certainly have something considerable; for every one knows how the impression a play makes on us when we see it acted may differ from the impression it makes when we read it in cold type. Is it to be argued from this that criticism, to be valid, must keep within the impression made by the play in the theatre? To some extent that may be argued. Look, for instance, at those time-schemes which some critics have made such a work about. It is entirely to the plays as reading-matter that their discrepancies and incoherences and uncertainties belong. In the theatre, time-schemes simply do not exist; the mere sequence and linkage of the events are enough to employ the sort of attention we exercise there. Shakespeare, writing for the theatre, did not worry about keeping to an accurate time-scheme, knowing very well that his audience would never notice whether he kept to it or not. Criticism which occupies itself with this matter may well be called irrelevant, since the matter is itself irrelevant to the kind of existence the art was designed to take. But do these time-schemes, often so vague and difficult, really trouble us when we read Shakespeare? I think not: not, at any rate, if we read a play, straightforwardly and without interruption, in order to take it in as a work of art. It is only when we pull it to pieces that the time-scheme may appear questionable. In straightforward reading, just as in the theatre, the sequence of events is all that matters. There is nothing so odd in Shakespeare as the time-scheme of the *Agamemnon*; yet for generations of readers no one noticed it. Indeed, to criticize time at all in a drama, so long as the action is sufficiently given by the mere sequence of the events, is equally irrelevant whether the play is read or acted. For, in spite of the notable differences between reading a play and seeing it acted, the two impressions are but two versions of the same work of art.

Shakespeare not only wrote for the theatre, but for a very peculiar kind of theatre. In many ways it seems to

have been the finest instrument which dramatic art has
ever devised for itself; and Shakespeare's technique is so
exactly adapted to this instrument, and shows such complete mastery of it, that one is tempted to call it waste
of time to produce him on any stage that does not
pretty closely correspond with the stage he wrote for.
But this fact is equally important in quite another way.
The effective existence of a play in the Elizabethan theatre
depended almost wholly on the acting; and the actors
depended very specially on their words, for their art was
rather to capture the imagination of the audience than to
produce anything that could be called an illusion. The
language of the play had in consequence to be of a highly
imaginative kind, for the most part: what is called poetic
language, whether in verse or not. And that response to
such language could be reckoned on, is one of the things
we do know for certain about an Elizabethan audience.
But it was very soon found that this highly imaginative
language could make its effect independently of the actors;
in fact, practically throughout the whole course of Elizabethan drama, plays had a dual existence—on the stage,
and in print. Those critics who exhort us never to forget
that Shakespeare's work belongs to the theatre, are apt to
forget that Shakespeare's public had no scruples at all
about taking his plays as reading-matter; and that Shakespeare himself approved of this dual existence for his own
plays cannot, I think, nowadays be doubted. Did he
calculate on it? It looks as if some of his contemporaries
had the reading public at least at the back of their minds
when they wrote their plays; and some (Chapman and
Jonson, for instance) seem to have kept more prominently
in their consciousness than that, the opportunity of appealing beyond the theatre. It is commonly assumed, however,
that Shakespeare thought of nothing but the stage. Is not
this rather a romantic notion? In the first place, we do
not know. In the second place, though obviously the stage
came easily first with him, is it humanly possible that he
could have been entirely oblivious of the public which

might read him? To take two very different instances: unless he had the reading public somewhere in his mind, I do not see how we are to account for *Hamlet* and *Troilus and Cressida*.

But my plea for liberty of interpretation does not depend on hypothesis. Ultimately, it simply demands recognition of the nature of a work of art. A work of art is not a book or a picture, not a medium or an instrument, not even the use of a medium or a performance on an instrument, unless it is taken in and understood. This is obvious enough. When we talk of *Macbeth*, say, as a book or a performance on the stage, what we really mean is the book when we read it, the performance when we witness it. A work of art does not exist until it is experienced by an individual mind. It will always be an individual experience; but at the same time it is an experience given to this individual mind by another mind, and wholly governed by the conditions under which it is given. Thus a play, like any other work of art, consists of a series of three terms: the author, his medium or technique, and the recipient. Of these three terms, the first is the only one that can never change; and the fact that this term is always the same gives us the sense in which it is possible to say, that through all its existences it is always the same play. But the third term, the recipient, changes every time the play comes into existence at all; and it is even possible for changes to occur in the middle term, the technique, provided the change conserves what the author committed to it. Thus a symphony may be transcribed as a pianoforte duet: a remarkable change, but one which, in the case of his own symphonies, Brahms himself carried out. And thus too the medium of *Macbeth* may change from the theatre to the printed page: perhaps an even more remarkable change, but one which, it appears, Shakespeare himself approved of, and may even to some extent have had in mind. He might very well approve of it, since the printed page merely gave him another way of making essentially the same appeal to imagination. So that, in spite of whatever differences there may be between them, whether we criticize the *Macbeth* we see in the theatre, or the *Macbeth* we read, it is still Shakespeare's *Macbeth* we are criticizing: in that sense, it is in either case the same *Macbeth*.

The existence of a work of art, in fact, is not material at all, but spiritual. It is a continually creative existence, for it exists by continually creating experience. In one sense, this means that it is a continually changing existence; for the experiences it creates must always be individual and therefore unique experiences. Yet in another sense it is always the same; for it always exists in unbroken connexion with its author, who *forms* the experience he gives. It will now appear why liberty of interpretation must necessarily be granted if Shakespeare's plays are regarded as works of art. Every reader or spectator is at liberty to say what the play means to him. The reason is a simple one: the play, as a work of art, has no other existence. To limit interpretation to what the play may have meant to Elizabethans is, frankly, to exclude the existence of the play as a work of art; for as a work of art it does not exist in what it may have meant to some one else, but in what it means to me: that is the only way it can exist. In any case, it had as many different existences in an Elizabethan theatre as there were heads in the audience. But, when I say a play exists in what it means to any one who will receive it, the implication is plain, that everything is excluded from that existence which is not given by the author's technique. The existence of a work of art is completed by the recipient's *attention* to what the author says to him; whatever may come in through *inattention* to that does not belong to the art at all. It is not liberty of interpreting when a critic sees the emancipation of women in Dido, or James the First in Hamlet; it is simply failure to attend to the poet, and thus does not come within the series of the three terms which constitutes a work of art—it has no part in that connexion between the mind of the poet and the mind of the recipient which is the essence of a poem. But when there is that connexion, when the response of individual imagination is wholly governed by the poet's technique, then poetry comes into existence. And liberty of interpreting necessarily comes too; for that is simply another way of saying, that the response, though governed by the poet, cannot in the nature of things be anything but individual. The rule tolerates no exceptions. The field of Shakespearian studies is a vast one, and almost every kind of talent can find occupation there. But it all exists because Shakespeare was a poet: all comes from that, and back to that everything goes at last. To regard Shakespeare as an artist is our first and last duty. But so to regard him is to admit what would never be denied in the case of any other poet. Whenever it is his art that is being criticized, liberty of interpretation must be allowed, in the sense in which I have tried to define it.

SHAKESPEARE'S ITERATIVE IMAGERY

(i) AS UNDERSONG (ii) AS TOUCHSTONE IN HIS WORK [1]

By CAROLINE F. E. SPURGEON

ITERATIVE imagery, that is the repetition of an idea or picture in the images used in any one play, is a marked characteristic of Shakespeare's art; indeed, it is, I think, his most individual way of expressing his imaginative vision.

It is quite clear that it is his habit of mind to have before him, as he writes, some picture or symbol, which recurs again and again in the form of images throughout a play, and I have already shown in an earlier paper [2] that these leading motives, for instance in the tragedies, are born of the emotions of the theme, and shed considerable light on the way Shakespeare himself looked at it.

Thus in *Romeo and Juliet* the beauty and ardour of young love is seen by Shakespeare as the irradiating glory of sunlight and starlight in a dark world. The dominating image is *light*, every form and manifestation of it. Each of the lovers thinks of the other as light: to Juliet, Romeo is 'day in night'; to Romeo, Juliet is the sun rising from the east; and, in the height of love's ecstasy, each sees the other as stars in heaven, dimming by their radiance the heavenly bodies themselves. The background, both of things seen, and of the imagery, is of light against darkness; sunshine, starlight, moonbeams, sunrise, and sunset, fire, candles, and torches, set off by quick-coming darkness, clouds, mist, rain, and night, forming a running accompaniment which augments unconsciously in us the picture

---

[1] First delivered 1931. Save for a few slight changes this lecture is here reprinted as originally published in 1931.

[2] *Leading Motives in the Imagery of Shakespeare's Tragedies*, Oxford University Press, 1930.

or sensation of an almost blinding flash of light, suddenly ignited, and as suddenly quenched, which was undoubtedly the way Shakespeare saw the story, in its swift and tragic beauty.

So also I have shown that the idea of a tumour, a hidden corruption, needing the surgeon's knife to release it, is the 'leading motive' in *Hamlet*, and throws light on Shakespeare's own view of the problem of Hamlet's dilemma, just as the imagery which plays round the figure of Macbeth, revealing him as a dwarfish and ignoble creature, clad in robes too large for him, is a good indication of at least one aspect of Shakespeare's own conception of his character, as he saw it pictorially.

The discovery of this 'undersong' was an early result of a piece of work on which I have been engaged for some years, which is the assembling, classifying, and cross-referencing of all Shakespeare's images, using the material thus collected as data upon which to base deductions and conclusions.

When I say 'images' I mean every kind of picture, drawn in every kind of way, in the form of simile or metaphor—in their widest sense—to be found in Shakespeare's work. Such a picture can be so extended as to take up a large part of a scene, as does the symbol of the untended garden in *Richard II*, or it can be suggested by a single word:

> Ripeness is all;

it may be a simple analogy from everyday things:

> They'll take suggestion as a cat laps milk,

or delicate fancy from a world of imagination:

> A lover may bestride the gossamer
> That idles in the wanton summer air
> And yet not fall; so light is vanity;

it may take the form of a personification drawn at full length—Time, the fashionable host, welcoming and speeding his guests; or it may be flashed on us in one vivid verb,

> Glamis hath murdered sleep;

and it may be every kind of metaphor—Lady Macbeth urging her lord to 'screw his courage to the sticking-place', Duncan, after life's fitful fever, sleeping well, Donalbain fearing the 'daggers in men's smiles', and Macbeth wading in blood or supping 'full with horrors'. For this purpose it is the picture that is important, not the particular way the picture is drawn, though that becomes of first interest when one studies Shakespeare's art and its development.

I embarked on this task of collecting and classifying the images, because it seemed to me that it might provide a new method of approach to Shakespeare, and I believe I have, by a happy fortune, hit on such a method, hitherto untried, which is yielding most interesting and important results. It not only throws light from a fresh angle, as we have seen in the tragedies, upon Shakespeare's imaginative and pictorial vision, upon his own ideas about his own plays and the characters in them, but it seems to me to serve as an absolute beacon in the skies with regard to the vexed question of authorship. It also enables us to get nearer to Shakespeare himself, to his mind, his tastes, his experiences, and his deeper thought than does any other single way I know of studying him.

I believe that a poet, and more especially a dramatic poet, to some extent unconsciously 'gives himself away' in his images. He may be, and in Shakespeare's case is, almost entirely objective in his dramatic characters and their views and opinions, yet, like the man who under stress of emotion will show no sign of it in eye or face, but will reveal it in some muscular tension, the poet unwittingly reveals his own innermost likes and dislikes, observations and interests, associations of thought, attitudes of mind and beliefs, in and through the images, the verbal pictures he draws to illuminate something quite different in the speech and thought of his characters.

Shakespeare's images have, of course, constantly been picked out and drawn upon, to illustrate one aspect or another of the poet's thought or mind, but the novelty of the procedure I am describing is that *all* his images are assembled, sorted, and examined on a systematic basis, the good with the bad, the disagreeable with the pleasant, the coarse with the refined, the attractive with the unattractive, and the poetical with the unpoetical.

They are not selected to point or to illustrate any preconceived idea or thesis, but they are studied, either as a whole, or in groups, with a perfectly open mind, to see what information they yield, and the result comes often as a complete surprise to the investigator.

In addition, it has been necessary, for purposes of comparison, to assemble and examine, on the same system, the images from a large number of plays by Shakespeare's contemporaries.

It takes a long time to assemble and classify the images. I do not believe any one could do it satisfactorily in less than several years' work; in the case of Shakespeare, it is essential gradually to grow familiar with his pictorial habit of thought, for, until one is fairly well saturated with this, it is very easy to overlook an image, often conveyed in a single word, which on a second, third, or fourth reading becomes quite clear. I have been at work on it now—intermittently—for over six years, and I am naturally far from satisfied yet. But when I have finished some of the deductions I am drawing from this material, I hope eventually to publish the material itself, so that other students can check and perhaps extend it, in order that it may serve as data and starting-point for other research of various kinds.

The undertone of running symbolic imagery, which I have described in the tragedies, I find to some extent in almost every play, contributing in various ways to the richness and meaning of the play, and profoundly influencing its effect upon us. In the tragedies it is closely connected with the central theme, and adds to and illuminates that theme; in the comedies as a whole, it contributes chiefly atmosphere and background; about its function in the histories it is less easy to generalize.

There is a simple but persistent running image through

all the early histories from the first part of *Henry VI* (where there are only touches of it) culminating in *Richard II*. The two parts of *Henry IV* are curiously free from any continuous imagery of this kind, while *King John* is a very interesting example of a most strong symbolism which powerfully affects us pictorially and emotionally. In the later plays, the romances, this symbolism becomes more subtle, and Shakespeare's tendency is to have an underlying idea rather than a concrete picture in the mind, an idea which he clothes in various kinds of imagery.

I will first give examples of what I call the 'undersong' of imagery within the limits of a single play, then as found recurring in many plays, and I will follow this by some illustrations of the way it seems to me this iterative imagery may serve as 'touchstone' of personality, and may help to reveal to us not only individual characteristics which mark the writer, but may even at times enable us to catch a glimpse of that fleeting and elusive entity, the man himself.

As simple examples of the way the imagery in the comedies supplies atmosphere and background, as well as emphasizes or re-echoes certain qualities in the play, let us look at *A Midsummer-Night's Dream* and *Much Ado*.

In *A Midsummer-Night's Dream* we know that what we feel overpoweringly is the woodland beauty of the dreaming summer night, and it is only when we look closer that we realize in some measure how this sensation is brought about.

The influence and presence of the moon is felt throughout, largely through the imagery, from the opening lines when the noble lovers impatiently measure the days to their wedding by the waning of the old moon and the coming of the new,

> like to a silver bow
> New-bent in heaven,

to the end, when Puck tells us the 'wolf behowls the moon', and that it is, therefore, the time of the night for the fairies' frolic.

Time and movement are both measured by her, for mortals as well as for Puck and the fairies: the lovers make their tryst for the moment on the morrow

> when Phoebe doth behold
> Her silver visage in the watery glass,

the fairies compass the globe 'swifter than the wandering moon'. She is the 'governess of floods', and controls not only the weather, but also the fiery shafts of love which at will she quenches in her 'chaste beams'; she symbolizes the barren air of the cloister, where the sisters live

> Chanting faint hymns to the cold fruitless moon;

she serves, as does the sun, for an emblem of steadfast constancy; and Hermia cries she would as soon believe a hole might be bored in the centre of the earth and the moon creep through it, as that Lysander should willingly have left her.

The word 'moon' occurs twenty-eight times, three and a half times more often than in any other play, partly, of course, owing to the prominence of Moonshine, often addressed as 'Moon', as a character in the comedy of the 'homespuns'. 'Moonlight', naturally, also occurs unusually often; indeed, Shakespeare only mentions moonlight in his plays eight times altogether, and six of these are in *A Midsummer-Night's Dream*, as is also his only reference to moonbeams. His single use of 'starry' is also here, when Oberon tells Puck to cover the 'starry welkin', and the sensation of starlight, which is constant (the fairies dance by 'spangled starlight sheen'; Puck accuses Demetrius of 'bragging to the stars'; if moonshine be gone Thisbe will find her lover by starlight, and so on), is largely owing to the many comparisons to the stars which come naturally to those who are looking at them, as when Demetrius assures Hermia that though she has pierced his heart, and is a murderer, she looks

> as bright, as clear,
> As yonder Venus in her glimmering sphere,

and Lysander declares that Helena

> more engilds the night
> Then all yon fiery oes and eyes of light.

This moonlit background then partly supplies the dreaming and enchanted quality in the play, which is reinforced by woodland beauty. This is drawn largely from two sources, closely allied and sometimes melting into one; the high proportion of poetical images—95 out of a total of 114—considerably higher than in any other comedy, and the very large number of nature-images, including animals and birds. These Shakespeare always has, but their number here is unusual, for in addition to those listed under 'nature', there are many which have to be classified under other headings, which really, all the time, are calling up country pictures before us. Thus the 'green corn' which

> Hath rotted ere his youth attain'd a beard,

which is really a personification, brings to the mind above all else the sight of the fields at the end of many a wet English summer, just as the description of the way

> the spring, the summer,
> The childing autumn, angry winter, change
> Their wonted liveries,

which comes under 'clothes', really presents us with a pageant of the swift succession of the seasons in their many-coloured garb.

Even the measurement of Time is made, not only by the moon, but also by the cock-crow, the 'middle summer's spring', and the 'lightning in the collied night', by the greening of the wheat and the coming of the hawthorn buds, by the mating of the birds and the swimming powers of the leviathan, by dawn and sunrise, by a shadow and a sound.

And the birds too, whose song and sound is heard throughout, as it should be in an English woodland play, the dove, the nightingale, the rook, and the lark—these are, as with Shakespeare always, used as a measure of all kinds of activities and sense-values: of light movement, 'hop as light as bird from brier', of sweet sound, 'more tuneable than lark to shepherd's ear', of colour-sense,

> high Taurus' snow,
> Fann'd with the eastern wind, turns to a crow
> When thou hold'st up thy hand,

or of headlong scattered flight, as when the wild geese or russet-pated choughs

> Rising and cawing at the gun's report,
> Sever themselves and madly sweep the sky.

Even in the farce of the rustics we get—as it were by chance—a splash of nature-beauty flung by the way such as:

> Of colour like the red rose on triumphant brier,

and in the play as a whole the succession of imaginative pictures crystallizing experiences, emotions, and sensations familiar to all English nature lovers has never been surpassed by Shakespeare himself. These are all well known, for they are among our greatest poetry, and a score of them could be named in this play alone, but two must suffice here.

We all know that delightful mid-season of early autumn when the night frosts nip the late summer flowers, and through which the hardy monthly roses persist in gaily blooming, but it is Shakespeare who has painted the poet's picture of it for ever with its exquisite mingling of sharp air and sweet scents, in the Fairy Queen's description of what was probably the experience of many a gardener at the end of the cold wet summer of 1594:

> we see
> The seasons alter: hoary-headed frosts
> Fall in the fresh lap of the crimson rose;
> And on old Hiem's thin and icy crown
> An odorous chaplet of sweet summer buds
> Is, as in mockery, set.

We have most of us seen a summer's sunrise over the sea, but Shakespeare has immortalized the pageant for us in a riot of colour and beauty when we watch with Oberon,

> Even till the eastern gate, all fiery-red,
> Opening on Neptune with fair blessed beams,
> Turns into yellow gold his salt green streams.

No wonder Keats underscored this play in parts almost continuously, for sheer poetry, nature and moonlight were his loves, and he found them all here together to his hand, as nowhere else in literature, in rich and joyous abundance. And these, largely through the imagery we have been analysing, have stamped their special impress on the play, which leaves us, as it has left myriads, over nearly three and a half centuries, amazed and bewitched by beauty and the strange power of the poet's pen.

In *Much Ado* we find ourselves in an entirely different atmosphere, gay, sparkling, unsentimental, witty, and we notice at once what a number of lively images there are in this play, of light sound and swift movement, which sustain this atmosphere, dancing (a Scotch jig, a measure, a cinque pace), music (the jesting spirit crept into a lute string, the clapper of a bell), song (in what key shall a man take you, to go in the song?), riding, galloping, ambling, shy swift birds (spirits 'coy and wild as haggerds of the rock'), the lightning-quick action of the hunting dog (wit as quick as the greyhound's mouth): these and others form a fitting accompaniment and setting for the gay and high-spirited girl born under a dancing star, in whose eyes 'disdain and scorn ride sparkling'.

Besides this note of gaiety, the dominant motive is English country life, but of a sort entirely different from the languorous moonlit atmosphere of the enchanted wood. It is a setting of active outdoor work and sport, at times contending against cold and storm, largely created indirectly through the imagery, in which the most noticeable and continuous idea is that of the country sports of bird-snaring and angling; both lovers being thought of as birds limed and caught in a net, or fish hooked by the 'treacherous bait'. This impression is confirmed by statistics of the images. For the only time in Shakespeare's plays, the images from 'Sport' head the list, and are therefore more numerous than those of either 'Nature' or 'Animals'. They include many from bird-snaring, riding, and fishing, as well as others from archery, shooting, tilting, hunting, fencing, bird's-nesting, and bear-baiting. Others, such as wrestling and dancing, listed under 'Bodily Action', might legitimately be added.

As compared with some plays, there are not a great many nature similes, but at times they run almost continuously. Thus, in the charming little scene of only slightly over a hundred lines, in the orchard (III. i), when Hero and Ursula bait their trap for Beatrice, we notice a succession of rural pictures—the pleached honeysuckle-bower, which, ripened by the sun, yet keeps it out; the lapwing running close to the ground couched in the woodbine; the pleasant angling

> to see the fish
> Cut with her golden oars the silver stream;

the young wild hawks, the vane 'blown with all winds', the 'covered fire' of weeds, the smoke of which so deliciously scents English gardens, the 'limed' trap, and the wild bird being tamed—all of which stimulate and sustain in us the consciousness of the background of active outdoor country life.

This is augmented by the repeated use of weather and seasons for purposes of comparison, as when Beatrice so wounds Benedick's pride by telling him he was 'duller than a great thaw', or Don Pedro exlcaims at his 'February face',

> So full of frost, of storm, of cloudiness,

as well as by touches like Dogberry's ewe that will not hear her lamb when it baas, the sound of Beatrice's dog barking at a crow, Don John's 'forward March-chick', or the secret of the rooting of crops, expounded by Conrade. To these may be added the many vivid country pictures drawn so easily and lightly by Benedick, such as the poor hurt fowl that creeps into the sedges, the melancholy lodge in a warren, the schoolboy who, overjoyed at finding a bird's nest, unwarily shows it to his companion, who steals it, the howling dog, or the honest drover who sells bullocks. All through, whatever the scene, the country outdoor atmosphere is kept before us, as when Don Pedro rounds off the rite of hanging Hero's epitaph on her tomb in church, by his picture, in delicate classical vein, of the coming of an English dawn:

> look, the gentle day,
> Before the wheels of Phoebus, round about
> Dapples the drowsy east with spots of grey.

In addition to this running imagery within a single play, there is also much repetitive imagery throughout the whole of Shakespeare's work, which supplies us with all kinds of information.

Thus, the repeated evidence of clusters of certain associated ideas in the poet's mind is one of the most interesting of studies, and throws a curious light on what I suppose the psycho-analyst would call 'complexes'; that is, certain groups of things and ideas—apparently entirely unrelated—which are linked together in Shakespeare's subconscious mind, and some of which are undoubtedly the outcome of an experience, a sight or emotion which has profoundly affected him.

I can best make this clear by giving an example, and I will choose a very simple and straightforward one. These groups are not all so easily interpreted as this is.

It is quite certain that one of the things which rouse Shakespeare's bitterest and deepest indignation is feigned love and affection assumed for a selfish end. He, who values so intensely—above all else in human life—devoted and disinterested love, turns almost sick when he watches flatterers and sycophants bowing and cringing to the rich and powerful purely in order to get something out of them for themselves. It is as certain as anything can be, short of direct proof, that he had been hurt, directly or indirectly, in this particular way. No one who reads his words carefully can doubt that he had either watched some one, whose friendship he prized, being deceived by fawning flatterers, or that he himself had suffered from a false friend or friends, who, for their own ends, had drawn out his love while remaining 'themselves as stone'.

Now whenever the idea of false friends or flatterers occurs we find a rather curious set of images which play round it. These are, a dog or spaniel, fawning and licking, candy, sugar or sweets, thawing or melting. So strong is the association of these ideas in Shakespeare's mind, that it does not matter which of these items he starts with— dog or sugar or melting—it almost invariably, when used in this particular application, gives rise to the whole series.

The simplest example is that in *Julius Caesar*, which starts with *thawing*. When Metellus Cimber prostrates himself before him, Caesar checks him, saying:

> Be not fond,
> To think that Caesar bears such rebel blood
> That will be *thaw'd* from the true quality
> With that which *melteth* fools, I mean, *sweet* words,
> *Low-crook'd court'sies* and *base spaniel-fawning*,
> Thy brother by decree is banished:
> If thou dost bend and pray and *fawn* for him,
> I spurn thee like *a cur* out of my way.

In *Hamlet* the image starts with *candy*. Hamlet tells Horatio he is the most just man he has ever known, and checks his friend's natural impulse to demur at this sudden and unlooked-for praise by saying 'Nay, do not think I flatter', for what have I to gain from you?

> Why should the poor be flatter'd?
> No, let the *candied tongue lick* absurd pomp,
> And crook the pregnant hinges of the knee
> Where thrift may follow *fawning*.

A touch of the idea recurs when Hotspur, speaking of Bolingbroke's attitude before he was king, cries:

> Why, what a *candy* deal of courtesy
> This *fawning greyhound* then did proffer me!

In *Antony* the first item of the image is *dog*, and the underlying idea is again false flattery, when Antony, thinking himself betrayed and deserted by Cleopatra and her followers, cries:

> the hearts
> That *spaniel'd* me *at heels*, to whom I gave
> Their wishes, do *discandy*, *melt* their *sweets*
> On blossoming Caesar.

Fragments of the same image recur when the original chord of '*flatterers*' is touched, as when Cassius tells Antony that his words

> *rob the Hybla bees,*
> *And leave them honeyless,*

and Antony then rounds on both Brutus and Cassius, crying

> Villians, . . .
> You . . . *fawn'd like hounds,*
> And bow'd like bondmen, kissing Caesar's feet;
> Whilst damned Casca, *like a cur*, behind
> Struck Caesar on the neck. O, you flatterers!

Here we begin with 'sweets', and, with the exception of 'melting', the rest of the series follows.

The explanation of this curious and repeated sequence of ideas is, I think, very simple. It was the habit in Elizabethan times to have dogs, which were chiefly of the spaniel and greyhound type, at table, licking the hands of the guests, fawning and begging for sweetmeats with which they were fed, and of which, if they were like dogs to-day, they ate too many, and dropped in a semimelting condition all over the place. Shakespeare, who was unusually fastidious, hated the habit, as he hated all dirt and messiness, especially connected with food.

So there come to be linked in his mind two things he intensely dislikes, one in the physical everyday world, the other in the world of mind and emotions: the fawning cupboard love of dogs, their greed and gluttony, with its sticky and disagreeable consequences, and the other fawning of insincere friends, bowing and flattering for what they hope to get, and turning their backs when they think no more is coming to them.

In one play, *Timon of Athens*, in which Shakespeare expressed some of his profoundest as well as his most bitter thoughts, we find that the whole subject is just this particular one about which he felt so acutely—a man betrayed by false friends and flatterers.

What do we find is the central image, the picture constantly before Shakespeare's eyes in this play? Dogs: dogs fawning and eating and lapping and licking, with 'gluttonous maws' devouring their lord's meat; hounds feasting on the blood of the animal they have killed; dogs being given food denied to men; dogs licking up remnants; dogs being stoned and spurned and kicked; a mangy dog, a sleeping dog, an unpeaceable dog, a beggar's dog.

Even Timon's imprecations are coloured by this picture, which is ever with him, 'Destruction *fang* mankind' he cries:

> And may diseases *lick up* their false bloods!

and the thought of Flavius is likewise tinged with it; why, he asks the servants of his ruined lord's creditors, did you not submit your bills,

> When your false masters eat of my lord's meat?
> Then they could smile and fawn upon his debts,
> And take down the interest into their gluttonous maws.

This constant preoccupation with dog-nature can be seen by any one on turning over the pages of the play; I will only remind you of the great central scene, practically every word of which I believe to be Shakespeare's, when Timon, found by Apemantus in the woods, rounds on the cynic and tells him he is but a rogue and a beggar who really scorns and envies those who are better off than he is, had he ever had a chance he would have rioted with the best; and he proceeds to expound his own position in a passionate speech.

It opens with 'dog' and ends with 'flatterer', but had we

not the key of the earlier group of images, we should
scarcely realize that it also is shot through with the picture
of dogs licking sweets, and with their mouths and tongues
melting the iced sugar on cake or sweetmeats.

'Thou', says Timon, 'art a slave',

>   whom Fortune's tender arm
> With favour never clasp'd, but bred a *dog*,

and the associative picture starts again:

> Hadst thou, like us from our first swath, proceeded
> The *sweet* degrees that this brief world affords
> To such as may the passive drugs of it
> Freely command, thou wouldst have plunged thyself
> In general riot, *melted* down thy youth
> In different beds of lust, and never learn'd
> The *icy* precepts of respect, but follow'd
> The *sugar'd* game before thee. But myself,
> Who had the world as my *confectionary*,
> The *mouths*, the *tongues*, the eyes and hearts of men
> At duty, . . . I, to bear this,
> That never knew but better, is some burden:
> . . . Why shouldst thou hate men?
> They never flatter'd thee: . . . Hence, be gone!

this curious group of images is but one example of many
such associated groups, which, when studied together,
throw a distinct light on Shakespeare's likes and dislikes,
physical sensations, experiences, and emotions, and sometimes on his deepest thought and feelings.

This habit of returning under similar emotional stimulus
to a similar picture or group of associated ideas is clearly
one of Shakespeare's characteristics which serves as a
'touchstone' of his authorship. Indeed, through his
images, Shakespeare seems to me often to have set his hall-
mark on a play or scene, as distinctly as ever goldsmith
stamped true metal.

Here, for example, are two pictures:

>   A thousand knees
> Ten thousand years together, naked, fasting,
> Upon a barren mountain, and still winter

> In storm perpetual, could not move the gods
> To look that way thou wert.
>
> Well could I curse away a winter's night,
> Thou standing naked on a mountain top,
> Where biting cold would never let grass grow,
> And think it but a minute spent in sport.

It is an unusual scene; the one of a vast company, the other of a single figure, naked, in biting winter cold on the summit of a barren mountain, and nothing remotely resembling it is to be found in a search of the work of twelve contemporary dramatists, although we find an echo of the same idea in Henry IV's indignant refusal to ransom Mortimer, 'No, on the barren mountains let him starve'.

The first picture comes from *The Winter's Tale*, a play which most people, except perhaps Pope and Mr. J. M. Robertson, believe to be wholly Shakespeare's, the second is from *Henry VI, Part II*, a play continuously doubted by critics of every kind, and of which Fleay said that Shakespeare probably never wrote a line.

Personally, I believe that if Fleay had looked a little closer, he would have allowed that Shakespeare wrote at least these four lines just quoted.

We may note that both pictures are used as a measure of time, both come with a hot gush of anger, and both are connected in the writer's mind with torment; in the one Paulina has just been asking Leontes

> What wheels? racks? fires? what flaying? boiling?
> In leads or oils?

he has in store for her, while, in the other, Suffolk is in the midst of wishing for his enemies poison and 'all the foul terrors in dark-seated hell'.

When it is found possible to multiply five, ten, twenty, or even thirtyfold such proof of likeness of idea and often of emotional stimulus or setting in images, between scenes or plays of disputed and of undoubted authenticity, the probability of the presence of Shakespeare's hand becomes very strong.

Another way in which the imagery test works I may illustrate from *Henry VIII*. Here we have a play which most critics agree was not all written by Shakespeare. They agree also that his collaborator was almost certainly Fletcher, but, of late, critical opinion has gone even farther, and the play has by some been reft from Shakespeare altogether, and handed over bodily to Fletcher and Massinger. There are in it undoubted likenesses to Massinger and he probably had some hand in it (though many parallels quoted in proof of his authorship apply with equal if not greater force to Shakespeare). In spite of these likenesses, however, I am one of those who still believe that Shakespeare wrote the greater part of the play, though I cannot now go into all my reasons.

I would just point out here that it has a very marked running symbol in the imagery, a continuous picture in the poet's mind of the human body seen in endlessly varied action, which seems partly summed up in Norfolk's description near the middle of the play of Wolsey's 'strange postures' (III. ii. 111–19).

Now this habit of seeing emotional or mental situations throughout a play in a repeatedly recurring physical picture seems to me to be peculiar to Shakespeare. I have up to now found it in no other writer, but this examination is not yet quite complete. I find in others an image *repeated*: thus in *The Faithful Shepherdess* Fletcher thinks of desire and love as *fire*, and repeats this again and again, 'consuming fires', 'wanton flames', 'hot flashes', and so on, but that is all there is to it; the image, which is a verbal commonplace, is entirely static, and you cannot feel there is any *picture* in the writer's mind. I find Chapman using a number of images of the body, as in *Byron's Conspiracy*, but there is no unity in them, no life, whereas Shakespeare's way is to conjure up a kind of 'moving picture', which is continually reappearing in different forms and from different aspects in the images.

He is particularly fond of the body as a running symbol, but it is always the body from some special aspect or angle, which is continuous throughout the play; thus in *Lear* it is a *tortured* body, in *Hamlet* a *diseased* one, in *Coriolanus* the different members and functions of the body, and so on.

There are three aspects of the picture of a body in the mind of the writer of *Henry VIII*: the whole body and its limbs, the various parts, such as tongue, mouth, eyes, and—much the most constant—bodily action of almost every kind; walking, stepping, marching, running, and leaping; crawling, hobbling, falling, carrying, climbing, and perspiring; swimming, diving, flinging, and peeping; crushing, strangling, shaking, trembling, sleeping, stirring, and, especially and repeatedly, the picture of the body or back bent and weighed down under a heavy burden.[1]

I may just slightly indicate how this symbol works. Buckingham thinks of the tourney on the Field of the Cloth of Gold as a body, and asks:

> Who did guide,
> I mean, who set the body and the limbs
> Of this great sport together?

He similarly pictures the plot against the King, so that when the nobles are arrested he exclaims:

> These are the limbs o' the plot: no more, I hope.

Norfolk, trying to restrain Buckingham's anger with the Cardinal, says:

> Stay, my lord,
> . . . to climb steep hills
> Requires slow pace at first . . .
> Be advised;
> . . . we may outrun,
> By violent swiftness, that which we run at,
> And lose by over-running.

[1] I know that this image is a very favourite one of Massinger's, but it is also often used by Shakespeare, and, so far as I have yet examined, it is never used by Massinger as part of a continuous picture, as here. At the same time, I believe that almost certainly Massinger had a hand in the play, and some of these 'body' images may be due to him.

We note as we read that many of the most vivid images in the play are of movements of the body, such as Norfolk's description of Wolsey diving into the king's soul, Cranmer crawling into the king's favour and strangling his language in tears, Katharine's

> sufferance panging
> As soul and body's severing,

or her picture of the great cardinal, with the king's aid, going swiftly and easily over the shallow steps, until mounted at the top of the staircase of fame.

Wolsey thinks constantly in terms of body movement; and among his images are those of a soldier marching in step with a squadron, a man scratched and torn by pressing through a thorny wood, or set on by thieves, bound, robbed, and unloosed; and in his last great speeches, which, in spite of rhythm, I incline to believe are Shakespeare's, he speaks of having '*trod* the ways of glory', see, Cromwell *carrying* peace in his right hand, urges him to *fling away* ambition, and pictures himself successively as a rash *swimmer* venturing far beyond his depth with the meretricious aid of a bladder, a man *falling headlong* from a great height like a meteor or like Lucifer, and finally, *standing* bare and *naked* at the mercy of his enemies.

The image of the back bent under the load recurs five times, and is obviously and suitably symbolic of Wolsey's state as well as of the heavy taxation. Wolsey complains that the question of the divorce was 'the weight that pulled him down', and, after his dismissal, sees himself as a man with an unbearable burden suddenly lifted off him, assuring Cromwell that he thanks the king, who has cured him, 'and from these shoulder's taken 'a load would sink a navy';

> a burden
> Too heavy for a man that hopes for heaven.

So also the king pictures himself as a man cruelly burdened, sweating under his load, when he turns to the Bishop with his query:

> my Lord of Lincoln; you remember
> How under my oppression I did reek,
> When I first moved you.

The idea of a man falling from a great height is constant in the case of both Wolsey and Cranmer; and the remonstrances made with their accusers are in each case exactly alike,

> Press not a falling man too far,

>   'tis a cruelty
> To load a falling man.

This 'undersong' of imagery, peculiarly Shakespearian, of a human body seen in every form of physical activity, seems to me to throw some fresh light on the problem of authorship, and the first question one asks is, 'Does this symbol run right through all the scenes, Shakespearian and those generally considered non-Shakespearian alike?' The answer is that it does not.

The generally accepted Shakespearian scenes, it will be remembered, are I. i. and ii, II. iii and iv, the early part of III. ii, and v. i. I find that the greatest number of these images occurs in Act I, scenes i and ii, Act II, sc. iv, and Act v, sc. i, that there are several in II, iii, and the early part of III. ii. Outside these, there are nine in the latter part of III. ii, two in v. iii, and two in II. ii. Now, curiously enough, quite apart from this fact, I already had found good reason to believe, from the point of view of images, as I shall show in a separate study, that Shakespeare had written more of Act III, sc. ii than is generally allotted to him, and that he had, at least, given some touches to v. iii and II. ii.

With these three exceptions, not one of these active 'body' images is to be found in any of the other nine scenes,[1]

---

[1] There is one 'burden' image in III. i. 111, but there is a subtle difference in it. It may be pure chance, but it does not carry with it the picture of a body *in action*, as all the other images do. Cf. III. ii. 407, v. iii. 76, II. iv. 208, or even III. ii. 380, where the word 'shoulders' vivifies the whole picture.

usually judged not to be Shakespeare's; that is I. iii and iv, II. i, III. i, IV. i and ii, and v. ii, iv, and v.

This is worth noting, for, in other cases, when an image is dominant—as, for instance, a tortured body is in *Lear*—it is to be found practically all through the play. Thus, in *Lear*, the only scene in which it is completely absent is the short business conversation of twenty-five lines between Cornwall and Edmund (v. iii). Everywhere else there are echoes and touches of the prevailing or 'floating' picture.

So that the entire breaking of the dominant thread of imagery in these particular scenes in *Henry VIII*, judged for quite other reasons not to be Shakespeare's, is, I think, significant, and points to another mind having been at work on them.[1]

I have said that in this play the images give me reason to think that Shakespeare's hand is visible in parts at least of scenes hitherto denied to him. Here is one instance of the kind of thing I build on, and there are many such. Towards the end of scene iii in Act v, generally thought not to be Shakespeare's, when Henry snubs Gardiner, who has just addressed him in terms of fulsome hypocrisy, the king uses these words:

> You were ever good at sudden commendations,
> Bishop of Winchester. But know, I come not
> To hear such flattery now, and in my presence
> They are too thin and bare to hide offences.
> To me you cannot reach, you play the spaniel,
> And think with wagging of your tongue to win me.

Does not this association of hypocritical flattery with the spaniel nature strike a familiar note when we remember the constant association of these two things in Shakespeare's mind? And when we add that no single image of fawning

---

[1] I do not for a moment offer this as a solution of the very puzzling riddle of the authorship of *Henry VIII*. There is a great deal more to be said about the evidence of the images, which by no means all points one way, and I think there are at least two possible explanations of this broken thread of imagery. But I do suggest that it is a factor which should be taken into account in any investigation of the problem.

dogs even without the association of flatterers is to be found in a search of nine of Fletcher's, and of Beaumont and Fletcher's plays, and that, out of fifty-seven plays by a dozen contemporary dramatists, the only association I find of fawning dogs with flatterers is once in Marlowe:

> We Jews can fawn like spaniels when we please
> (*Jew of Malta*, ii. iii. 781.)

and once in Ben Jonson, who speaks of parasites,

> With their court-dog-tricks, that can fawn and fleer,
> (*Volpone*, iii. i. 59.)

it would seem as if the odds were heavy in favour of this image being Shakespeare's.

And finally, to pass to my last point, I believe, as I said earlier, that we can detect, unerringly, many of Shakespeare's personal characteristics, experiences, and even points of view as it were obliquely in and through the verbal pictures he draws in such profusion to illustrate quite other emotions and thoughts in the hearts and minds of his characters. I believe that when these pictures are all assembled, and can be studied in proportion, it is possible to build up from them a fairly trustworthy picture, not only of the peculiarities of his bodily senses and organism, of his tastes and interests, of things seen and deeply felt, especially in youth, but also to some extent a picture of his attitude of mind, his opinions and beliefs such as you could never gain with any certainty from opinions or beliefs expressed directly as such by any one of his characters. I can, perhaps, illustrate by two or three examples how this seems to me to work.

When Othello brings out the horror of the contrast between the fair looks of Desdemona and what he believes her deeds entirely by means of *smell*, lamenting

> O thou weed,
> Who art so lovely fair and smell'st so sweet
> That the sense aches at thee, would thou hadst
> ne'er been born!

and answering her piteous query, 'Alas, what ignorant sin have I committed ?' with the agonized cry

> What committed!
> Heaven stops the nose at it;

we not only realize Othello's torture, racked between love and repulsion, but we also know incidentally that Shakespeare had a sensitive nose.

And when in addition we find that he repeatedly expresses disgust and loathing through the medium of revolting smells, chiefly of unwashed humanity and decaying substances, and that to his imagination sin and evil deeds always *smell foully*, we are justified in assuming that he himself intensely disliked bad smells.

Further, if we are to judge by his images, it would seem that he is more sensitive to the horror of bad smells than to the allure of fragrant ones. It is not possible now to demonstrate this in detail, but it is significant that, in his most sustained and exquisite appreciation of the rose (Sonnet 54), what chiefly appeals to him is the fact that, unlike other flowers, roses even when faded never smell badly, but that

> Of their sweet deaths are sweetest odours made,

What he shrinks from above all is a fair flower with 'the rank smell of weeds' (Sonnet 69), or a sweet-smelling flower which turns very much the reverse when dead, and we can sense the deep repulsion in the words,

> Lilies that fester smell far worse than weeds.

In this kind of way we can glean much information indirectly about his senses. His colour-sense as seen through his images is so interesting and so individual that it deserves far more time than we can give it to-day. The same is true of his marvellously acute touch-perception, his quick consciousness of the texture of the skin, Desdemona's 'smooth as monumental alabaster', Perdita's hands 'soft as dove's down', the hard horniness of the palm of a ploughman. We have constant evidence of his sensitiveness to the surface-quality of various substances, the smoothness of ice or of oil, the pleasant softness of rain, the cold hardness of stone, and the smooth imperviousness of marble, and it does not surprise us that some of the most vivid and haunting of his metaphors are drawn from this delicate sense of touch.

Can we not *feel* Falstaff manipulating the wax till he gets it to precisely the right degree of softness when he remarks complacently of Shallow, 'I have him already tempering between my finger and thumb, and shortly will I seal with him'? And is not Angus's satisfaction that Macbeth is reaping the reward of his deeds expressed in what is surely one of the most terrible and haunting pictures in a play already replete with them, terrible, because of the substance *suggested by its texture*, but not named,

> Now does he feel
> His secret murders sticking on his hands?

Or again, as throwing light on his tastes and interests, look at Jaques's good-natured advice to Touchstone dissuading him from being married by Sir Oliver 'under a bush like a beggar', and telling him to get to church, 'and have a good priest that can tell you what marriage is: this fellow will but join you together as they join wainscot; then one of you will prove a shrunk panel, and like green timber warp, warp'. We see the force of Jaques's argument, so vividly illustrated, that the Puritan preacher cannot marry them legally, and that then being but loosely joined in a way which can only be successful if their own characters are perfectly straight and upright, one of them will probably bend and twist out of it, which was indeed precisely what Touchstone intended to do. But we also see that Shakespeare had closely observed carpenters joining oak panelling and dovetailing it together, and had experienced how important it was for the success of that particular job that the wood should be perfectly dry and well seasoned. And when in addition we find that of all the many trades and crafts and their processes upon which

Shakespeare draws so constantly for his similes—the smith shaping the molten iron in his forge, the butcher in his slaughter-house, the potter tempering clay and whirling his wheel, the tailor cutting out by his pattern, the weaver at his loom, the glover, the printer, the solderer, the dyer— that of all these and others, the craft he seems by far the most familiar with, and in the terms of which he thinks most often and most easily is that of a village carpenter and joiner; when we discover that the number of images from screwing, nailing, riveting, hooping a barrel with ribs of metal, the action of wedges, the tendency of wood to shrink and warp, and general joinery and carpentry is remarkable, as well as the number of those from specific tools—a hammer, a mallet, a handsaw, a file, an auger or a vice, and the sharpening of knives and implements on a whetstone—we may surmise that Shakespeare himself had some knowledge of this craft. When, moreover, we find that nearly all these carpentry images are peculiarly vivid or real, showing exact and precise knowledge, we are, I think, justified in going farther and assuming that Shakespeare had a personal taste for and pleasure in carpentry, and that, contrary to our idea of most poets, he was probably a practical, neat, and handy man about the house, as we know that he was a 'Johannes Factotum' about the stage.

So, by the same indirect means, we can follow his interest in and knowledge of other crafts, especially of needlework, for the small details of which he seems to have had a peculiarly observant eye.

Or, to take a question of individual temperament, Shakespeare's intense sympathy with the feelings of animals is illustrated again and again in his similes, and most especially his feeling for and love of birds, and his hatred of their sufferings when limed or snared. But let us choose something less obviously appealing than the snared or netted bird, and look at what he says about snails, and how much it reveals of the strange 'fluidity' of his own poet's character. He concentrates on their outstanding qualities and characteristics so unerringly that, as Keats says in commenting on it, 'he has left nothing to say about nothing or anything'.

Most people, asked suddenly to name the outstanding quality of the snail, would answer 'its slow pace'. Not so Shakespeare, who assigns that second place only. The snail seems to him an example of one of the most delicately sensitive organisms in nature; it is 'love's feeling' only that

is more soft and sensible
Than are the tender horns of cockled snails.

The marvellously sensitive simile in *Venus and Adonis*, describing this peculiarity, also incidentally reveals the poet's acute appreciation of the point of view of the other person, when he describes the feelings of the

snail, whose tender horns being hit,
Shrinks backward in his shelly cave with pain,
And there all smother'd up in shade doth sit,
Long after fearing to creep forth again.

Notice how he emphasizes the greater poignancy of mental than physical pain, even in a snail, and remember how appositely he applies the same sensation and action years afterwards when describing Aufidius,

Who, hearing of our Marcius' banishment,
Thrusts forth his horns again into the world;
Which were inshell'd when Marcius stood for Rome,
And durst not once peep out.

Had we nothing but these three similes to guide us, we should realize that the author of them had the most exquisitely sensitive apprehension of the feelings of others, not only of men but of animals. As we know, because he himself tells us so, that Keats took part in the existence of a sparrow when it came and picked in the gravel before his window, so surely do we know, because Shakespeare tells us so in another way, that he took part in the existence of the snail and its feelings when he inadvertently touched it on the garden path.

I claim, moreover, that we can go even farther than this,

and that we can obtain quite clear glimpses into some of
the deeper thoughts of Shakespeare's mind through this
oblique study of his imagery. Take, for instance, the
subject of Death, of which we have upwards of eighty
images and personifications; it is impossible to study all
these without gaining at least a glimmer of light on Shakespeare's own attitude towards it.

There is, of course, much well-known and intensely
suggestive discussion and reflection on death in his work,
especially in those three closely related plays *Hamlet*,
Measure for Measure, and *Timon*, but it is all strictly the
outcome of the dramatic situation and the view of the
character who speaks.

Hamlet's obsession with and revolt from the physical
horror of death, his fears and doubts as to the death of
the mind, and his final realization that death, not life, is
'felicity', the Duke's arguments to prove that the best of
life is sleep, and death itself no more, Claudio's natural
horror of the unknown, Timon's certainty that for him the
'nothingness' of death is liberation and fulfilment—all this
and much more Shakespeare himself may have felt and
believed, but we do not know that he did.

What we do know is that when he thought of death
certain sets of pictures flashed into his mind, and these we
can look at with him, and, by virtue of his own genius,
we can see them almost as vividly as he did.

These pictures reveal a highly sensitive imagination
which realizes to the full that 'cowards die many times
before their death', and that the sense of death 'is most in
apprehension', yet which shrinks intensely from its physical
side and the horrors of it, and in that mood sees Death as
an 'ugly monster', a 'rotten carcase' in rags, an 'odori-
ferous stench'. This side of Shakespeare is very conscious
of the greed and destructiveness of Death, especially in
war or tragic accident, as in *King John* and *Romeo and
Juliet*, and pictures him as a warrior with jaws of steel
'mousing the flesh of men', a skeleton feasting upon
soldiers by the thousand, a 'carrion monster', a proud and

mighty being, who to supply food for his feasts strikes down kings, queens, and princes 'at a shot', and a mouth gorged with food.

Viewed thus, as the destroyer of youth untimely, by accident or battle, Death is frightful and repellent to look at, a

> Hard-favour'd tyrant, ugly, meagre, lean,
> . . . . . .
> Grim-grinning ghost.

It is sometimes suggested, however, that what we see is not Death as he really is, but a mummer or actor, 'thou antic death, which laugh'st us here to scorn'; a bogy masked to frighten children, as when the messenger after the battle of Shrewsbury cries:

> . . . hateful death put on his ugliest mask
> To fright our party.

Yet we cannot feel that anything of Shakespeare's own hope or experience is expressed in the words of Northumberland in an earlier play,

> even through the hollow eyes of death
> I spy life peering.

When Death takes toll of youth and beauty, he is thought of sometimes as a lover, especially in the case of Juliet and Cleopatra; Constance, in her grisly picture, greets him as husband and lover; while Claudio in despair, Lear in his frenzy, and Antony in set determination, each resolve to greet death bravely and with zest, as a bridegroom running to meet his bride.

The power of Death, and man's helplessness in his grip, is constantly kept before us, and Shakespeare shows us Death as a wrestler, a tilter, an antagonist against whom we fight a losing game, and whom we can at most hold 'awhile at the arm's end'; a hound dogging us at the heels, a hunter, a fowler, an archer with an ebon dart; a fell sergeant, 'strict in his arrest'; a soldier, laying siege to the mind, pricking and wounding it; a king boldly keeping his Court within the very confines of the crown of a mortal king; a jester scoffing and grinning at the pomp with which he humours a monarch's vanity, while, at his own time, with a little pin he bores his castle wall and claims him for his own; and life itself is seen but as Death's fool or dupe, ever vainly trying to escape him, while ever irresistibly drawn towards him.

These are, for the most part, aspects of Death seen under special circumstances, the terrible and hungry feeder in war, and the ravisher of youth, beauty, and strength, who mockingly plays with and dominates not only kings and princes but even life itself; and we realize that Shakespeare is here merely presenting to his audience the figure of the grim yet semi-jocular skeleton with which he and they alike were familiar in medieval jest and picture.

May we dare to conjecture from his many other images something of Shakespeare's own view of death? I believe we may.

Even a glance at his pictures of life gives us some clue to its opposite. Thus, life is a voyage, uncertain and bound in shallows and miseries, a journey, a pilgrimage; death is a journey's end, sometimes a shipwreck, but never a haven or harbour. Life is a fever, a dream; death is the sure physician and a sleep; life is merely a breath and death the mirror which proves this to us; life is a light, a candle, a lamp, a fire, a spark; death the extinction of all these. Life is a spring flower, death a frost; life is a prison, death a release; life is a thread, a knot, death is the thread cut, decayed, or cracked, and the knot untied.

In general it would seem he does not rebel against death, but accepts it as a natural process, a debt we owe to God, the cancelling of the bond of life, and he thinks of it fairly constantly as the end of all we know, sometimes coming abruptly and harshly, as the untimely frost on a flower, a winter that kills, an axe set to a tree, or more gradually, as a canker or over-ripeness; but on the whole, most often, in spite of Hamlet's questionings and Claudio's ravings, an end wholly peaceful, merciful, and restful.

Most constantly of all he sees it as a sleep when 'the

long day's task is done', or it is a window closing, shutting out the daylight, a black veil, very often a cloud over the sun, or, as I have said, the extinguishing of light, a burnt-out torch or candle, a spent lamp and the coming of night, when

> the bright day is done,
> And we are for the dark.

It is the key that unlocks the shackles of trouble and disease by which we are held fast in this world, that shuts up and makes an end of the day, but it is never the key that unlocks the door to a new life.

On the other hand, it is a way to freedom and liberty, a jailer releasing a prisoner to 'enlarge his confine', the kind umpire of men's miseries, who 'with sweet enlargement doth dismiss' them hence.

Only once does Shakespeare in his own person seem to tell us directly what he himself thinks about Death, and that is in the grave 146th Sonnet, addressed to the soul of man. Here we see the medieval picture reversed, and the greedy feaster on the flesh of men subdued and annihilated in his turn by the spirit of man grown strong, and here Shakespeare points out to us the way of life, and so of the defeat of death. This way is to concentrate on the nurture of the soul or spirit rather than the body, even at the expense of the body, which is but the 'fading mansion' of the soul, its servant and inferior, and here for the first and only time we find a note of hope and triumph, markedly absent from all his other pictures of man in his relation to 'that dark spirit':

> Then, soul, live thou upon thy servant's loss,
> And let that pine to aggravate thy store;
> Buy terms divine in selling hours of dross;
> Within be fed, without be rich no more:
> So shalt thou feed on Death, that feeds on men,
> And Death once dead, there's no more dying then.

If we examine in this way Shakespeare's many pictures of other abstractions, of love and hate, of sin, evil and good, of time, of fear, and so on, we can, I submit, gradually assemble and create a fairly reliable picture of the general attitude of his mind, and in some cases of his very passionate feeling.

Thus, as we collect and examine our material, there seems gradually to emerge a very definite figure of an intensely alive, incredibly sensitive, and amazingly observant man. Probably a quiet one—he does not like noise —and not, it would seem, a dreamer, but practical and watchful, all the time absorbing impressions and knowledge like a sponge, registering them like a sensitive plate.

We see he is a country man through and through, that it is the sights and sounds of boyhood which chiefly remain with him, and that half a lifetime spent in a great city has never deflected by one iota his interest from the pageant of the English countryside to that of the streets, which latter, indeed, he seems hardly to notice. What he does notice are the sky and clouds, the seasons, the weather and its changes, rain, wind, sun, and shadow, and of all the outdoor occupations what he loves most is to work and saunter in his garden or orchard, and to note and study the flight and movements of the wild birds.

Next to this we find him most interested in the homely indoor occupations and routine, eating, drinking, sleeping, the body and its clothes, candles, fire and lamps, birth and death, sickness and medicine, parents and children, and especially he delights in watching the women's work continually going on in a cottage kitchen, preparing food, cooking, washing up, dusting, knitting, darning, and patching.

We see that in that kitchen, as well as enjoying much, he has also suffered from many things, from smoky chimneys, stopped-up ovens, guttering evil-smelling candles, and ill-trimmed lamps, as well as from greasy badly-cooked food and tainted or musty meat.

We can watch some of his tastes and opinions gradually developing; it is amusing, for instance, to see his interest in food and cooking and his fastidiousness beginning to grow in early middle age, whereas there is evidence even in his early work of his disgust at surfeit, as well as of his curiously modern belief that we bring upon ourselves a great deal of our own bad health by ill-regulated living, and especially by over-eating.

So the central figure gradually emerges, not an outline sketch merely, but full of detail, a living, breathing, and intensely human being, with marked individuality and tastes.

I believe that these pictures of Shakespeare's brain—I have over six thousand of them now collected—form an as yet almost unread and unstudied volume, packed with information as to the nature, experiences, and thoughts of the man about whom, I suppose, above all others, the world as a whole is most eager to learn. For generations we have striven pathetically and vainly to follow and study his mind and doings through the dry records of legal documents and law-suits, while all the time there has lain open before us a book full of facts, fragmentary perhaps, but sometimes dovetailing together in the most satisfactory way, a book ablaze with sidelights, not only on the man himself but also on his surroundings, and on the rich and many-coloured background of his thought and vision. I suggest that through these pierced lancet windows of the mind we can, if we will, listen to the sounds of the world he lived in, and learn which most affected and charmed him; we can catch vivid glimpses of the life he saw and the figures in it which specially enchanted him; we may even form some estimate as to how far he himself shared in or was affected by current beliefs and points of view: and all this information, and much more, we can gather direct from the person best qualified to give it us—Shakespeare himself.

PRINTED IN GREAT BRITAIN AT THE UNIVERSITY PRESS, OXFORD
BY JOHN JOHNSON, PRINTER TO THE UNIVERSITY